DIDEROT'S *SELECTED WRITINGS*

DIDEROT'S
Selected Writings

SELECTED AND EDITED,
WITH AN INTRODUCTION AND NOTES, BY
Lester G. Crocker

TRANSLATED BY
Derek Coltman

THE MACMILLAN COMPANY, *NEW YORK*
COLLIER-MACMILLAN LTD., *LONDON*

Library of Congress Catalog Card Number: 65-17831

FIRST PRINTING

This book is part of a series, Classics in the History of Thought, prepared under the general editorship of Crane Brinton and Paul Edwards.

The Macmillan Company, New York
Collier-Macmillan Canada Ltd., Toronto, Ontario

Printed in the United States of America

CONTENTS

Introduction

THE life of Denis Diderot, like his thought, was not without its aspects of turbulence and drama. He was born on October 5, 1713, the eldest child of a respected artisan of Langres, in the province of Champagne. Traditionalism and piety, clannishness and middle-class conservatism were the hallmarks of the town and of the family. Much of Diderot's life, much of his thought were to be in rebellion against these; but still another part was to be their continuance and their defense.

For some years he expected to follow the example of others in his family and enter the church. Due to rather mysterious and perhaps adventurous circumstances, he was sent to Paris in the autumn of 1728. There he acquired a Master of Arts degree in 1732. Meanwhile, he had been falling under the influence of a bohemian milieu of students and freethinkers. The moment of rebellion was at hand. Refusing to bow to the pressures put on him by his father to follow an honorable career, he broke off with his family and his past and settled down to years of hand-to-mouth living in the garrets of the Latin Quarter. Many are the stories of his hardships and adventures. He eked out an existence by giving mathematics lessons, writing sermons on commission, borrowing under false pretenses. All the while, he read voraciously and caroused with youthful libertinism when he could.

In the early 1740's, Diderot formed a close friendship with another unknown, disreputable, and aspiring young man—Jean-Jacques Rousseau. It was at this time, too, that he made a great mistake and eloped with Antoinette Champion, in the teeth of his father's opposition—which went so far as to have him imprisoned by means of a *lettre de cachet.* Antoinette was uncultured and shrewish; worst of all, she had no understanding of his need for other liaisons and carried on about his infidelities in violent domestic scenes.

Income from hackwork was now supplemented by respectable translations from the English, a language Diderot knew well, along with Latin, Greek, and Italian. They included a version, with commentary, of Shaftesbury's *Essay on Merit and Virtue* (1745). This was his introduction to moral philosophy, which was to be, together with all problems relating to the human adventure, his central preoccupation. His motto might well have been: "*Homo sum; humani nihil a me alienum puto.*" From Shaftesbury, Diderot borrowed another motto: "The good, the true, and the beautiful." It was always before him and recurs frequently in his writings. But this passionate love of virtue, mingled with sentimentality and weepiness, betrays the persistence of fundamental bourgeois traits typical of his time. These were to clash with an implacable logic which impelled him ever more to materialism and to the questioning of the bases of moral values.

The next year, Diderot tried his own wings; it was a short flight, and not into uncharted regions. The *Pensées philosophiques (Philosophic Thoughts)* was written in the vein of numerous clandestine manuscripts, but with a style, a fire that belonged to him alone. An attack on Christianity and a defense of deism, it combines cosmological speculations with moral considerations and includes a passionate defense of the passions.

The *Pensées philosophiques* was, not unexpectedly, burned by the censorious authorities, and the police set on Diderot's trail. In 1747, a surprise visit to his apartment netted them another antireligious manuscript *La Promenade du sceptique (Skeptic's Stroll)*, which was not published until 1830; but even this failed to frighten the hothead. Besides, he was now concerned with something far more serious. He had accepted the job of editing, with d'Alembert, a vast new project to be known as an *Encyclopédie*. He was far from realizing that it was to absorb him for twenty years, bring him unforeseeable trials and tribulations, or that it would turn out to be his most important and influential work.

For the moment, however, there was time for other endeavors.

The year 1748 saw the appearance of *Les Bijoux indiscrets (The Indiscreet Jewels)*, a bawdy tale with philosophic interludes. For this indecency, Diderot sought to make amends by publishing five mathematical memoirs. Then, in the spring of 1749, came the *Lettre sur les aveugles, à l'usage de ceux qui voient (Letter on the Blind, For the Use of Those Who See)*. It was a highly original and suggestive exploration of the effects of our senses on our moral and metaphysical ideas. Deism now gave way to frank atheism. A mechanical and evolutionary view of the universe was combined with the beginnings of a mechanistic biology. But whatever this important work may have done for his reputation as a philosopher, it did little for his personal well-being and equanimity. He was seized by the police on the twenty-fourth of July and carted away to a dungeon in the thick-walled prison of Vincennes. Not until his spirit was broken and until he penned a most unheroic letter of confession, followed by an oath never again to write against religion, under pain of life imprisonment, was he taken to less cramped quarters. And not until November 3 was he set at liberty, to return to his family and friends, his books, and his *Encyclopédie*.

The *Lettre sur les sourds et muets, à l'usage de ceux qui entendent et qui parlent (Letter on the Deaf and Dumb, For the Use of Those Who Hear and Speak)*, which came out in 1751, contained nothing to arouse the authorities. It is a brilliant analysis of language and rhetoric and, aside from a significant article in the *Encyclopédie*, "Du Beau" ("On the Origin and Nature of the Beautiful"), his first venture into aesthetic philosophy.

Diderot's "Prospectus" for the *Encyclopédie* had appeared late in 1749, d'Alembert's important *Discours préliminaire (Preliminary Discourse)* in 1751, and in July of that year, the first beautiful folio volume was distributed to its subscribers. It immediately aroused much hostility among the devout. Already it was quite clear that the object of this work was not only to bring all important and useful knowledge together. The hope for a better and a freer society, for a world of rationality and progress was contained in its pages. Attacks on political abuses and religious tyranny, though artfully concealed by a variety of devices, were scattered among the most innocuous-sounding titles and paragraphs. The church saw itself menaced, and many high persons in government were uneasy. Most fearful of all, and most determined to crush the enterprise, were the Jesuits. The second volume of the *Encyclopédie* added fuel to the fire. Its offensiveness was compounded by the scandal over the Abbé de Prades; this young theologian had published a most unorthodox thesis, and Diderot had the imprudence to help him write his no less scandalous *Apology*. The Privy Council soon issued a decree suppressing both volumes of the *Encyclopédie* and ordering seizure of the manuscripts. Diderot was urged by his friends to run to a foreign land. He refused and stood firm. Finally, aided by powerful anti-Jesuit influences at court, the enterprise was allowed to continue under a "tacit license."

Meanwhile, Diderot's personal life was changing. At home, a daughter, born in 1753—the first of his children to survive—was to turn him increasingly toward his latent bourgeois impulses. The rupture with his family at Langres was healed; all was forgiven, and the prodigal son welcomed back into the fold—a new version of the classic story he was to admire so much in the paintings of Greuze. Melchior von Grimm had become his dearest friend, and as he fell more and more under his ascendancy, Diderot's ties with Rousseau—whose own thought was leading to an inevitable break with the Encyclopedia group—were growing looser. He more and more frequented the brilliant, atheistic society that gathered around the Baron d'Holbach, who was called "*le maître d'hôtel de la philosophie*." And then began the great love affair of his life, one destined to last for years, with an intellectual spinster, Sophie Volland. Posterity is grateful for the magnificent correspondence which was its chief literary result. Diderot also found time to enter a famous musical quarrel, between the partisans of French and Italian opera ("La querelle des bouffons"), on the side of the Italians.

A final work in his first group of philosophical writings dates from 1753: the *Pensées sur l'interprétation de la nature (Thoughts on the Interpretation of Nature)*. This series of "thoughts," modeled partly on Bacon and the Baconian outlook, describes and prescribes scientific methodology and then goes on to a long series of "conjectures." Some of these now seem utterly quaint or fantastic. Others bear the mark of Diderot's forward-looking, synthetical mind. Among other things, he is apparently impressed by the need for working toward a theory of organic evolution—an idea with which a few advanced thinkers were then flirting.

Then Diderot laid philosophical speculation to rest for a time. While more volumes of the *Encyclopédie* came off the presses—with a resultant rise in income; while the thunderous quarrel with Rousseau was breaking out—a quarrel that was to shake literary Europe for years and is still being fought by scholars—Diderot turned to the arts. In 1757, he published *Le Fils naturel (The Natural Son)*, a new kind of play which he called "drama," together with a discussion of its theory, in a series of *Conversations*. The play itself is not very true to the theory, but instead anticipates nineteenth-century melodrama. The following year a second play, *Le Père de famille (The Father)*, proved another instance of his theatrical taste and ability. Both works represent the sentimental, middle-class taste of the period; both create an atmosphere dripping with virtue and moral preaching, with plots punctuated by *coups de théâtre* and overdramatic ranting.

Not long after this, Diderot became intensely involved in the problems of painting and sculpture. To please his friend Grimm, he wrote detailed commentaries on the biennial Salons, to be published in Grimm's secret newspaper, *La Correspondance littéraire*, which was distributed to foreign nobility. He also wrote an *Essay on Painting* and other pieces. As time went on, he became more and more knowledgeable about techniques and developed the first important method of aesthetic criticism. His criticism was personal; the canvas often served as a stimulus to his own imagination and creativity. He possessed a gift for making the pictures he described live; at times, dissatisfied, he "remade" them. Practical criticism was accompanied by theorizing. Both his theory and taste tended to make of the arts an extension of literature and a vehicle for preaching the moral virtues. Occasional philosophical digressions enliven the great Salons of 1765 and 1767. Here, as in *Le Rêve de d'Alembert* and *Le Paradoxe sur le comédien*, Diderot discusses various aesthetic problems, including imagination and creativity.

The year 1760 saw Diderot's first important sally into the novelistic genre. *La Religieuse (The Nun)*, which was based on an actual incident, told of the desire of a girl, whose parents had compelled her to take vows, to recover her freedom. This dramatic work is more than a satire of convents and the monastic system. It is an interesting experiment in technique and an exploration of female psychology and sexology, with the accent on the abnormal. It combines a most telling realism of detail with an effort to achieve emotional impact through a variety of devices (light and darkness, tableaux, torture) which have qualities that partly recall Richardson (whom Diderot worshiped) and partly foreshadow the Gothic novel of horror. *La Religieuse* also breaks new ground by its rather precise descriptions of lesbianism. Unfortunately, none of this was to influence his time, for Diderot dared not publish his story, which did not appear until 1796.

There were more turbulent episodes that punctured these relatively peaceful undertakings of Diderot. Together with the "treason" of Rousseau and their scandalous quarrel came the vicious attacks on him and his friends by writers in the service of the "devout party," as it was called. Most dramatic of all was the final condemnation of the *Encyclopédie* and the revocation of its license in 1759. This disaster was partly brought on by the publication, in the year preceding, of *De l'Esprit (On the Mind)*, by Diderot's friend Helvétius, a work which developed the most extreme consequences of the sensationist philosophy, especially that selfishness is the sole law of man and of all beings and that education and government have the power to mold men as they will—all this leading to the first systematic philosophy of utilitarianism. The *Encyclopédie* and its authors were publicly denounced as the root of the evil. At first, the Parlement of Paris merely ordered the seven published volumes to be completely revised. But a month later, on March 8, a decree of the Privy Council completely outlawed the work. The publishers were forbidden to sell the volumes that had already appeared or to print any new ones, under pain of exemplary punishment. It looked as if the *Encyclopédie*, the great work of Diderot's life, was never to be finished.

D'Alembert and many other collaborators abandoned the sinking ship or had already done so with the first signs of a storm. Voltaire urged continuing the enterprise under the aegis of his protector Frederick the Great, a tyrant whom Diderot detested, despite his pretension to being a fellow philosophe. Alone, he stood firm, regrouped his cohorts, and when he had instilled his courage in them and in the publisher, it was finally decided to complete and print the remaining volumes in secrecy and then to throw them all at once into the hands of the thousands of subscribers, a *fait accompli.* The government, in fact, connived in this solution because of the important financial interests involved and fear of foreign competition.

And now, while the last volumes were being readied, and a decade after the *Pensées sur l'interprétation de la nature*, Diderot's inquiring mind turned back to speculative philosophy. This time he was to find the form in which he would excel: the dialogue. In the give-and-take of imaginary discourse, his characteristic bent, of exploring both sides of a question, of finding some truth on both sides, of carrying speculation to the test of the most extreme conclusions, could express itself with all the liveliness of his own brilliant conversation. This time, too, he was to compose stories and novels, mingling the problems of aesthetic creation—and the benefits of its reality—with those of philosophic speculation.

He began with a masterpiece, *Le Neveu de Rameau (Rameau's Nephew)*, largely written in 1762. Here character creation, scintillating and lifelike dialogue, and an entirely original use of pantomime supply the aesthetic texture for a subtle discussion of the world, of ways of life, of moral values—a sometimes bitter satire in which moral nihilism appears as the effective, ruling law of life, and moral values as secondary, even as hypocritical pretense.

Again, the impact of Diderot's radical thought was nullified by his fear of persecution, and not until 1823 was *Le Neveu de Rameau* revealed to the French public. It waited even longer for his most important philosophical work, the tripartite *Rêve de d'Alembert (D'Alembert's Dream)*, which was written in 1769 but not printed until 1830. This brilliant, imaginative dialogue, the most complete and far-ranging philosophy of materialism in the eighteenth century, contains the essence and ultimate reach of Diderot's radical thought.

Beginning in 1770, Diderot embarked on a series of works which can best be described as a combination of moral experiments and aesthetic experiments. (*Le Neveu de Rameau*, though earlier, fits into this group.) His purpose was to test the extreme possibilities of character, of behavior, of moral theory and judgment. The results, philosophically, reveal the shaky nature and uncertainty of the latter two, the fundamental immorality of human life and character and, paradoxically, their capacity for moral heroism. For Diderot, the most admirable quality is greatness of soul, greatness *in being*, regardless of whether it inclines the protagonist to good or evil according to conventional terms. These writings take on a variety of forms: tales—*Les Deux amis de Bourbonne (The Two Friends from Bourbonne)*, *Ceci n'est pas un conte (This Isn't a Story)*, *Mme de la Carlière;* dialogues —*Entretien d'un père avec ses enfants (A Father's Talk with His Children)*, *Supplément au voyage de Bougainville (Supplement to Bougainville's Voyage);* a most curious and rich novel, partly modeled on *Tristram Shandy*, entitled *Jacques le Fataliste (Jacques the Fatalist)*, 1773, published in 1796; and a play, *Est-il bon, est-il méchant? (Is He Good, Is He Bad?)*, 1781. With the exception of the first, all remained locked in Diderot's drawer or in those of close friends. This lover of paradox, this uncompromising searcher for truth, ever ready to follow reason's torch as far as it would lead him, was also a preacher of sound morality. He loved virtue—and social order—too much to publicize what he aristocratically termed "a doctrine for the few." Virtue and moral values are real, he maintained, even if it is not easy, or even possible, to substantiate and justify them—or to practice them. Nothing is more characteristic of Diderot than his own confession of rage at being "entangled in a devilish philosophy which my heart rejects and my reason cannot help approving."

Nevertheless, his reason did disapprove, and rebel, to a significant extent. Outraged by Helvétius' posthumous work *De l'Homme (On Man)*, 1773, Diderot composed a point-by-point rejoinder, which was not published until 1875, *Réfutation de l'Homme d'Helvétius (Refutation of the Work of Helvétius Entitled On Man)*. While this provocative, often angry piece is by no means an abandonment of scientific materialism, it makes clear the limits of such a philosophy and demands throughout the recognition of what is peculiar to man as paramount. Although nature is an all-embracing continuum, it develops discrete levels. The human phenomenon is characterized by the emergence of consciousness, which is self-causative and self-directive toward selected ends. This was truly the revenge of humanism against an antihumanistic variety of naturalism. And yet, so typically of Diderot, even as he wrote and revised his *Réfutation*, he was also composing a scintillating dialogue in defense of his antireligious views, the *Entretien d'un philosophe avec la Maréchale (Conversation with a Christian Lady)*, 1774, published in 1796.

But we have allowed the course of Diderot's intellectual activity to carry us chronologically beyond the other events of his life. In January, 1766, the *Encyclopédie* was completed, and its last two volumes released, under the spurious imprint of Neuchâtel. Not long after, its distribution was prohibited by the police and the defiant publisher sent to the Bastille. Once more Diderot was urged to flee, and once more he refused. The storm died down. The Encyclopedists' worst enemies, the Jesuits, had been expelled from France in 1764. Powerful figures at court and in the government quietly used their influence to allow distribution of the remaining sets, and the long battle was won, with an anticlimactic lack of drama and spectacle. It had been Diderot's victory.

The remaining years were largely taken up with family matters, such as the marriage of his daughter and the joys of being a grandfather. But there was one eventful interlude: a journey to St. Petersburg, to pay homage to Catherine the Great, who had heavily subsidized him. We need not tarry over the details of this journey or his five-month stay at court, piquant though they are. Diderot enjoyed friendly and informal relations with Her Majesty and did not hesitate to sermonize her about good government. Part of his time, both coming and going, was spent in the Netherlands. There, and upon his return to Paris in 1774, after an absence of fifteen months, Diderot composed a number of pieces for Catherine, in which he set forth his ideas on government and laws and on public education. They were not published until long after his death, but they clearly place him—contrary to Rousseau—in the liberal tradition.

In this final period, he also wrote *Elements of Physiology;* his best play, *Est-il bon, est-il méchant?;* and a long defense of Seneca, *Essai sur les règnes de Claude et de Néron (Essay on the Reigns of Claudius and Nero)*, 1778–1782, which contained a vitriolic attack on his former friend Rousseau.

The last years were quiet. The battles were over, the *compagnons d'armes* dead or dispersed, and Diderot prepared for what he called "the great voyage" with no religious faith but a tranquil conscience. He enjoyed the firm conviction that his life had been, all in all, a good and a useful one. Posterity, he was certain, would recognize his merits and accord him the place that was due to him. He died quickly on July 31, 1784, in a small apartment opposite the present Comédie-Française.

Note on the Texts

ALL selections have been specially translated for this volume.

The standard French edition of Diderot's works is by Assézat and Tourneux, Garnier Frères, Paris, 1875. It will hereafter be referred to as A-T. Its text is not, however, always complete or accurate, and many of the translations in this book were prepared from more recent critical French editions.

L.G.C.

DIDEROT'S *SELECTED WRITINGS*

Philosophic Thoughts

[1746]

The Pensées philosophiques, *Diderot's first original work, was written and published (and burned by order of Parlement) in the spring of 1746. It was highly successful, went through several editions, and provoked numerous refutations. The "dialogue" between the atheist and the deist is the really original part of the book, the rest consisting of more striking formulations of ideas that were already being spread by opponents of Christian attitudes which no longer obtained in real life.*

The Pensées philosophiques *is to be found in the first volume of the standard edition.*

Philosophic Thoughts

I

People are continually inveighing against the passions; we impute all man's troubles to them and forget that they are also the source of all his pleasures. They are an element in his constitution of which it is impossible to speak either too well or too ill. But what makes me angry is that no one ever considers anything but their bad side, as though it would be an insult to reason to say a single word in defense of its rivals. And yet it is the passions alone, great passions, that can raise the soul to great deeds. Without them, there would be an end of sublimity both in human actions and in art; the fine arts would return to their infancy, and virtue would become a quibble.

II

Sober passions make commonplace men. If I wait for the enemy to attack when the safety of my country is at stake, then I am but a poor sort of citizen. My friendship is merely prudence if my friend's peril does not make me forget my own. And if my own life is dearer to me than the woman I love, then I am but an everyday sort of lover.

III

Extraordinary men lose their eminence when their passions become dulled. Restraint destroys the greatness and energy of nature. Consider that tree; you owe the cool spread of its shade to the luxuriance of its branches, and you will enjoy that shade until winter comes to strip away their foliage. When superstition is allowed to perform the task of old age in dulling the human temperament, we can say good-bye to all excellence in poetry, in painting, and in music.

IV

In that case, you will reply, we should account ourselves fortunate if we are endowed with strong passions. Yes, certainly, provided they are all in accord with one another. Once establish a just harmony between them and you need fear no disorders. In a society where hope is balanced by fear, love of honor by love of life, and the inclination to pleasure by a proper care for health, there can be neither libertines, rash fools, nor cowards.

V

To attempt the destruction of our passions is the height of folly. What a noble aim is that of the zealot who tortures himself like a madman in order to desire nothing, love nothing, feel nothing, and who, if he succeeded, would end up a complete monster!

XV

I say there is no God; that the creation is a myth; that the eternity of the world is certainly no more difficult to believe than the eternity of a spirit; that it is ridiculous, simply because I cannot conceive how motion could have given birth to a universe that it so evidently has the power to maintain, to remove this difficulty by positing the existence of a being I can't conceive of either; that the glories we perceive in the physical sphere do reveal the existence of an intelligence, but that the chaos prevailing in the sphere of morality destroys all possibility of a Providence. I say that if everything is the work of a God, then everything should be as perfect as possible; for if everything is not as perfect as possible, this implies either impotence or a will to evil on the part of God. . . . Those, says the atheist, are my objections. And what is your answer to them? You say that I am a scoundrel and that I dispute God's existence only because I have reason to fear Him. But let us leave such turns of phrase to the hack sermon writers. . . . Because a man is wrong not to believe in God, are we therefore right to abuse him? Abuse is ever the refuge of those who lack proofs. I would wager a hundred to one that out of two men in an argument, the one who loses his temper is the one in the wrong. "You reach for your thunder instead of answering," Menippus said to Jupiter; "that means you are in the wrong."

XVII

All the airy nonsense of the metaphysicians is not worth a single argument *ad hominem*. To convince someone of a truth, it is sometimes enough merely to awaken a physical or moral feeling in him. A stick sufficed to persuade the Pyrrhonist of his error in denying his own existence. And Cartouche,[1] pistol in hand, could have taught Hobbes a similar lesson: "Your money or your life; we are alone, I am the stronger, and there can be no question of equity between us."

XVIII

It is not the metaphysicians who have dealt atheism its severest blows. All the sublime meditations of Malebranche[2] and Des-

[1] Cartouche (Louis-Dominique Bourguignon, 1693–1721), a famous highwayman.

[2] Malebranche (1638–1715), French philosopher and theologian, author of *De la Recherche de la vérité* and other works.

cartes had less power to shake the foundations of materialism than a single one of Malpighi's observations. And if this dangerous hypothesis is losing ground today, it is to experimental science that the honor is due. It is in the works of Newton, Musschenbroek,[3] Hartsoeker,[4] and Nieuwentyt[5] alone that we have found satisfactory proofs of the existence of a sovereignly intelligent being. Thanks to the work of these great men, the world is no longer a God:[6] it is simply a machine, with its wheels, its ropes, its pulleys, its springs, and its weights.

XIX

The subtleties of ontology have at best made skeptics; the creation of true deists was reserved for natural science. The discovery of germ cells alone has completely destroyed one of the atheist's most powerful objections. Whether motion be essential or accidental in matter, I am now persuaded that its effects are limited to developments of what already exists. All observations concur to prove that putrefaction alone can produce no organized life. I can admit that the mechanism of the lowest insect is no less marvelous than that of man without fearing any inference that since an internal agitation of molecules produced the one, it is therefore likely that it also produced the other. If an atheist had suggested two hundred years ago that we should one day see men springing fully formed from the bowels of the earth as today we see a cluster of insects emerging from a mass of heated flesh, I should very much like to know what the metaphysicians would have had to say in reply.

XX

. . . It follows that if the universe—what do I mean, the universe?—if a butterfly's wing reveals traces of an intelligence

[3] Musschenbroek (1692–1761), Dutch physicist and experimentalist.

[4] Hartsoeker (1656–1725), Dutch physicist and doctor, discoverer of spermatozoa.

[5] Nieuwentyt (1654–1718), Dutch mathematician and doctor. He attempted to prove the existence of God by the wonders of nature.

[6] What Diderot evidently means here is that the world is an entity requiring God for its explanation.

that are a thousand times clearer to me than the signs that tell you your fellow man is endowed with the faculty of thought, then it would be a thousand times more insane for me to deny the existence of God than for you to deny that your fellow man thinks. And that this is in fact the case, I call upon your knowledge and your conscience to attest: have you ever observed more intelligence, more order, more wisdom, or more logic in the actions and behavior of any man alive than you have in the mechanism of an insect? Is divinity not as clearly imprinted in the eye of a mite as the faculty of thought in the works of the great Newton himself? What! Is the formation of the world inferior as a proof of intelligence to an explanation of the world? What an assertion! . . .

"But," you reply, "I am the more willing to admit the faculty of thought in another because I am a thinking being myself. . . ." That, I agree, is a line of argument I cannot use; but am I not compensated for this disadvantage by the superiority of my proofs over yours? Is the intelligence of a primal being not better demonstrated by his works, by the nature he created, than a philosopher's ability to think by his writings? Remember that I opposed you with no more than a butterfly's wing and a mite's eye, when I could have crushed you beneath the weight of the entire universe. Either I am gravely mistaken or this proof is quite the equal of any taught by the academic philosophers. It is on this argument, and on one or two others of like simplicity, that I base my acceptance of God's existence, and not on those tissues of dry and metaphysical ideas that are less apt to unveil the truth than to cloak it in an appearance of falsehood.

XXI

I open the notebooks of a famous professor and read: "Atheists, I grant you that motion is essential in matter; but what conclusion do you draw from that? That the world was produced by atoms being scattered at random like dice? I would as soon you told me that Homer's *Iliad* or Voltaire's *Henriade* was produced by a random scattering of type."

I shall take good care not to use this argument against an atheist myself: to use such a simile would be to deal him every trump in the pack. According to the laws of probability, he would reply, the occurrence of a possible event should cause me no surprise; and the improbability of the event can be compensated for by the number of throws. There exists a certain number of throws that would enable me to wager with advantage that I could throw a hundred thousand sixes at the same time with a hundred thousand dice. Whatever the finite sum of letters with which I might be asked to give random birth to the *Iliad*, there would always be a corresponding finite number of throws that would make the wager to my advantage; and my advantage would even be infinite if the number of throws allowed were infinite too. You are willing to agree with me, I suppose, he would continue, that matter has existed from eternity and that motion is of its essence. As a means of repaying this favor, I shall suppose, as you do, that the universe is limitless, that the innumerable atoms that compose it are infinite in number, and that this order you find so astonishing is nowhere belied. Now these reciprocal admissions of ours can lead to only one possible conclusion: that the possibility of the universe having been created by chance is very small, but that the number of throws allowed was infinite. In other words, the improbability of the event was more than sufficiently compensated for by the number of throws. Therefore, since matter has been in motion from all eternity and since there may have occurred in that time an infinite number of marvelous arrangements proceeding from the infinite number of possible combinations, if anything should be repugnant to reason, it is the supposition that not one of those marvelous arrangements was in fact included among the infinite multitude of those that matter did successively assume. It follows, then, that the mind ought to be astonished less by the actual birth of the universe than by a hypothetical continuation of the original chaos.

XXII

I distinguish three classes of atheists. There are those who tell you quite clearly that there is no God and who really think this to be true: *these are the true atheists*. There are a fairly large number who are not sure what to think and who would be quite willing to decide the question by the toss of a coin: *these are the skeptical atheists*. And there are a great many who would like to believe that there is no God, who put on a pretense of believing that there isn't, and who live as if they believed there isn't: *these are the braggarts of the party*. I detest the braggarts because they are false; I pity the true atheists because they are beyond all possibility of consolation; and *I pray to God* on behalf of the skeptics because they want enlightenment.

XXIII

The deist proclaims the existence of a God, immortality of the soul, and all that follows from this. The skeptic has not made up his mind about these matters. The atheist denies their existence. The skeptic therefore has one more motive for being virtuous than the atheist and rather less reason than the deist. Were it not for his fear of the lawmaker, the natural inclination of his temperament, and his awareness of the present advantages of virtue, the atheist's probity would lack foundations, and the skeptic's would be built on a "perhaps."

XXIV

Skepticism is not suited to everyone. It presupposes a deep and disinterested inquiry into things: a man who doubts because he cannot see the reasons in favor of belief is merely ignorant. The true skeptic has counted and weighed the reasons. But the appreciation of such arguments is no inconsiderable matter. Which of us knows their exact value? Even if someone produced a hundred proofs of the same truth, each of them would have its partisans. Every mind contains its own telescope. The objection that looms to me like a colossus may count for nothing in your eyes; and you may dismiss as trivial an argument that I find overwhelming. If we are divided over intrinsic value, how are we to agree on relative importance? Tell me, how many moral proofs are needed to outweigh a metaphysical conclusion? Are my lenses deficient, or are yours? And if it is so difficult to weigh our reasons, if there are no questions without their pros and cons, and these almost in equal measure, why then do we decide so quickly? How is it we speak in such decided tones? Have we not ourselves experienced a hundred times how repulsive dogmatic arrogance is in others? . . .

L

A single rational demonstration impresses me more than fifty facts. Thanks to the extreme confidence I place in my powers of reasoning, my belief is not to be won by the first charlatan who comes along. High priest of Mohammed, you may make the lame walk, the dumb speak, and the blind see; you may cure paralytics, resuscitate the dead, and even restore their missing limbs to the maimed—a miracle still so far unattempted—and yet, to your great astonishment, my faith will remain unshaken by these things. Do you really want me to become your proselyte? Then lay all these conjuring tricks aside, and let us reason. I have more faith in my judgment than I have in my eyes.

If the religion you proclaim is true, then its truth can be proved by evidence and demonstrated by invincible arguments. Find those arguments. Why bother me with prodigies, when all you need to bring me to my knees is one good syllogism? Do you mean to tell me that it is easier for you to cure a cripple than to enlighten me?

Additions to the *Philosophic Thoughts*

[1762]

XV

If there are a hundred thousand souls damned for every one that is saved, then the Devil still has the advantage, without having given up his only son to death.

Mortals, worship God, love your brothers, and make yourselves useful to your country.

There was a man who had been betrayed by his children, his wife, and his friends; faithless business associates had sapped his fortune and plunged him into poverty. Filled with hatred and profound contempt for mankind, he took his leave of the world and sought solitary refuge in a cave. Once there, grinding his fists into his eyes and meditating a vengeance proportionate to his resentment, he cried, "Oh, scoundrels! What shall I do to punish them for their injustice and make them as unhappy as they deserve to be? Oh! If it were only possible to imagine . . . to fill their heads with some vast fantasy that would become more important to them than their very lives and about which they would find it impossible ever to agree! . . ." Upon the instant, he rushed out from the cave, crying, "God! God!" Innumerable echoes took up his words on every side. "God! God!" This terrifying name was carried from one pole to the other and heard in all parts of the globe with consternation. At first, men threw themselves upon the ground in fear; then they rose to their feet, questioned one another, fell to arguing, grew bitter, began to curse one another, hate one another, cut one another's throats—and the deadly wish of our misanthropist had been fulfilled. For such has been in the past, and such will be in the future, the history of a being fated to be forever important and incomprehensible in equal degree.

XVII

Take away a Christian's fear of hell and you also take away his faith.

LVII

Hearing a theologian exaggerate the actions of a man whom God has made a whoremonger and who has slept with his neighbor's wife (whom God made not only pretty but obliging), you might be excused for thinking that the end of the world was upon us. Oh, my friend, listen to Marcus Aurelius, and he will tell you that you are invoking your God's anger for nothing but the pleasurable and illicit friction of two membranes.

The Indiscreet Jewels

[1748]

Published in 1748, Les Bijoux indiscrets *belongs to the tradition of licentious novels, which were one aspect of the revolt against Christian morality and, in some extreme cases, against culture itself. Diderot's novel, however, is interlaced with chapters bearing the mark of his persistent inquiry into philosophical and literary questions. The "novel" part of the book is stereotyped and tedious. (See A-T, Vol. 4.)*

The Indiscreet Jewels

CHAPTER XXXVIII

Conversation About Literature

". . . What a difference, madame," Ricaric interrupted, "between an author such as Tuxigraphe, who was brought up on a diet of the Ancients, and most of our modern writers."[1]

"But these Moderns you are criticizing so high-handedly are not as despicable as you claim they are," Selim put in. "Do you mean to say that you have never found genius, inventiveness, spirit, detail, characterization, or telling speeches in their works? And in any case, what do I care for rules as long as a work gives me pleasure? It is certainly not the observations of the wise

[1] The discussion refers to the famous "Quarrel Between the Ancients and the Moderns." The "Saracens" are, of course, the French.

Almudir or the learned Abaldek, nor the Poetics of the erudite Facardin, which I have never read, that make me admire the plays of Aboulcazem or Mubardar or Albaboukre or any of those by a great many other Saracens! What other rule is there but the imitation of nature? And don't we observe her with the same eyes as the writers who have studied her?"

"Nature shows us different aspects of herself at different times," Ricaric replied. "All of them are true, but not all of them are equally beautiful. It is in the works of the past, which appear to hold a very low place in your esteem, that we should learn how to choose between these different aspects. Such works are compendia of those writers' experiences and of their predecessors' experiences too. However clever we may be, we can only perceive things successively; and one man, in the short space of life allotted to him, cannot hope to see all the things that have been discovered in previous centuries. Otherwise, you would be forced to argue that a whole science might be conceived, developed, and perfected all in the mind of one man, and that would be contrary to experience."

"Monsieur Ricaric," Selim replied, "your argument leads us toward only one possible conclusion: that the Moderns, since they enjoy possession of all the treasures that have been amassed until their time, must be richer than the Ancients; or, if this comparison displeases you, that the Moderns, having climbed up onto the shoulders of their giant predecessors, must be able to see farther than the latter could. And, indeed, what are their physics, their astronomy, their navigation, their mechanics, their mathematics when compared to ours? Why, then, should our eloquence and our poetry not be superior to theirs also?"

"Selim," the Sultana replied, "one day Ricaric shall deduce the causes of this difference for you. He shall tell you for what reasons our tragedies are inferior to those of the Ancients. And I, for my part, will gladly undertake to demonstrate for you that such is in fact the case. I won't accuse you of not having read the Ancients," she went on. "Your mind is too cultivated for you to have remained unacquainted with their theater. Now, if you will set aside certain ideas you have about their customs, their way of life, and their religion—which shock you only because the circumstances of our lives are different from theirs—you must admit that their subjects are noble, well chosen, and interesting; that the action always develops as though of itself; that their dialogue is simple and extremely close to nature; that their denouements are not contrived; that the interest is never divided; and that the action is never weighed down with superfluous episodes. . . ."

"By the head of Brahma," the Sultan exclaimed with a yawn, "Madame has given us an academic dissertation."

"I don't at all understand the rules," the favorite continued, "and still less the learned language in which they have been formulated; but I do know that only what is true can please or move us. I also know that the perfection of a play consists in imitating an action so exactly that the spectator, being constantly deceived, imagines that he is watching the action itself. Now, is there anything at all like that in the tragedies you are crying up to us?

"Do you admire their plots? They are usually so complicated that if so many things were really to happen in so short a space of time, it would be nothing less than a miracle. The ruin or the preservation of an empire, the marriage of a princess, the destruction of a prince—all these things sometimes happen in the twinkling of an eye. If there is a conspiracy afoot, then it is sketched out in the first act, strengthened and sworn to in the second, and in the third, every precaution has already been taken, all the obstacles overcome, and each conspirator is ready to perform his task—upon which there instantly follows a rebellion, a fight of some kind, perhaps even a set battle. Can you call that a plot? Can you really find such things interesting, exciting, credible? I hope not, for I could never forgive you for it, you who know how difficult it can be to bring even the most contemptible little intrigue to a successful conclusion and how time-consuming even the smallest political matter can be in the way of overtures, discussions, and deliberations." . . .

"But you will not deny, madame," Selim replied, "that if the incidents they depict destroy our sense of illusion, at least the Moderns restore that illusion with their dialogue. No one understands dialogue better than the writers of today, it seems to me."

"Then no one understands anything about it all," Mirzoza broke in. "The bombast, the wit, and the pinchbeck glitter that characterize the style of the Moderns are a thousand miles from nature. It is in vain that the author tries to conceal himself; my eyes pierce through the facade, and I am constantly aware of him behind his characters. Cinna, Sertorius, Maxime, and Émilie are never anything but mouthpieces for Corneille. That is not how people talked in the works of our Ancient Saracens. . . ."

"After what Madame has just said about the action and the dialogue in our modern plays, it is unlikely," Selim said, "that she is going to spare their denouements."

"I certainly shall not," the favorite continued, "for there are a hundred bad ones for every good one. When they are not completely unprepared, they are usually nothing short of miracles. You find authors suddenly embarrassed by a character they have been dragging from scene to scene for five acts, and all they can do is dispatch him with a dagger thrust; whereupon everyone begins to weep, and I, for my part, start to laugh hysterically. And, then, has anyone ever talked the way their characters declaim? Do kings and princes walk any differently from any man who walks well? Have they ever gesticulated like madmen or creatures possessed? Do princesses hiss when they talk? It is generally supposed that we have brought tragedy to a high degree of perfection, but I consider it as more or less proven that of all the literary genres the Africans have practiced in recent times, tragedy is the most imperfect." . . .

"I do admit," Selim replied, "that your argument carries a great deal of weight, but would it not be possible to object that we go to the theater already fully aware that it is the imitation of an event we are going to see and not the event itself?"

"But," Mirzoza continued, "is that awareness any reason for not representing the event in the most natural possible way?"

"Which is to say, madame," Mangogul broke in, "that you are in the vanguard of the anti-Moderns party." . . .

Letter on the Blind
For the Use of Those Who See

[1749]

The Lettre sur les aveugles, à l'usage de ceux qui voient *appeared in 1749 and resulted in Diderot's imprisonment in a dungeon of Vincennes. The work is divided into three parts: investigation of the psychology of the blind and of the effect of the absence of one sense on metaphysical and moral ideas; the blind man's reactions to the teleological proof of God and his concept of a self-creative universe; a discussion of the Molyneux problem, dealing with the origin and formation of ideas. In this, his first mature work, Diderot finally discards the deism to which he had been precariously clinging. (See A-T, Vol. 1.)*

Letter on the Blind, For the Use of Those Who See

. . . THE external signs of power that have such a strong effect upon us make no impression at all on the blind. Our blind man appeared before the magistrate as though he were no different from any other fellow man. Nor could he be intimidated by threats. "What will you do to me?" he asked M. Hérault. "I shall throw you into a black dungeon," the magistrate replied. "Ah, monsieur," the blind man answered, "I've been in one for twenty-five years already." What an answer, madame! And what a text, too, for one who likes to moralize as much as I! We say farewell to life as though we were leaving a delightful spectacle; the blind man takes his leave as though from a dark cell; and though we have more pleasure in life than he, you must admit that he has much less regret at the thought of death.

The blind man of Puiseaux judges his proximity to a fire by the intensity of the heat, the fullness of a vessel by the sound of the liquid he pours into it, and the nearness of bodies by the movements of the air against his face. He is so sensitive to the least changes in atmosphere that he can tell a street from a dead end. He has a marvelous ability for judging the weights of solid bodies and the capacity of vessels; he has made his arms and fingers into scales and compasses of such accuracy that on any occasion when the laws of statics are in question, I would always put my money on our blind man, even if he were pitted against twenty people who could see. He can distinguish scarcely fewer nuances in the texture of bodies than in the sound of voices, and there is no reason to fear that he would ever mistake his wife for another woman, unless it were to his own advantage. Though it is extremely likely that women would be held in common if there were a whole race of blind people or else that their laws against adultery would be extremely harsh. For wives would find it so easy to deceive their husbands by making prearranged signals to their lovers.

He judges beauty by his sense of touch—which is understandable. But what is less easy to grasp is that diction and voice tone also enter into this judgment. . . . He can also judge duration of time much more accurately than we, by the succession of his actions and thoughts. The qualities he esteems most highly in others are beauty of skin, firmness of flesh, plumpness, pleasingness of shape, sweetness of breath, and the charms of voice and diction. . . .

"I am perfectly well aware that you are not blind, gentlemen," he said to us. "And you are surprised at the things I can do. But why are you not astonished as well by the fact that I can speak?" I think there is more of philosophy in this remark than he himself intended. The ease with which we learn to speak is quite surprising. There are many terms incapable of representation by perceptible objects and which have no body, as it were, so that we succeed in attaching ideas to them only by a succession of deep and delicate combinations of the analogies we perceive between the nonperceptible objects themselves and the ideas they arouse in us. It must therefore be admitted that a person born blind must experience greater difficulty in learning to speak than sighted people, because the number of nonperceptible objects is always larger for him, and he must consequently have a smaller field of opportunity for comparison and combination. How, for example, can the words "facial expression" be expected to become fixed in his memory? It is a kind of pleasurable percept that consists of objects so difficult of apprehension by a blind man that, because they are not easily perceived even by ourselves, who are able to see, we should be quite embarrassed by the task of explaining exactly what "facial expression" is. Since it resides principally in the eyes, the sense of touch is of no help. And, besides, what can it convey to a blind man if we talk about "dull eyes," "lively eyes," "eyes sparkling with wit," etc.?

From this I conclude that we certainly draw considerable benefits from the cooperation of our senses and our sense organs. It would be yet another matter still if we were to use them separately or if we never used two on occasions when the aid of one would suffice. To add touch to sight when our eyes are adequate is to add a trace horse, pulling in a different direction, to two horses that are already quite lively enough.

Since I have never doubted that the state of our organs and of our senses has a great influence on our metaphysics and our ethics and that our most purely intellectual ideas, if I may express it thus, are very much dependent on the structure of our body, I began to question the blind man about his attitude toward the vices and virtues. I perceived, first of all, that he had a prodigious aversion to theft. This aversion sprang from two causes: firstly, the ease with which people could steal from him without his knowing it and then, even more perhaps, the ease with which he could be apprehended if he himself were to steal. And this second cause does not spring from any lack of awareness on his part of how to guard against the additional sense that he knows we have or from ignorance of how to cover up a theft. He places little value upon modesty, and were it not that clothing protects him from the potentially injurious elements, he would scarcely comprehend its use at all. He admits frankly that he cannot grasp why we should cover up one part of the body rather than another and even less what strange caprice in us gives priority among those that are covered to certain parts whose functions, and the discomforts to which they are subject, would seem to require that they be left exposed. Although we live in an age that has been freed of a great many prejudices by the spirit of enlightenment, I do not think we shall ever reach the point of ignoring the claims of modesty quite so completely as this blind man of mine. To him, Diogenes would not have been a philosopher at all.

Since the blind are affected by none of the external demonstrations that awaken pity and ideas of grief in ourselves, with the sole exception of vocal complaints, I suspect them of being, in general, unfeeling toward their fellow men. What difference is there to a blind person between a man urinating and a man bleeding to death without speaking? Do we ourselves not cease to feel compassion when distance or the smallness of the object produces the same effect on us as lack of sight does on the blind? Thus do all our virtues depend on our way of apprehending things and on the degree to which external objects affect us! I feel quite sure that were it not for fear of punishment, many people would have fewer qualms at killing a man who was far enough away to appear no larger than a swallow than in butchering a steer with their own hands. And if we feel compassion for a horse in pain though we can crush an ant without a second thought, are these actions not governed by the selfsame principle? Ah, madame! How different is the morality of the blind from ours! And how different again would a deaf man's be from a blind man's; and how imperfect—to put the matter kindly—would our own system of morality appear to a being who had one more sense than we ourselves!

Nor do our metaphysics tally with theirs any better. Think how many of the principles they hold are sheer absurdities to us—and vice versa! I could furnish you with certain details on this point that I am sure you would find very entertaining, but the sort of people who are ready to see criminal intentions everywhere would certainly condemn me as irreligious if I did so—as though it were in my power to make the blind perceive things otherwise than they do. I shall limit myself to a single observation, and one with which everybody, I think, must agree—namely, that the great argument we are accustomed to derive from the marvels of nature is a very weak one for the blind. The ease with which we can create new objects, as it were, with the aid of a little mirror is something even more incomprehensible to them than the stars above, which they have been doomed never to see. That vast and luminous globe advancing from east to west across the sky is a matter of less astonishment to them than a tiny fire that they themselves are able to augment or diminish at will: since they perceive matter in a more abstract way than we, they also find it less difficult to believe that it is endowed with thought.

If a man who had possessed the gift of sight for only one or two days were to find himself among a people who were blind, he would either have to make up his mind to remain silent or else resign himself to being taken for a madman. Every day he would reveal some new mystery to them, a mystery that would be such only to them and that the skeptics would congratulate themselves on not believing. Such an incredulity, so stubborn, apparently so just in many ways, and yet so unfounded, could surely be turned to good use by the defenders of religion as an example. If you will allow yourself to imagine this situation I have described for a moment, it will recall to you, in another form, the fate and the persecutions of those who were unfortunate enough to stumble across the truth in an age of darkness and who were then imprudent enough to reveal that truth to their blind contemporaries, among whom they had no crueler enemies than those people whom one would have expected at first glance, because of their rank and education, to have found it least difficult to understand their feelings. . . .

There is a kind of abstraction of which so few men are capable that it seems to have been reserved for pure intellects alone; I mean that kind of abstraction by which everything is reducible to numerical units. It must be admitted that the results of such a geometry would be extremely accurate and its findings very generally applicable; for there are no objects, whether in nature itself or in the realm of the possible, that these simple units would not be able to represent: points, lines, surfaces, solids, thought, ideas, sensations. . . . And if this was in fact the fundamental intent of Pythagoras' doctrine, as it may perchance have been, then one may say of him that he failed in his project because this way of reasoning is too far above us and too close to the methods of the Supreme Being, who, according to the apt and ingenious expression of one English geometrician, is "geometrizing" perpetually, throughout the universe.

A pure and simple unity is too vague and general a symbol for us. Our senses lead us back perpetually to signs more suited to the limited scope of our minds and the conformation of our organs. We have even succeeded in making these signs common among us and in making them serve, so to speak, as a storage depot that permits us to trade ideas with one another. We have established some for the eyes—letters and figures—and some for the ears—articulated sounds—but we have none for the sense of touch, even though this sense, too, has its own particular method of speaking and of eliciting responses. In default of such a language, all communication between ourselves and those who are born deaf, blind, and dumb is broken. They grow physically, but they remain in a state of imbecility. Perhaps they would acquire ideas if we could make ourselves understood to them while they were still children, in some fixed, determinate, and consistently uniform way; in a word, if we were to trace the same letters on their hands that we ourselves draw on paper and if the same meaning were invariably attached to them. . . .

When he[1] was about to die, an extremely able minister of religion, the Reverend Gervaise Holmes, was summoned to his bedside. They conversed together about the existence of God, and I shall translate for you here the few fragments of their

[1] The blind English mathematician Nicholas Saunderson. The anecdote related here was invented by Diderot himself and caused considerable resentment in the Royal Academy.

conversation that have come down to us, for they are certainly worthy of our attention. The minister began by using the marvels of nature as an argument for God's existence.

"Oh, sir," the blind philosopher replied, "let us not talk of that great and beautiful spectacle which was never made for me! I was condemned to pass my life in darkness, and you are citing such marvels to me as I can never understand. For these things are proofs only to those who can see, like you. If you desire me to believe in God, then you must make me touch and feel him."

"Sir," the minister adroitly continued, "place your hands upon your own body and there you will sense the divinity that resides in the admirable mechanism of your own organs."

"Mr. Holmes," Saunderson replied, "I tell you again, nothing of all that can be as beautiful to me as it is to you. And even if the physical mechanism of animals is as perfect as you claim—and I am certainly willing to believe it is, for you are an honest man and incapable of any attempt to deceive me—what has that to do with a sovereignly intelligent being? If it is a matter of astonishment for you, then that may possibly be because you are in the habit of treating everything that is beyond your comprehension as a miracle. I myself have been an object of wonder to you so often that my opinion of what surprises you is inevitably a low one. People have been drawn to see me from all over England merely because they could not conceive how I was able to do geometry; you must admit that those people did not have very exact notions as to what is or is not possible. We encounter some phenomenon that is, in our opinion, beyond the powers of man, and immediately we say, 'It is the work of God.' Our vanity will admit no lesser explanation. Can we not reason with a little less pride and a little more philosophy? If nature presents us with a knot that is difficult to untie, then let us leave it as it is; let us not insist on cutting it there and then and on employing for the task the hand of a being who thereupon becomes a knot even more difficult to untie than the first. Ask an Indian why the globe remains suspended in the air and he will reply that it is borne on the back of an elephant. And on what does the elephant rest? On a tortoise. And the tortoise, who supports that? . . . This Indian fills you with pity, and yet one might answer, to you as to him: Mr. Holmes, my friend, confess your ignorance right away, and spare me the elephant and the tortoise."

Saunderson broke off for a moment; he seemed to be waiting for the minister to reply. But what method of attack could he use to convince a blind man? Mr. Holmes took advantage of the good opinion Saunderson had conceived of his own honesty and of the learning of Newton, Leibniz, Clarke,[2] and some others among his compatriots—the leading geniuses of the world, all of whom had been deeply impressed by the wonders of nature and recognized that they had been created by an intelligent being. This was, beyond a doubt, the strongest argument that the minister could present to Saunderson. And, indeed, the good blind man did admit that there would be some temerity in denying what a man such as Newton had not disdained to accept. Nevertheless, he went on to point out to the minister that Newton's evidence in this matter was not as strong for him, being blind, as that of nature in its entirety had been for Newton; and that whereas Newton's belief was based on the Word of God, he himself was reduced to taking the word of Newton.

"Just think, Mr. Holmes," he added, "to what extent I am forced to place my trust in your word and in Newton's. I cannot see anything, yet I am admitting that there is a wonderful order in the universe, though I hope that you will require no more of me. I am yielding to you on the present state of the universe so that you will permit me, in return, to think as I please about its former and first state, in regard to which you are no less blind than I. It is a matter in which you can produce no witnesses against me and in which your eyes are of no use to you whatever. You may imagine, then, if you wish, that the order you find so impressive has always existed. But please allow me to believe that such is not the case; that if we went back to the origin of things and time, if we were to sense matter as it first began to move and perceive chaos start to take some shape, then we should discover a whole multitude of monstrous, un-

[2] Samuel Clarke (1675–1729), English philosopher and theologian, author of a *Demonstration of the Existence and Attributes of God.*

formed shapes for every properly organized one. For though I cannot argue with you about the present state of things, I may at least question your beliefs on their former state. I may ask you, for example, who it was that told you or Leibniz or Clarke or Newton that during the short time when animals were first formed, some were not without a head and others without feet? I am in a position to maintain that some had no stomachs and others no intestines; that certain others, to whom the possession of a stomach, a palate, and a set of teeth seemed to promise longer life, ceased to exist because of some defect in the heart or lungs; that such monsters all died out, one after the other; that all the defective combinations created by matter have now disappeared and that only those have remained whose physical equipment included no important contradiction and who were therefore able to subsist unaided and perpetuate themselves.

"If we suppose all this, then if the first man had been born with a blocked larynx or had lacked suitable food or had possessed defective organs of generation or had not encountered a female or had combined with another species, then what, Mr. Holmes, would have become of the human race? It would have been included in the general purging of the universe; and this proud creature who calls himself man, dissolved and dispersed among the molecules of all matter, would have remained, perhaps forever, among the number of the possibles.

"If no ill-formed creatures had ever existed, then you would not fail to claim that there never will be any and that I am indulging in fantastic hypotheses; but the order of things is not so perfect," Saunderson went on, "that monstrous beings are not still produced from time to time." Then, turning his face to the minister, he added, "Look well at me, Mr. Holmes. I have no eyes. What did we do to God, you and I, that one of us should possess those organs and the other be deprived of them?"

Saunderson's air as he uttered these words was so sincere and so intense that the minister and the rest of the people present could not help but share his grief, and they began to weep bitterly over his fate. The blind man sensed this. "Mr. Holmes," he said, "the kindness of your heart was well known to me before, and I am very sensible of the proofs you are giving me of your goodness in these my last moments; but if I am dear to you, do not begrudge me upon my deathbed the consolation of never having been a cause of grief to anyone."

Then, in a firmer voice, he added, "I conjecture, then, that in the beginning, when fermenting matter was hatching out the universe, men such as myself were quite common. And why should I not assert what I believe about animals to be true of worlds also? How many maimed and botched worlds have melted away, re-formed themselves, and are perhaps dispersing again at any given moment, far away in space, where I cannot touch them and you cannot see them, but where motion still goes on, and will always go on, combining conglomerations of matter until they have attained a state of organization that will permit them to endure? Oh, philosophers, transport yourselves with me to the borders of the universe, beyond the point where I can still touch or you can still see organized entities; wander across the face of this new ocean and seek amidst its uncoordinated motions for some vestiges of that intelligent being whose wisdom you so much admire here on earth!

"But what need is there of taking you out of your own element? What is this world, Mr. Holmes? A composite entity subject to revolutions, all of which display a continuous tendency toward destruction; a rapid succession of beings that follow one another, thrust one another aside, then disappear; a passing symmetry; a momentary order. A short while ago, I was blaming you for judging the perfection of things according to the measure of your own abilities; I could accuse you now of measuring their duration according to the measure of your own lives. You are judging the discontinuous existence of the world as the ephemeral mayfly judges ours. The world is eternal for you in just the same way as you are eternal for the being that lives only an instant. Yet even so, the insect is more reasonable than you. Think of the tremendous succession of mayflies, generation after generation, that attests to your eternity! What an immense tradition! Yet we shall all pass away one day, and without any possibility of measuring either the real space that we once occupied or the exact time that we have lived. Time, space, and matter are perhaps only a point."

Saunderson grew somewhat more agitated during this discussion than his condition would permit of. He was overcome by an attack of delirium that lasted for several hours and from which he emerged at last only to cry, "*O God of Clarke and Newton, pity me now!*" and to die.

Such was Saunderson's end.

Those who have argued that a person born blind would be able to distinguish between a cube and a sphere have begun by supposing a fact that should perhaps have been questioned—namely, that a person blind from birth whose cataracts were removed would be in a condition to use his eyes immediately the operation was over. They have said only, "Upon comparing the ideas of a sphere and a cube that he has received from his sense of touch with those he obtains of them from his sight, a person blind from birth will necessarily recognize that they are the same; and it would be extremely odd in him to declare that it is the cube, when he sees it, that gives him the idea of a sphere and that he formerly received the idea of a cube from the sphere. He will therefore term 'sphere' and 'cube,' when he sees them, the same objects that he termed 'sphere' and 'cube' when he knew them only by touch."

But what arguments did their opponents use in reply to this? They too supposed that the person blind from birth would be capable of sight as soon as his organs were healthy; they imagined that it would be exactly the same with an eye freed from its cataract as with an arm that has ceased to be paralytic: the latter, they said, needs no exercise in order to feel, consequently the former can need no exercise in order to see. And they added, "Let us grant the blind man a little more capacity for thought than you do, and after carrying the argument to the point at which you left it, he will go on to say, 'Yes, but what assurance do I have that when I approach these bodies and place my hands on them, they will not suddenly belie my expectations—that the cube will not give me the sensation of a sphere and the sphere that of a cube? Only experience can teach me whether there exists a conformity of relations between sight and touch.

These two senses could be contradictory in their relation to things without my knowing. Perhaps I might even believe that what now presents itself to my sight is merely an appearance, unless I had already been informed that these are indeed the same two bodies that I had touched before.' " . . .

Such, madame, in brief, are the arguments that have been employed on both sides of this question. And as I proceed with my own analysis of them, you will soon perceive how far those who claimed that a man blind from birth would indeed be able to see shapes and distinguish between bodies were from realizing why they were right and how many good reasons those of the opposite persuasion had for thinking that they could not be wrong.

The question of the man born blind, considered somewhat more generally than Molyneux[3] set it out for us, comprises two others that we shall consider separately. We may ask: (1) whether the blind man will be able to see directly after the operation; (2) in the event that he should be able to see, whether he will be able to see sufficiently to discern shapes; whether he will be in a condition to apply to them with certainty, when he looks at them, the same names he gave to them when he touched them; and whether there will be proof available to him that those are in fact the correct names.

Will the man born blind be able to see immediately after his eyes have been operated upon? Those who claim that he will not be able to do so say, "As soon as the person blind from birth is in possession of the ability to use his eyes, the whole scene within the range of those organs will immediately be depicted at the back of them. This picture, composed of an infinity of objects collected together into an extremely small space, will appear to him as nothing but a confused conglomeration of shapes that he will be in no condition to distinguish one from another. Almost everyone agrees that only experience can teach him to judge the distance of objects and that he must even go over to them, touch them, move back from them, approach them again, and touch them again before he can so much as be certain

[3] William Molyneux (1656–1698), philosopher, astronomer, friend of Locke, and author of *Dioptrica nova.*

that they are not a part of himself, that they are in fact foreign to his own being, and that he can sometimes be near to them and sometimes farther away. Why, then, should experience not also be necessary in order for him to perceive them at all?

"When objects move away from a man without experience who is perceiving objects for the first time or when he moves away from them so that they are beyond his range of vision, he ought to suppose that they have ceased to exist; for it is only the experience we have of permanent objects, the fact that we can return and find them still in the place where we left them, that makes us aware of their continued existence while we are not there. Perhaps this is why children are so quickly consoled for the loss of toys that are taken away from them. We cannot say that they forget them quickly; for if we consider that there are children of two and a half who already know a considerable portion of the words in a given language and that it is more difficult for them to pronounce those words than to remember them, we cannot fail to be convinced that childhood is the age of memory par excellence. Would it not therefore be more natural to suppose that children imagine that what they no longer see no longer exists? Especially since their joy always appears to be mingled with wonder when the objects they have lost suddenly reappear? Their nurses help them to acquire the notion that absent beings can still continue to exist, by exercising their imaginations with a little game that consists simply in covering up one's face and then suddenly showing it again. In this way, they are able to experience a hundred times in a quarter of an hour the fact that what is no longer visible has not ceased to exist. From which it follows that we owe the notion of the continuous existence of objects to experience; that we acquire the notion of distance by touch; that the eye may possibly have to learn how to see, just as the tongue learns how to talk; that it would not be astonishing if the aid of one sense was necessary to another; and that touch, which proves the existence of external objects to us when they are before our eyes, may also be the sense whose role it is to make us aware not only of their shapes and other modifications but even of their presence itself."

In addition to these arguments, there are also the famous

experiments made by Cheselden.[4] The young man whose cataracts were removed by this gifted surgeon was for a long while unable to distinguish either size, distance, position, or even shape. An object an inch high placed in front of his eyes so as to cut off his view of a house appeared to him as large as the house. . . .

We are compelled to admit, therefore, that we must perceive an infinity of things in the objects we look at that neither a child nor a person blind from birth can perceive, even though their eyes are receiving identical images; that it is not enough for objects to strike us, but that we must also concentrate our attention on the impressions they leave; that consequently no one sees anything the first time he uses his eyes; that the only effect produced by the first few instants of sight is a multitude of confused sensations; that these are clarified only with the passage of time and by habitual reflection on what takes place within us; that experience alone can teach us to compare the sensations we receive with the objects that give rise to them; and that since sensations contain no essential resemblance to objects, we can become acquainted with the analogies between them only by a process of learning, a process in which experience can be our only teacher. . . .

I am nevertheless far from thinking that the eye is unable to teach itself or, if I may so express it, to experiment with itself. . . . It is not difficult to conceive how the use of one of the senses may be perfected and accelerated by the observations of another, but it is completely inconceivable that there should be an essential interdependence of their two functions. It is certainly true that there are qualities in bodies that we could not perceive in them without the sense of touch: it is touch that alerts us to the presence of certain modifications that remain imperceptible to the eyes until they have been informed of them by our sense of touch; but these services are reciprocal, and in those people whose sight is keener than their sense of touch, it is the former that informs the latter of the existence of objects and modifications that might escape it because of their smallness. . . .

[4] William Cheselden (1688–1752), noted surgeon, who removed the cataracts from a boy who had been born blind, and author of a widely used book on anatomy.

Here, then, is my own opinion on the two preceding questions. I think that the first time the eyes of a person blind from birth are opened to the light of day, he will perceive nothing whatever; that his eyes will need some time to acquire experience, but that they will eventually acquire this experience by themselves, without the help of touch, and that they will succeed not only in distinguishing colors but in discerning at least the approximate limits of objects. Now let us consider, supposing that he acquires this aptitude in a very short time or that he achieves it by attempting to use his eyes in the darkened room, where, after urging him on to such exercises, we should have taken care to enclose him for some time after the operation and before the experiments—let us consider, I repeat, whether he will recognize with his eyes the bodies we have given him to touch and whether he will be able to assign their proper names to them. This is the last question that remains for me to solve.

In order to acquit myself of the task in a manner that will please you, for I know you like to be methodical, I shall first make distinctions between the several kinds of people on whom the experiments might be carried out. If they are from the lower classes, without education or culture, and unprepared, I hold that when the cataract operation has completely eliminated the defect from their organs and the eyes are healthy, objects will be represented in them quite distinctly; but that these persons, being unused to any kind of reasoning, having no notion of what a sensation or an idea is, possessing no means of comparing the images they have received from their sense of touch with those that are now coming to them through their eyes, will say, "That is a circle, that is a square," without there being any reliable basis for their judgment; or they may even admit quite candidly that, apart from their position, they can perceive nothing in the objects now presented to their view that in any way resembles the ones they have already touched.

There are other people who will compare the shapes they now see the bodies to possess with the shapes they felt previously with their hands, project their touch mentally onto the bodies over the intervening space, and then say of one that it is a square and of the other that it is a circle, but without really knowing why—the comparison of the ideas they received from their sense of touch with those they are receiving from their eyes being insufficiently distinct in their minds to convince them of the truth of their judgment.

I shall now pass, madame, without digression, to the outcome of such an experiment made upon a metaphysician. I have no doubt whatever that from the very first moment he began to see objects distinctly, he would begin to apply his reason to them as though he had been seeing them all his life; and that after comparing the ideas now impinging on him through his eyes with those he has already acquired by touch, he would say, with the same assurance as you or I, "I am extremely tempted to believe that this is the body I have always referred to as a circle and that this other is the one I have always called a square; but I shall be extremely careful not to say that such is in fact the case. How do I know for certain that if I went over to them they would not vanish as I attempted to touch them? How do I know whether the objects of my sight are also destined to be the objects of my sense of touch? I am ignorant whether what is visible is also tangible; and even if I were not in this uncertainty, even if I took the word of the people around me that what I now see is indeed what I formerly touched, that would still not be of very much help. Those objects could very well transform themselves in my hands and provide sensations to my sense of touch quite different from those I am experiencing through my eyes. Gentlemen," he would add, "this body seems to me to be the square, and that one the circle; but I have no certain knowledge that they are the same to the touch as to sight."

If we substitute a geometrician for the metaphysician, Saunderson for Locke, he too will say that of the two shapes he can now see, the one, if he is to believe his eyes, is the one he used to call a square, and the other is the one he used to call a circle. "For I perceive," he would add, "that it is only in the first that I could arrange the threads and position the large-headed pins that marked the four corner points of the square and that it is only on the second that I could inscribe or circumscribe the threads I was once obliged to use when demonstrating the properties of the circle. That, therefore, is a circle! And that a square! But," he would have continued, with Locke, "it is possible that when I apply my hands to these shapes they will each be transformed into the other, so that the same figure might serve me to demonstrate the properties of the circle to the blind and the properties of the square to those who can see. Perhaps I should see a square and at the same time feel a circle. No," he would have continued, "I am mistaken there. Those to whom I demonstrated the properties of the circle and the square did not have their hands on my abacus, nor did they touch the stretched threads that I employed to delimit my figures, and yet they understood me. Therefore they were not seeing a square when I felt a circle; for if they had, we should never have understood one another. I should have been giving them the outline of one figure while demonstrating the properties of another; I should have been presenting them with a straight line and calling it an arc, then with an arc and calling it a straight line. But since everyone did in fact understand me, all men see alike; from which it follows that I now see as a square what they saw as a square then, and as a circle what they too saw as a circle. Therefore, this is what I have always termed a square, and that is what I have always termed a circle."

. . . However, I do not think that the outcome would be the same with other, more composite objects. It seems reasonable to believe that M. de Réaumur's[5] blind woman could in fact distinguish between the various colors, but I should lay thirty to one that her choice between the sphere and the cube was a random one; and I am quite certain that without some sort of divine revelation, she could never have recognized her gloves, her dressing gown, or her shoe.

[5] René-Antoine de Réaumur (1683–1757), French naturalist and physicist, had observed the reactions of a blind woman whose cataracts had been removed.

Letter on the Deaf and Dumb For the Use of Those Who Hear and Speak

[1 7 5 1]

The Lettre sur les sourds et muets, à l'usage de ceux qui entendent et qui parlent *was published in 1751. It has little relation to the earlier* Letter on the Blind, *except for Diderot's continuing interest in questions of psychology. It is concerned with aesthetic experience, rhetoric, and the role of language in thought and in the function of ideas. (See A-T, Vol. 1.)*

Letter on the Deaf and Dumb, For the Use of Those Who Hear and Speak

. . . AFTER such a successful effort of perception, you will agree that a deaf-mute would be justified in feeling fairly pleased with himself; but mine did not stop there: suddenly, in a flash of inspiration, it came to him that he had grasped what music and musical instruments were. He thought that music was a special means of communicating thoughts and that the instruments, the hurdy-gurdies, the violins, and trumpets, became, in our hands, additional organs of speech. Precisely what one would expect, you will say, from a man who had never heard the sound of instruments or music. But I would ask you to consider that the construction he placed upon the available facts, though it is obviously false to you, is almost the only logical conclusion for a deaf-mute. When he reflects on the degree of attention we pay to music and to those who play on musical instruments, the signs of joy or sadness apparent on our faces and in our gestures when we are moved by a beautiful harmony, and when he compares these effects with those produced by speech and other external objects, how can he help but suppose that there is some sense in those sounds, whatever it may be, and that both voices and instruments are awakening some distinctly intelligible perception in us?

And do you not find, sir, that this piece of deduction is a faithful likeness of our own thoughts, our own way of reasoning, our own logical processes, or, in a word, of those concepts that have made the reputations of so many philosophers? Every time these latter have ventured a judgment upon things that, if they were to be properly understood, seemed to require the aid of an organ they did not have—a frequent occurrence, I might add—they have shown less wisdom and ended up further from the truth than the deaf-mute I am talking about at the moment; for, after all, though we may not speak so intelligibly through a musical instrument as we do with our mouths and though musical sounds do not reproduce thought as faithfully as speech, nevertheless they are saying something. . . .

If I were dealing with someone who had not yet acquired a facility with abstract ideas, I should lay great stress upon this theory of human understanding, and I should say to him: Sir, think of man as an automaton, as a sort of walking clock; let the heart represent its mainspring, and the other organs inside his chest the other principal pieces of the movement. Imagine in his head a bell furnished with little hammers and from these hammers an infinite multitude of threads stretching out in every direction and terminating at points all over the case. Then place on top of this bell one of those little figures we use to ornament the tops of our clocks, and let it have its head bent a little to one side, like a musician listening to hear whether his instrument is properly tuned or no: that little figure will be the *soul.* If several of the little threads are pulled at the same instant, the bell will be struck by several hammers, and the little figure will hear several sounds at once. Now, suppose that among all these strings there are some that are being pulled continuously: just as our only proof of the noise that is made in Paris by day is the silence we are aware of at night, so there will be sensations inside us that will often elude us precisely because they are always there—such as the sensation of our existence. The soul cannot perceive its own existence except by turning in upon itself, especially when we are in good health. No part of our body reminds us of its existence when we are healthy; if one of them should do so, with a sensation of pain, then this is a certain sign that we are unwell; and even if the sensation it sends us is one of pleasure, it is not always certain that our health is any better.

It would be easy for me to extend this comparison and to add that the sounds given out by the bell do not fade immediately; that they possess duration; that they form harmonies with the sounds that follow them; that the little listening figure compares them and forms an opinion as to whether they are concords or discords; that our memory at any given moment, the power of recall that we need in order to form opinions and to express them, is represented by the vibrations of the bell, our power of judgment by the formation of concords, and our discourse by their sequence; and that it is not without good reason that we describe some people's brains as being "cracked." . . .

In examining the language provoked in different circumstances by the sensations of hunger or thirst, men were frequently made aware that identical expressions were being employed to render differing ways of looking at these phenomena; whereupon they invented the signs *you, him, me, it,* and innumerable others, which enabled them to be more specific. Because language required a certain degree of precision, the state of the soul in one indivisible instant was necessarily represented by a multiplicity of terms, and these terms split up the total impression into parts. But because these terms were spoken in sequence and were apprehended successively, as they were spoken, men were led to believe that the affects of the soul which the terms represented were also occurring in sequence. But such is by no means the case. The state of our soul is one thing, the account we give of it—whether to ourselves or to others—is another; the instantaneous totality of sensations that constitute that state is by no means the same thing as the sequential and itemized attention that we are forced to apply to it in order to analyze it, communicate it, and make ourselves understood. Our soul is a moving picture of which we are ceaselessly attempting to make a copy. We need a great deal of time if we are to render it faithfully, but the original exists in its totality at any given moment: the mind does not function step by step as our expression of it does. The brush can execute only after a considerable lapse of time what the painter's eye takes in at a single glance. The formation of language demanded itemization: but to *see* an object, to *decide* that it is beautiful, to *experience* a sensation of pleasure, and to *desire* possession of that object are all parts of a single and instantaneous state of the soul, and one that Greek and Latin express with a single word. And once that word has been spoken, everything has been said, everything is understood. Ah, sir, how much our apprehension is modified by the signs we use! And how cold a copy is even the most vivid speech of what takes place within us! . . .

I would exhort you, sir, to consider these things at length if you wish to grasp the full complexity of this question of inversions. As for myself, since I prefer to spend my time creating clouds rather than dispersing them, questioning opinions rather than forming them, I am going to prove to you, in addition, that if the paradox I have just advanced is not true, if we do not in fact apprehend more than one thing at the same time, then it is impossible for us to use our reason or to converse, for to converse or to use our reason is also to make a comparison between two or more ideas. And how is it possible to compare ideas if they are not present in the mind at the same time? You cannot deny that we are able to receive more than one sensation at the same time, such as those of color and shape when we look at an object; and I do not see why sensations should be considered more privileged than abstract and intellectual ideas.

In your opinion, does memory not presuppose the simultaneous presence of two ideas in our mind when we make a judgment: the idea we are conceiving at the moment and the recollection of an idea we have conceived in the past? For my own part, I think that this is the reason why good judgment and a good memory are rarely found together. A good memory presupposes a great facility in entertaining a great many ideas at once or in rapid succession; and this facility is an obstacle to the tranquil comparison of a small number of ideas that the mind ought to be gazing at, so to speak, with great concentration. A head crammed with a great number of unrelated objects is rather like a library made up only of odd volumes. It is like one of those Germanic compilations that bristle, in defiance of all reason and taste, with passages of Hebrew, Arabic, Greek, and Latin, that are already vast, that are continually being made vaster still, that are fated to go on growing even vaster forever, and that are all the worse for it. It is like one of those periodicals stuffed with analyses and estimates of works that analysis has entirely failed to comprehend—warehouses full of assorted goods, where only the inventory has any relevance. It is like a series of glosses in which one can, for the most part, find nothing but things one doesn't want and only very rarely what one is looking for and in which the things that one does need are almost always lying buried amid the heaps of useless things. . . .

Consequently, since the principal object of language is the communication of thought, it is my opinion that our own tongue is of all languages the most refined, the most exact, and the most estimable; the language, in short, that has retained least of those defects that I am tempted to refer to as the vestiges of primitive *stammerings*. And to continue the comparison, without partiality, I should say that by having no inversions in our language, we have gained in exactness, in clarity, and in precision—qualities essential to rational discourse—and that, by the same token, we have lost in warmth, in eloquence, and in energy. I am tempted to add that the didactic and measured gait to which our language is subjected makes it more suitable for dealing with the sciences and that because of the turns of phrase and the inversions permitted by Greek, Latin, Italian, and English, those languages have the advantage in literature; that we can express thought better than any other people, so that French would always be the choice of good sense, but that imagination and the passions will always prefer the ancient languages and those of our neighbors; that French should be spoken in society and in schools of philosophy; Greek, Latin, and English in the pulpit and on the stage; that our tongue will be the language of truth, should truth ever return to the earth, and that Greek, Latin, and the others will be the languages of fiction and lies. The French language is made to teach, to enlighten, and to convince; Greek, Latin, Italian, and English, to persuade, to move, and to deceive. Speak Greek, Latin, and Italian to the masses; but to the wise, speak French.

Another disadvantage of the languages that employ inversion is the great powers of concentration and memory that they demand of the reader or listener. Think how many cases, how many objects, how many endings there are to work out in a single Latin or Greek sentence of any length! We understand almost none of it until we reach the end. French does not tire one in this way; it is possible to understand it word by word, as it is spoken. . . .

In all speech, considered generally, we must distinguish between thought and expression; if the thought is rendered with clarity, purity, and precision, that is sufficient for everyday conversation; add to these qualities a nice choice of words, together with rhythmic and harmonious phrasing, and you have a style suitable for use in the pulpit, though you will still be a long way from poetry, especially from that kind of poetry employed in the descriptive passages of epic poems and odes. At such times there is a spirit flowing through the poet's words that gives life and emotion to every syllable. What is this spirit? I myself have sometimes felt its presence; but I know no more of it than that it is the cause whereby things can be spoken and represented simultaneously, so that the mind apprehends them, the soul is moved by them, the imagination sees them, and the ear hears them all at one and the same time; so that the language used is no longer merely a succession of linked and energetic terms expressing the poet's thought with power and nobility, but also a tissue of hieroglyphics, all woven inextricably together, that make it visible. I might say that all poetry is, in this sense, emblematic.

But an understanding of poetic emblems is not something that is granted to everyone; we must almost be capable of creating them in order to experience them deeply. The poet says:

> *Et des fleuves français les eaux ensanglantées*
> *Ne portaient que des morts aux mers épouvantées.*[1]
> Voltaire, *Henriade*, II, 357

But how many readers do in fact see those waters swollen with corpses in the first syllable of "*portaient*," or the flow of the rivers being dammed up, as it were, by the piles of bodies? How many see the massed waters and corpses collapsing, then flowing down toward the sea, on the second syllable of that same word? The terror of the seas is made visible to every reader by the word "*épouvantées*," but an emphatic pronunciation of its third syllable further reveals to me the vastness of their extent.

The poet says:

> *Soupire, étend les bras, ferme l'oeil et s'endort.*[2]
> Boileau, *Lutrin*, II, 164

Everyone exclaims, "How beautiful!" But will the reader, or that kind of reader who is given to checking the number of syllables in a line with his fingers, be aware how fortunate it is for a poet, when he has a sigh to express, that there exists in his language a word of which the first syllable is muffled, the second tenuous, and the last one mute? We read, "*étend les bras*," but we scarcely take in the way in which it was possible to represent all the length and the lassitude of those arms in one plural monosyllable; the stretched-out arms fall so softly at the end of that first hemistich that almost no one realizes it, any more than we catch the sudden drop of the eyelid in "*ferme l'oeil*" or the imperceptible passage from wakefulness to sleep in the fall of the second hemistich: "*ferme l'oeil et s'endort*."

The man of taste will certainly remark that the poet has four separate actions to depict and that his line is divided into four parts; that the last two actions are so close to each other that there is almost no interval discernible between them; that of the four parts of the line, the last two, joined by a conjunc-

[1] "And the bloody waters of the French rivers
Bore only corpses to the frightened seas."

[2] "Sighs, stretches out his arms, closes his eyes, and falls asleep."

tion and by the speed of the prosody in the penultimate part, are likewise almost indivisible; that each of these actions takes up exactly that quantity of the total duration of the line that accords with its nature; and that by including all four of them in a single line, the poet has faithfully rendered the promptness with which they do habitually follow one another. There, sir, we have one of those problems that poetic genius solves without even formulating them to itself. But is this solution within the grasp of all his readers? No, sir, indeed it is not; and I fully expect all those who failed to grasp these hieroglyphics when they first read this line for themselves (and there will be a great many of them) to laugh at my commentary . . . and call me a visionary.

I used to think, like everyone else, that one poet could be translated by another; it was an error, and I am now disabused of it. You may translate the thought; you may perhaps be so fortunate as to find the equivalent of a turn of phrase; . . . that is something, but it is not everything. The subtle emblem, the artful hieroglyphic that holds hidden sway over an entire description, that depends for its power on the distribution of long and short syllables in languages with quantitative prosody and on the distribution of vowels and consonants in the words of any language—all that necessarily disappears in even the best translation. . . .

To compare the beauties of one poet with those of another is something that has been done a thousand times. But to bring together all the beauties common to poetry, to painting, and to music; to show the analogies between them; to demonstrate how the poet, the painter, and the musician render the same image; to seize the fugitive emblems of their expressions; to determine whether there may not be some similarity between those various emblems, etc.—that is what now remains to be done and what I advise you [the Abbé Batteux[3]] to add to your *The Fine Arts Reduced to a Single Principle.* And, furthermore, do not neglect to insert at the beginning of that work a chapter on what you mean by "beautiful nature," for I know there are people who agree with me that without the second of these two things, your

[3] Charles Batteux (1713–1780), French littérateur and aesthetician, author of *Les Beaux-Arts réduits à un seul principe.*

treatise lacks a foundation; and that without the first, it has no application. Instruct them, sir, once and for all, how each art imitates nature in one and the same object; show them that it is false to say, as they do, that all nature is beautiful and that there can be no ugliness in nature except in what is misplaced. Why, they ask me, is an old, gnarled oak, one that has lost most of its branches and that I should have cut down if it were growing at my door, precisely the one that the painter would plant there if he were to paint my cottage? Is the oak beautiful, or is it ugly? Who is right, the owner of the cottage or the painter?

Natural Right (*Encyclopedia*)

[1755]

The article "Droit naturel" ("Natural Right") appeared in the fifth volume of the Encyclopedia, *which came out in 1755. Although Diderot believed in a universal natural law, his concept of that law was naturalistic—based on human structure, needs, and experience; it was not the traditional innate or God-given natural-law doctrine. This article is an attempt to defend the legitimacy of the cultural imposition of moral value against the claims of radical egoism or nihilism. One of its important ideas is that of a "general will," whose nature and function are not, however, the same as Rousseau's. "Natural Right" was written partly in reply to certain ideas in Rousseau's* Discourse on the Origin of Inequality *(1755) and perhaps to ideas in Rousseau's article "Political Economy," but Diderot may also have had La Mettrie and others in mind. (See A-T, Vol. 14.)*

Natural Right (Encyclopedia)

WE are so accustomed to using this expression that there is almost no one who is not convinced in his own mind that he understands it immediately, without any need for thought. This inner conviction is shared by the philosopher and the unthinking man alike, with this single difference: that upon hearing the question "What is right?" the latter, immediately bereft of all words and ideas, will refer you to the tribunal of conscience and remain mute; whereas the former will be reduced to silence and deeper reflection only after having turned in a vicious circle that either brings him back to the same point from which he set out or throws him into some other problem no less difficult of resolution than the one from which he had thought to free himself by his original definition.

The philosopher, when questioned, says, "Right is the foundation or prime reason of justice." But what is justice? "It is the obligation to render to each exactly what is due to him." But what is there that belongs to one rather than another in a state of things in which everything belongs to everyone and in which a distinct idea of obligation does not yet exist? And what would a man owe to others if he allowed them everything and asked nothing of them in exchange? It is at this point that the philosopher begins to feel that *natural right* is of all our moral notions both one of the most important and one of the most difficult to determine. We shall therefore consider that we have accomplished a great deal in this article if we succeed in establishing clearly a few principles with whose aid the most considerable objections ordinarily raised against the notion of *natural right* may be resolved. In order to achieve this, we must begin our argument again from the very beginning and take care not to advance any argument that is not established by evidence—by the kind of evidence, that is, of which moral questions are capable and that will satisfy any reasonable man.

1. It is evident that if man is not free or if his instantaneous decisions or even his vacillations are caused by some material thing external to his self, so that his choice is not the pure act of an immaterial substance and of a simple faculty of that substance, then there can be no rational goodness or wickedness, even though there may be animal goodness and wickedness: there can be neither moral good nor moral evil, neither justice nor injustice, neither obligation nor rights. From which it is at once apparent, we may add in passing, how important it is to establish solidly in our minds the reality not merely of *free will* but also of *liberty*, which is only too often confused with *free will.*

2. Our existence is mean, contentious, and full of care. We have passions, and we have needs. We wish to be happy, and yet the unjust and passionate man is constantly feeling himself impelled to do unto others what he does not desire they should do

unto him. This is a verdict he pronounces in the depths of his own soul, and one from which he cannot escape. He sees his wickedness, and he must either admit it to himself or else allow everyone else the same authority he arrogates to himself.

3. But what reproach can we make to the man who is tormented by such violent passions that life itself becomes an unbearable burden to him if he does not satisfy them and who, in order to acquire the right of doing as he pleases with the existence of others, gives up his own into their hands? What shall we answer if he has the audacity to say, "I realize that I am bringing terror and confusion to the human race; but I must either be unhappy or the cause of unhappiness in others, and no one is dearer to me than I myself. Do not blame me for this abominable predilection; it is not a matter of free choice. It is the voice of nature, which never argues more strongly within me than when it is speaking on my own behalf. But is it only in my heart that it makes itself heard with such violence? Oh, men! I call you all to witness: which of you, when at the point of death, would not buy back his life at the expense of the majority of the human race, if he were sure he could do so with impunity and in secret? And yet," he will continue, "I am equitable and honest. If my happiness demands that I rid myself of all the existences obstructing my desires, then any other individual must be able to rid himself of mine if it obstructs his. Reason requires as much, and I subscribe to it. I am not so unjust as to demand from another any sacrifice that I am not prepared to make for him"?

4. There is one thing I perceive at the very outset that seems to me to be acknowledged by the good man and the wicked man alike—namely, that we must, in all things, make use of our reason, because man is not merely an animal, but an animal with the power of reason. It follows, therefore, that means of discovering the truth of the present problem do exist; that whoever refuses to seek that truth has forfeited his right to be called a man and should be treated by the rest of his kind as a wild beast; and that once the truth has been discovered, whoever refuses to conform to it is either insane or morally evil.

5. What, then, shall we reply to this savage reasoner of ours before we deprive him of speech forever? That his whole

speech may be reduced to a single question, namely, whether or not he acquires any right over the lives of others by abandoning his own life to them; for he does not merely wish to be happy, he also wishes to be equitable and to use his equity as a means of protecting himself from the epithet "wicked"; for if he did not so wish, then we should have to hang him without answering him. We shall point out to him, therefore, that even if what he yields up to others belonged to him so completely that he was able to dispose of it as he pleased and even if the condition he is proposing to the others was actually to their advantage, he would still have no legitimate authority to make them accept it; that he who says, "I wish to live," has just as much right on his side as he who says, "I want to die"; that the latter has only one life and that by abandoning it, he is making himself the master of innumerable lives; that the exchange he wants to make would scarcely be equitable even if there were only himself and one other evil person on the face of the earth; that it is absurd to assume that others want what he wants, since it is uncertain that the peril to which he is exposing his fellow men is equal to the peril to which he is consenting to expose himself; that the value of what he is risking may not be proportionate to the value of what he is forcing me to risk; that the question of *natural right* is much more complicated than it appears to him; that he is constituting himself both claimant and judge; and that his court may not perhaps be competent to judge this case.

6. But if we deny the individual the right to decide about the nature of justice and injustice, from whom are we to seek a judgment on this great question? From whom? From mankind; it is for mankind alone to decide this question, because the good of all is its only passion. Private wills are not to be trusted: they can be either good or evil; but the general will is always good: it has never deceived, and it never will deceive. If the animal order were more or less on a level with ourselves; if there existed reliable means of communication between them and us; if they could transmit their feelings and thoughts to us clearly and be made aware of ours with equal certainty; in a word, if they were capable of voting in a world parliament, then they would have to be summoned to take part in it, and the question

of *natural right* would then be debated not merely by *mankind* but by *animalkind*. But the animals are cut off from us by unchangeable and eternal barriers, and we are dealing here with an order of knowledge and ideas peculiar to the human species, things that both emanate from and constitute its station in the world.

7. In order to know how far he ought to be a man, a citizen, a subject, a father, or a child and when it is proper for him to live or die, the individual should address himself to the general will of mankind. It is for the general will alone to fix the limits of every duty. You have the most sacred *natural right* to everything that is not forbidden to you by the species as a whole. And it is the general will that must enlighten you as to the nature of your thoughts and your desires. Everything that you conceive, every course of action you consider, will be good, great, noble, sublime if it is in accordance with the general and common interest. There is no quality essential to your species other than the one you require in all your fellow men for your own happiness and theirs. It is the degree of this conformity between you and all of them and between all of them and you that will make it clear to you when you are transgressing the bounds of your species and when you are remaining within them. So that you must never lose sight of it; for if you do, you will perceive that the notions of goodness, of justice, of humanity, of virtue begin to decay in your understanding. Say to yourself often, "I am a man, and I possess no truly inalienable *natural rights* other than those possessed by all mankind."

8. But, you will say, where is the depository of this general will; where can I consult it? . . . In the principles embodied by the written law of every civilized nation; in the social behavior of savage and barbarous peoples; in the tacit agreements obtaining among the enemies of humankind; and even in indignation and resentment, those two passions that nature seems to have placed even in animals to compensate for a lack of social law and public vengeance.

9. If you reflect carefully on all the preceding sections, you will stand convinced: (1) that the man who heeds only his personal wishes is the enemy of mankind; (2) that the general

will is in each individual member of mankind a pure act of the understanding, which reasons in the silence of the passions as to what a man may demand from his fellow man and what his fellow man has the right to require of him; (3) that this attention to the general will of the species and its common desire is the rule that must govern the conduct of one individual toward another in the same society, of the individual toward the society of which he is a member, and of the society of which he is a member toward other societies; (4) that submission to the general will is the bond that holds all societies together, even including those created by crime. Alas, virtue is so attractive that robbers will respect its image even in the depths of their caves! (5) that laws must be made for all men and not for one, otherwise that solitary being would be no different from the violent reasoner we hanged in section five; (6) that since of the two wills, the general and the private, the general never errs, there is no difficulty in perceiving to which of them the legislative power should belong for the sake of mankind's happiness or what veneration we owe to those august mortals whose private will unites both the authority and the infallibility of the general; (7) that even if we supposed the notion of species to be in perpetual flux, the nature of *natural right* would not change, since it would always be dependent on the general will and on the common desire of the entire species; (8) that equity is to justice as cause is to effect, or that justice can be nothing but the utterance of equity; (9) lastly, that all these consequences are evident to anyone who uses his reason and that anyone who refuses to use his reason, thereby forfeiting his status as a man, ought to be treated as an unnatural being.

Political Authority (*Encyclopedia*)

[1751]

The article "Autorité politique" appeared in the first volume of the Encyclopedia *(1751). It contained a strong attack against tyranny and a defense of legal rights. But these radical-sounding, rhetorical phrases were quite abstract, and Diderot really was defending the monarchy, trusting to hope that kings would be limited by natural law and a sense of responsibility. (See A-T, Vol. 13.)*

Political Authority (Encyclopedia)

No man has received from nature the right to give orders to others. Freedom is a gift from heaven, and every individual of the same species has the right to enjoy it as soon as he is in enjoyment of his reason. If nature has established any authority, it is that of paternal power; but paternal power has its limits, and in the state of nature it would end as soon as the children were capable of fending for themselves. All other authority originates elsewhere than in nature. Upon close examination, it can always be traced back to one of two sources: either the strength and violence of the man who has seized it or the consent of those who have submitted themselves to it in accordance with an actual or hypothetical contract between them and the man on whom they have conferred it.

Power acquired by violence is a mere usurpation and lasts only as long as the strength of the man in authority remains greater than that of those who are obeying him; so that if the latter become stronger in their turn and shake off the yoke, they have as much right and justice on their side as the other had when he imposed it on them. The same law that created the authority is thus unmaking it again: it is the law of the strongest.

Sometimes, authority established by violence changes its nature—that is, when it is continued and maintained by the express consent of those who have been subjugated. But then it enters into the second category, of which I am going to speak, and he who at first seized it by force, now becoming a prince, ceases to be a tyrant.

Power deriving from the consent of the peoples subject to it necessarily presupposes conditions that render the wielding of it legitimate, useful to society, advantageous to the state, and restricted within certain fixed limits. For man should not and cannot give himself entirely and unreservedly to another man, because he has a greater master above all, to whom alone he belongs completely. I mean God, whose power over his creatures is always direct, a master as jealous as he is absolute, one who can never lose his rights and who never delegates them. For the common good and for the maintenance of society, he permits men to establish a hierarchical order among themselves and to obey the commands of one of their own number; but he wishes this subordination to be reasonable and moderate, not blind and unconditional, so that no created being shall ever arrogate to himself the rights of the Creator. Any other form of submission must properly be termed idolatry. To bow the knee before a man or an image is merely an external ritual, and one the true God, who requires our hearts and minds, sets very little store by. It is a ceremony he relinquishes freely to human institutions, in order that they may use it, according to their needs, as the outward mark of a civil and political cult or of a religious cult. It is not, therefore, such ceremonies in themselves, but the spirit in which they are established, that makes the practice of them either innocent or criminal. An Englishman has no scruples about attending his king on bended knee; the ceremony signifies no more than what it is intended to signify. But to yield up one's heart, one's mind, and the right to determine one's own actions, to abandon these unconditionally to the will and the caprice of someone who is no more than another created being, to make such a being the sole and final motive of one's actions, is assuredly and essentially a crime of divine lese majesty. If this were not so, then that power of God we hear so much about would be no more than an empty phrase that human policy would twist to its every whim and that the spirit of irreligion might even trifle with in its turn, so that as all our ideas of power and subordination became confused, we should see the prince flouting the authority of God, and the subject the authority of the prince.

True and legitimate power is therefore necessarily limited. Indeed, the Scriptures tell us: "Let your submission be reasonable." "All power that comes from God is an orderly power." For that is how we must understand those words, in accordance with right reason and their literal meaning and not in accordance with the interpretation put upon them by baseness and flattery, which claim that all power, of whatever kind, comes from God. For what can such an interpretation mean? Are there no unjust powers, then? Are there no "authorities" that, far from coming from God, have established themselves against his orders and against his will? Do usurpers have God on their side? And must we pay total allegiance to persecutors of the true religion? . . .

The prince holds from his subjects themselves the authority that he has over them, and this authority is limited by the laws of nature and the laws of the State. The laws of nature and the laws of the State constitute those conditions according to which they have submitted themselves, or are regarded as having submitted themselves, to his government. And since he has no power or authority over them except by their choice and their consent, one of these conditions is that he may never use that authority to break the act or contract by which it was conferred on him; for he would then be acting against himself, since his authority can continue to be upheld only by the bond that first established it.

Whoever annuls the one destroys the other. The prince cannot therefore dispose of his power and of his subjects without the consent of the nation and without regard to the choice indicated by the contract of submission. If he were to act otherwise, then all that he had done would be automatically nullified, and the laws would disengage him from any promises and oaths he might have made, as they do in the case of a minor who has acted in ignorance, since he would have been claiming to dispose of what he held only in trust and as an entail as though he were the full and unconditional owner of it.

Besides which, the power of government, although hereditary in one family and placed in the hands of one person, is not a private property but a public one. Consequently, it can never be taken away from the people, to whom alone the full ownership of it essentially belongs. And therefore it is the people that leases out this power: they are always party to any contract awarding the right to exercise it. It is not the State that belongs to the prince; it is the prince who belongs to the State. But it is the prince's function to govern in the State, because the State has chosen him for that function, because he has made a pledge to the people that he will administer their affairs, and because they, on their side, have pledged themselves to obey him in accordance with the laws. He who wears the crown may renounce it absolutely if he so wishes, but he has no power to place it on the head of another without the consent of the nation that placed it upon his. In a word, the crown, the power of government, and public *authority* are goods of which the nation is the owner and of which princes are life tenants, ministers, and depositaries. Although a prince is the head of a State, he is nonetheless a member of it also, the first member, to be sure, the most venerable and the most powerful, with complete power to govern, but unable to do anything legitimately that would change the established government or to give his place as the head of the State to another. The scepter of Louis XV must necessarily pass to his eldest son, and there is no power that can oppose this—neither the power of the nation, because that is the condition of the contract, nor that of the young prince's father, for the same reason.

Authority may sometimes be leased out for limited periods only, as in the Roman republic. Sometimes it is leased out for the lifetime of a single man, as in Poland; sometimes for the entire life-span of one family, as in England; sometimes for the life-span of a family but transmitted through its male line only, as in France. . . .

The conditions of this pact are different in different States. But everywhere in the world, the nation has the right to maintain the contract that it has made against all opposition; no power may change it; and when it is no longer operative, the nation recovers full right and liberty to enter into a new contract howsoever and with whomsoever it pleases. That is what would happen in France if, by the greatest of misfortunes, the entire ruling family were to die out even to the least of its branches; the scepter and the crown would then return to the nation.

Only slaves whose minds were as limited as their hearts were vile could possibly think otherwise, it seems to me. Such people were born neither for the glory of their prince nor for the advantage of society; they have neither virtue nor greatness of soul. Fear and self-interest are the springs of their actions. Nature produces them only in order to serve as a foil to the luster of virtuous men; and Providence makes use of them to create those tyrannical powers with which it ordinarily punishes peoples and sovereigns who have offended against God—the latter by usurping, the former by granting overmuch to a mere man, that supreme power over his creations which the Creator has reserved to himself.

The observance of laws, the preservation of liberty, and a love of one's country are the fecund sources of all that is great and admirable in men's works and actions. In them are to be found the happiness of peoples and the true renown of the princes who rule over them. With them, obedience is a thing of glory, and authority revered. While flattery, self-seeking, and slavishness of spirit, on the other hand, are the origins of all the ills that can overwhelm a State and of all the despicable weakness that can dishonor it. Where such things are common, the subjects are wretched and the prince is hated; the submission of the former is shameful, the domination of the latter cruel. If I consider France and Turkey from this point of view, both together, I perceive, on the one hand, a society of men united by reason, their actions prompted by virtue, governed according to the laws of justice by a ruler who is equally illustrious and wise; and, on the other, a herd of animals kept together only by habit, goaded forward only by the law of the rod, and led by an absolute master who knows no law but his own caprice. . . .

On the Origin and Nature of the Beautiful (*Encyclopedia*)

[1752]

The article "Du Beau" appeared in the second volume of the Encyclopedia *(1752). Diderot had already given evidence of his interest in aesthetics, and this article reveals his broad knowledge of contemporary publications in that field both in England and France. "Du Beau" is first of all a critique of earlier aesthetic systems and then an original exploration of the nature of the aesthetic experience, especially of its subjective and objective elements. (See A-T, Vol. 10.)*

On the Origin and Nature of the Beautiful (Encyclopedia)

. . . We are born with the faculties of feeling and of thinking. The first step taken by the faculty of thought is to examine its perceptions, to unify them, to compare them, to combine them, to apprehend the propriety or impropriety of the relations between them, etc. We are also born with needs that oblige us to employ a variety of expedients, among which, according to the effects we expected of them and to the effects they in fact produced, it was repeatedly demonstrated to us that there can be some that are good, some bad, some swift, some brief, some complete, some incomplete, etc. Most of these expedients were tools, machines, or some other invention of that kind; but every machine supposes the combination and arrangement of several parts tending to a single end, etc. And so our needs and the most immediate exercise of our faculties conspire together as soon as we are born to provide us with ideas of order, arrangement, symmetry, mechanism, proportion, and unity—all ideas proceeding from the senses and therefore artificial. But we have moved on from the concept of a multiplicity of artificial and natural entities, all arranged, proportioned, combined, and symmetrically disposed, to the abstract and negative concept of disproportion, disorder, and chaos.

These concepts are formed by experience, like all others; they too have come to us by way of our senses; even supposing there were no God, they would still have come to us, since they were formed in us long before the concept of his existence; they are quite as positive, as distinct, as clear, and as real as those of length, width, depth, quantity, and number. And since they have their origin in our needs and in the exercise of our faculties, even if there existed somewhere on the surface of the earth a people in whose language these concepts had no names, they would nonetheless exist in the minds of that people to a greater or lesser extent, in a more or less developed state, based on a greater or lesser number of experiences, applied to a greater or lesser number of things. For there is no other kind of difference possible between one people and another or between one man and another belonging to the same people. For however sublime the expressions we may employ to designate the abstract concepts of order, proportion, relation, and harmony, whether or not we choose to term them "eternal," "original," "sovereign," or "the essential rules of beauty," they have reached our understanding by way of the senses, taking the same path as the very basest notions; and they are nothing but abstractions made by our minds.

But scarcely had the exercise of our intellectual faculties and the necessity of providing for our needs by inventions, machines, etc., sketched in our minds these notions of order, relation, proportion, connection, arrangement, and symmetry than we found ourselves hedged around by entities in which the same notions were, so to speak, repeated to infinity. It was impossible for us to take a single step in the world without encountering some object that stirred up these notions in us; they made inroads upon our soul at every moment and from every side; everything taking place inside us, everything in the world outside, everything that had subsisted from previous ages, all that industry, reflection, and the discoveries of our contemporaries presented to our gaze, continued the process of inculcating in us the notions of order, relation, arrangement, symmetry, propriety, impropriety, etc., and there is no other notion, unless it be that of existence, that can have become as familiar to men as the one now in question.

If, then, the notion of the *beautiful*, whether absolute, relative, general, or particular, is composed of nothing but the notions of order, relation, proportion, arrangement, symmetry, propriety, and impropriety and if these notions sprang from no other source than the one that gave rise to those of existence, number, length, width, depth, and an infinity of others about which there can be no dispute, we can, in consequence, it seems to me, employ this first series of notions in a definition of the *beautiful* without being accused of substituting one term for another and of therefore moving in a vicious circle.

"Beautiful" is a term we apply to an infinite number of entities; but whatever the differences between those entities may be, it must follow, provided we are not applying the term "beautiful" erroneously, that there exists a common quality in all these things of which the term "beautiful" is the sign.

This quality cannot be among those that constitute their specific difference, for this would mean either that there was only a single *beautiful* entity in existence or, at the most, only one class of *beautiful* entities.

But among those qualities common to all the entities we term "beautiful," which shall we select as being the thing for which the term "beautiful" is the sign? Which one? It is obvious, it seems to me, that it can be only that one whose presence renders them all *beautiful;* that quality whose frequency or rarity (if it is susceptible of frequency or rarity) makes them to a greater or lesser degree *beautiful*, whose absence causes them to cease being *beautiful*, which cannot change its nature without making the *beautiful* different in kind, and of which the opposite would make the most *beautiful* things unpleasant and ugly; that quality, in short, by means of which *beauty* first comes into being, augments, achieves its infinite variety, declines, and disappears. And only the concept of *relation* is capable of these effects.

I therefore term "beautiful," independently of my existence, everything that contains the power of awakening the notion of relation in my mind; and I term "beautiful" in direct relation to myself everything that does awaken that notion.

When I say "everything," however, I am making exception of those qualities related to the senses of taste and smell; for although these qualities may awaken the notion of relation in us, we do not term the objects in which they reside "beautiful" when considered only in regard to those qualities. We say an "excellent" dish, a "delicious" smell, but not a "beautiful" dish or a "beautiful" smell. So that when we say, "That is a beautiful turbot," or "That is a beautiful rose," we are considering other qualities in the turbot and the rose than those relative to the sense of taste or smell.

When I say "everything that contains the power of awakening the notion of relation in my mind" or "everything that does awaken that notion," it is because we must distinguish carefully between the forms residing in the things themselves and the notion that I have of them. My understanding puts nothing into things and takes nothing from them. Whether I am thinking of the facade of the Louvre or not, all the parts of which it is composed still have such and such a form nonetheless and are arranged together in such and such a way; whether there were men there to see it or whether there weren't, it would still be *beautiful*, though only for hypothetical beings with bodies and minds like ours; in relation to other beings, it might be neither *beautiful* nor *ugly*, or even *ugly*. From which it follows that although there exists no *absolute beauty*, there do exist two different kinds of *beauty* in relation to us: *real beauty* and *perceived beauty*.

When I say "everything that does awaken in us the notion of relation," I do not mean that in order to call a thing "beautiful" it is necessary to evaluate exactly what the relations are prevailing within it; I do not require that a person looking at a piece of architecture should be able to state definitely things that the architect himself may be ignorant of, that such and such a part is to another as such and such a number is to another number; or that the person listening to a concert should know, as sometimes the composer himself does not, that such and such a sound is to another sound in the relation of two to four or four to five. It is enough for him to perceive and sense that the various parts of the building or the sounds of the piece of music are in fact related, either among themselves or with other objects. It is the indefiniteness of these relations, the ease with which we grasp them, and the pleasure that accompanies their perception that have made us imagine that the *beautiful* was rather a matter of feeling than of reason. I dare assert that whenever a principle has been known to us from earliest childhood, so that we are accustomed to applying it immediately and easily to external objects, we suppose that we are judging according to our feelings; but we shall be forced to admit our error on every occasion when the complexity of the relations and the novelty of the object delay the application of the principle. Then pleasure must wait, before it is felt, until the understanding has pronounced the object *beautiful.* Though the judgment, in such cases, is almost always concerned with *relative beauty* and rarely with *real beauty*.

Either we consider the relations apparent in men's actions, and we have *moral beauty;* or in works of literature, and we have *literary beauty;* or in musical compositions, and we have *musical beauty;* or in the works of nature, and we have *natural beauty;* or in the mechanical creations of man, and we have the *beauty of artifice;* or in the likenesses provided by works of art or of nature, and we have *imitative beauty:* according to the object and according to the aspect from which you are considering the relations within the same object, the *beautiful* will assume different names.

But a single object, whatever it may be, can be considered either in isolation and in itself or as it exists in relation to other objects. When I say of a flower that it is "beautiful" or of a fish that it is "beautiful," what do I mean? If I am considering the flower or the fish in isolation, then I mean simply that I perceive its various parts as being ordered, arranged, symmetrical, and related (for all these words merely designate different ways of considering the fundamental relatedness). In this sense, every flower is *beautiful,* and every fish too. But with what kind of *beauty?* With what I call *real beauty.*

If, however, I am comparing the flower and the fish with other flowers and fishes, then when I say that they are "beautiful," this means that among other things of their own kind, this particular flower and this particular fish awaken in me the strongest ideas of relation and the largest number of a certain sort of relations: for I shall demonstrate before long that since all relations are not of the same nature, so the contribution they each make to *beauty* can be larger or smaller. But I can state with certainty that when considered in this latter fashion, objects can be *ugly* as well as *beautiful.* But with what kind of *beauty* or what kind of *ugliness?* With what is termed *relative beauty* or *relative ugliness.*

What, then, do we mean when we say to an artist, "Imitate the beauty of nature"? Either we don't know what it is we are asking of him or else we are saying: If you have to paint a flower and if there are no other reasons determining your choice, then select the most *beautiful* of flowers as your model; if you have to paint a tree and if your subject does not require that it should be an oak or elm that is withered, broken, blasted, stripped of its branches, then select the most *beautiful* tree; if you have to paint any natural object and have no other reasons to influence your choice, then select the most *beautiful.*

From which it follows: (1) That the principle of imitating the beauties of nature demands the profoundest and most far-ranging study of all the various kinds of natural phenomena;

(2) That even if one had acquired the most perfect knowledge of nature and of the limits she has prescribed for herself in the creation of each being, it would still be no less true that the number of occasions on which the most *beautiful* could be employed in imitative art would be to the number of occasions in which we ought to prefer the less *beautiful* as unity is to infinity;

(3) That although there is indeed a maximum of beauty in every work of nature considered in itself (although, for example, the most *beautiful* of roses can never have the stature or the spread of an oak), nevertheless there can be neither *beauty* nor *ugliness* in any work of nature if we are considering it solely with regard to the use we can make of it in the imitative arts. . . .

We can therefore assure the reader that whether he takes his examples from nature or whether he borrows them from painting, morality, architecture, or music, he will always find himself applying the term "real beauty" to whatever has the inner power to awaken the idea of relation and the term "relative beauty" to whatever awakens a sense of proper relations with those things to which it ought to be compared.

I shall content myself with one example, taken from literature. Everyone knows that sublime phrase from the tragedy *Horace:* "*Qu'il mourût.*" ["He should have died."] Suppose I ask someone who is unacquainted with Corneille's play, and who has no notion of what old Horatius' answer means, what he thinks of this phrase. It is obvious that since he does not know what this "*Qu'il mourût*" is, since he cannot tell whether it is a complete sentence or merely a fragment of one, and since he can only with difficulty make out any grammatical relation between the separate words, the person of whom I ask this question will reply that to him the phrase appears neither *beautiful* nor *ugly*. But if I tell him that it is the reply of a man who has been consulted on what another man should do in combat, then he will begin to apprehend a kind of courage in the speaker, one that will not allow him to believe it is always better to go on living than to die, and this "*Qu'il mourût*" begins to interest him. If I add that this combat involves a nation's honor, that the combatant is the son of the person being questioned, that he is his last remaining son, that the young man was confronting three foes who had already taken the lives of his two brothers, that the old man is talking to his daughter, and that he is a Roman, then the reply "*Qu'il mourût,*" at first neither *beautiful* nor *ugly*, acquires beauty in proportion as I develop its relation to the circumstances and eventually becomes sublime.

Change that relation and those circumstances, transpose the "*Qu'il mourût*" from a French theater to an Italian stage, from the mouth of the venerable Horatius to the mouth of Scapin, and this "*Qu'il mourût*" will become burlesque. . . .

Relations derive, in general, from an operation of the understanding. They arise when the understanding considers either a being or a quality as presupposing the existence of another being or another quality. Example: When I say that Peter is a "good father," I am considering in him a quality presupposing the existence of another quality, that of being a son; and so with all other relations, whatever they may be. From which it follows that although the relation exists only in our understanding, as far as the perception of it is concerned, it is nonetheless derived fundamentally from things. I may say, therefore, that a thing contains real relations within itself whenever it possesses qualities that a being of my physical and mental constitution could not consider without supposing the existence either of other beings or of other qualities, either in the thing itself or outside of it; and I shall classify these relations as *real* or *perceived*. But there exists a third kind of relations, the *intellectual* or *fictitious:* those which the human understanding itself seems to put into things. A sculptor looks over a block of marble; his imagination, swifter in its action than his chisel, strips away all the superfluous portions and discerns a figure in it; but this figure is properly speaking imaginary and fictitious. . . .

The *beauty* that results from the perception of a single relation is generally less than that resulting from the perception of several relations. The sight of a *beautiful* face or a *beautiful* painting affects us more than that of a single color, a star-studded sky more than a blue curtain, a whole landscape more than a flat stretch of field, a building more than a piece of land, a musical composition more than a single sound. Though the relations must not be multiplied to infinity, for *beauty* does not follow any such progression; we can admit in *beautiful* things only such relations as a good mind can clearly and easily grasp. But what constitutes a good mind? Where are we to find that point in works of art below which their lack of relations renders them too simple and beyond which they are overloaded by excess? This is the first source of diversity in judgments on such matters. This is where disputes first arise. Everyone agrees that *beauty* does exist and that it is the result of perceived relations, but it must depend on the extent of one's knowledge and experience, on how far one is accustomed to judging, contemplating, and observing, and on the natural scope of one's mind, whether one says that an object is either poor or rich, confused or complete, skimped or overloaded.

But there are so many compositions in which the artist is forced to use more relations than the majority can grasp and in which almost no one except those who practice the same art—which is to say, all those least disposed to do him justice—can wholly understand the merit of what he has done. What becomes of the *beautiful* then? . . .

Unpleasant ideas may become attached to the most *beautiful* of objects by accident. We may like Spanish wine, but it is only necessary to take some with a little emetic added in order to hate it; from then on we are no longer free to choose whether or not we shall feel nauseated by the sight of it: the Spanish wine is still good, but our condition is not the same in relation to it. . . .

But despite all these causes of diversity in our judgments [Diderot has listed twelve[1]], there is no reason at all to think that *real beauty*, which consists in the perception of relations, is a creation of fantasy. The application of this principle may vary endlessly, and its accidental modifications give rise to dissertations and literary battles, but the principle remains nonetheless invariable. There are perhaps not two men on earth who perceive exactly the same relations in one and the same object and who judge it to be *beautiful* in the same degree. But if there did exist a man who remained unaffected by relations of any kind, then he would be a perfect example of stupidity; and if he were insensitive to certain kinds only, then this phenomenon

[1] Diversity in ability to perceive relations and the artist's need to use more relations than the tests of his time can handle; perception of part instead of all of the relations; differences in value scales; personal and environmental differences; diversity of talent and knowledge; lack of awareness of "simple ideas" necessary to abstraction; semantic confusions; prejudice and prejudgment; constant change in our feelings and perceptions; accidental associations of ideas; habitual associations of ideas; prejudice in favor of a famous name.

would be an indication of some defect in his animal economy: we should still be prevented from taking a skeptical attitude by the general condition of the rest of the race.

The *beautiful* is not always the product of an intelligent cause; often physical motion alone can produce a prodigious number of remarkable relations, both in objects considered in isolation and among several objects susceptible of comparison. Natural-history museums provide a great many such examples. And in these cases, the relations are the result of fortuitous combinations, at least in relation to us. There are a hundred instances of how nature's caprices can imitate the productions of art. And we may well ask not, perhaps, whether that philosopher who was cast up by a storm onto the shores of an unknown island was right to exclaim, upon remarking a few geometrical shapes, "Courage, my friends, here are the footsteps of men," but certainly what the number of relations is that we must observe in a thing before being completely certain that it is the work of an artist; in what case a single fault of symmetry would prove more than the entire given sum of relations; what is the relation between the time that the fortuitous cause has taken to produce its effect and the relations observed in the effects produced; and whether, excepting the works of the Almighty, there are cases in which the number of relations could never be compensated for by the number of throws of the dice.

Apology for the Abbé de Prades

[1752]

The publication of Prades' thesis for his doctorate in theology, Jerusalem coelesti *(1751), occasioned a storm of protest which became a factor in the first condemnation of the* Encyclopedia. *It was sensationist in its psychology, tinged with a defense of "natural religion," and interlarded with Biblical criticism. Diderot's* Suite de l'Apologie de M. l'Abbé de Prades *(1752) was ostensibly written by Prades himself and is a reply to the pastoral instruction on Prades' thesis issued by the Jansenist Bishop of Auxerre. Diderot's refutation testifies to his polemical skill in theological disputation. It is a defense of freedom of thought and of sensationism and also touches on a variety of subjects of contemporary philosophical interest. (See A-T, Vol. 1.)*

Apology for the Abbé de Prades

"The great disease of our age," says M. d'Auxerre [the bishop who attacked the thesis of the Abbé de Prades, in which Diderot had had a hand], "is the wish to appeal from the tribunal of faith to that of reason . . . ; as though that sovereign reason which is alone incapable of ignorance and error has not merited the sacrifice of our own, whose narrow bounds so often halt our progress. . . . This cast of mind, which contains the germ of incredulity, reveals itself openly in the very first pages of the thesis we are discussing."

I know of nothing so improper or so injurious to religion as this vague sort of declamation that some theologians indulge in against reason. To hear them talk, you might think that men cannot enter the Christian fold unless they become like a herd of cattle going into a cow shed and that we are bound to renounce all common sense in order either to embrace our religion or to continue in it. To establish such principles, I say again, is to pull man down to the level of the brute beast and to place falsehood and truth on an equal footing. The Christian religion is founded on so large a number of proofs, and those proofs are so solid, that if there is anything at all to be feared where they are concerned, it is not that they may be discussed, but that they may be forgotten. It seems to me, therefore, that any person who decided to acquire a solid knowledge of this matter would certainly be able to distinguish between the truths that form the object of our faith and the intellectual arguments that serve as the basis for our religious practices. The proofs we find in the Gospels cannot be examined with too much rigor, and it would be a blasphemy to suppose them incapable of withstanding analysis on the part of man. But such commentaries and such analyses are equally the province of both the theologian and the philosopher. If we are to be exact, it is merely a matter of applying dialectics to the proofs of religion, the rules of Aristotle to the divinity of Jesus Christ. And this application cannot be too rigorous, for its object is too important. Not to devote a considerable part of one's life to this study is to be a Christian merely by chance, as one might have been a Mohammedan elsewhere.

Only a very bad theologian would confuse the certainty that follows revelation with the truths that are revealed. They are entirely different things. Before the understanding can submit itself entirely to the one, it must have been completely satisfied as to the other. But how is it to achieve this satisfaction other than by a free and honest exercise of its faculties?

". . . The writer of this thesis has not expressed himself clearly on this point. One is left in doubt, after reading what he says, whether the man he envisages is without ideas, like a blank slate on which nothing has been written, or whether he does have ideas, but only unformed, cloudy, and confused ones."[1]

I leave the choice to M. d'Auxerre. . . . And though I might perhaps be a bad philosopher if I accepted the second of these opinions, still I should be no less a good Christian.

"The first reflection that presents itself is that this is far from being the man whose creation is described in Genesis."

No, it was not of Adam that I spoke; and where is the heresy in that? Since it was my design to follow the gradual growth of our knowledge, it would have been absurd to choose the first man as an example, since all his was infused into him instantaneously by God.

"It is not specified in the thesis where the man discussed in it came from, nor who made his body."

There are a great many other things too that are not specified in it; but after expressing myself so clearly on the fact that the soul is a gift from God, I would never have imagined that anyone could have had any doubts as to my orthodoxy concerning the formation of the body.

"The Biblical expression that God breathed life onto his face (or gave him a reasoning soul) is retained; but after that we are told that he was left without knowledge, without thoughts, without distinct ideas, and, in short, little more than a brute beast, an automaton, a machine endowed with motion. Where can the chimerical idea of such a man have come from?"

From nature. Yes, my lord, for I believe very sincerely, and without thinking myself any the less a Christian for it, that man brings neither knowledge, thoughts, nor ideas with him into this world. I am certain that he would indeed remain like a brute beast, like an automaton, like a machine endowed with motion if the use of his material senses did not stir the faculties of his soul to action. Such is the opinion of Locke; it is the opinion of experience and truth. . . . [Most philosophers would not permit] this prelate to accuse them of materialism simply because they claim, with the English philosopher, that we progress from the

[1] Passages within quotation marks are taken from the Bishop of Auxerre's criticism.

positive notion of the finite to the negative notion of the infinite; that without sensations we could have no knowledge either of God or of moral good and evil; in a word, that there is no innate principle within us, whether speculative or practical.

"What an aberration of the mind is this, to create a factitious and imaginary man, who never did exist, in order to seek for the origin and progression of his knowledge in metaphysical speculations, while completely ignoring the real, the actual man who was created by God!"

The man to whom notions preceding the use of his senses are attributed is the factitious and imaginary one, the illusory being who haunted Plato, St. Augustine, and Descartes. It was the latter who restored this way of thinking among us; and we have still not forgotten that his proof of God's existence, based on the notion of innate ideas, caused him to be accused of atheism. What verdict ought they to have pronounced, then, against those who considered a belief in God to be indissolubly linked with Aristotle's conclusions? And what should we think today of those who treated the old axiom "*Nihil est in intellectu quod non prius fuerit in sensu*"[2] as impious and who seem to make the truth of our religion depend upon the existence of innate ideas? What indeed, unless that the more vehemently and the more furiously these theologians feel themselves compelled to condemn those who disagree, the more they make it clear, as I have already agreed with M. Bossuet in pointing out, not that the opinion they are proscribing is heretical or erroneous, but that they themselves are extremely ignorant and rash? . . .

. . . The *state of nature* is not that of Adam before the Fall; that momentary state ought to be the object of our faith, not of our reasoning. It is a question, among philosophers, of the present condition of his descendants, considered as a *herd* and not as a *society;* a condition not only possible but, since it is that of almost all savages, still in existence, and one that it is quite legitimate to choose as a starting point when one is undertaking to explore philosophically, not the eclipsed grandeur of human nature, but the origin and continuous progress of human knowl-

[2] "There is nothing in the mind that has not been previously in the senses."

edge; a condition in which we recognize man as possessing certain special qualities that raise him above the beasts, others that he shares with them and that keep him on the same level with them, and, finally, defects—or less energetic qualities, if you prefer—that make him lower than the beasts; a condition that lasts for a greater or lesser length of time, according to the opportunities men may find to establish law and order and to pass from the herd state to the social state. I mean by *herd state* that condition of life in which men, brought together only by the simple promptings of nature, like monkeys, deer, rooks, etc., have made no covenants that subject them to duties, nor constituted any authority that obliges them to abide by those covenants; a condition in which resentment (that passion which nature, in its care for the preservation of all beings, has placed in each individual in order to make him formidable to his fellows) is the sole check to injustice. . . .

. . . "What is this!" [M. d'Auxerre] cries. "Do you mean to say that self-preservation merits the first place in our concerns? St. Augustine thought very differently. . . . If we were discussing man as a child, it might be different perhaps; but the man in the thesis is an adult. . . . It almost seems as though the writer's aim was to lead us to the school of Epicurus, by turning our first thoughts toward the needs of our bodies."

What nonsense this is! What an effort is needed to reply to these puerilities, and what moderation to reply to them seriously! What, my lord? Have you not perceived that I did begin with man in his cradle and then, having explained how his ideas originated in the sensations he received from the objects surrounding him, that I observed how his own body is of all these objects the one that affects him most? Where is the heresy in that? And what does the evidence of St. Augustine have to do with it? The Scriptures and all the Church Fathers put together can never change the laws of nature or make the knowledge of God and notions of moral good and evil in man precede an awareness of his own existence or of his own corporal needs. . . .

"Since if each man," he says, "limits himself to pursuing his own interest, it is impossible that the interest of one should not frequently be contrary to the interest of another; to propose the pursuit of self-interest as a goal to all men is necessarily to set them all at one another's throats. What man does not know and feel that the principal goal of society should be the common interest and that private interest can be only a result of the common good? Who will not be amazed at the eccentricity of a man who offers us as the basis and fundamental bond of society what can cause only its ruin and its destruction? . . . What, in fact, would it be like, a society in which everyone had only his own private interest in view? Would that not be an unquenchable source of quarrels, divisions, jealousies, hates, wars, violence, and a greater evil than if all men were to live in isolation? . . . But God made man for society. It is in divine law that a theologian, and even a philosopher, should seek for its origins, instead of taxing his brain, as M. de Prades does, by attempting to discover them in the material advantages that each member derives from it or in the fear that men feel for one another and for everything that may do them harm, according to the notions of another modern philosopher [Montesquieu]. . . . Let us open the book of Genesis, and there, in the second chapter, we shall find the origins of human society and the reasons for its establishment, set out in the words of God himself: 'It is not good that the man should be alone; I will make him an helpmeet for him like unto himself.' "

. . . [Now] what did I say in my thesis? After following the mental progress of one of Adam's nephews as he gradually became acquainted with the objects that surrounded him, I added that among those objects he becomes aware of, there are a great many that seem entirely similar to himself ("I will make him an helpmeet for him"), that he is inclined to believe that they have the same needs as himself, and that it will probably be greatly to his advantage if he joins forces with them ("I will make him an helpmeet"). My assertion is therefore no more than a paraphrase of the passage from Genesis that M. d'Auxerre has used, as inappropriately as it is possible to do, as an argument against me. The Scriptures suggest no other foundation for the future bond between Adam and Eve than identity of needs and the hope of mutual aid. "I will make him an helpmeet": this identity of needs and this hope are presumed from their external resemblance and the similarity of their shapes. "I will make him an helpmeet for him like unto himself": words that must either mean nothing at all or else signify the conjunction of two motives of *self-interest*....

So that we now behold men living side by side, forming a *herd* rather than a *society*, and attracted to this corporate existence only by their own self-interest and the similarity of their outward appearances. "I will make him an helpmeet," "I will make him an helpmeet for him like unto himself": what will happen? Not being bound as yet by any law, all animated by violent passions, all seeking to acquire personal ownership of the common advantages produced by the union, according to the talents, strength, wisdom, etc., that nature has endowed them with, all in unequal measure, the weak will become the victims of the stronger, the stronger may in their turn be surprised and massacred by the weak, and soon this inequality of talents, strength, etc., will destroy among men the beginnings of the bond that their own self-interest and their external resemblances had suggested to them for their mutual self-preservation. And how will they overcome this terrible difficulty? After having been drawn together, after having lived side by side, after having stretched out their hands as a sign of friendship, are they now to end up by devouring one another like wild beasts and by exterminating one another? No, they will feel the danger and the barbarousness of this law based upon the inequality of talents, of this law so fatal alike to the weak, whom it oppressed, and to the strong, whose ruin it necessarily brought in its train—a condign recompense for their injustice and their tyranny—and they will make covenants among themselves that will make good the natural inequalities between them or that will forestall their harmful effects. After which, an authority of some sort will be charged with supervising the observance and continuation of these covenants. Then men will no longer be a *herd* but a political society; they will no longer be unruly and vagrant savages, but men, as we see them today, enclosed in cities and recognizing the authority of government. . . . If there existed in any human society a citizen so lacking in reason that he failed to recognize the disadvantages of *original anarchy*, attempted to shake off the yoke of the covenants that had been drawn up, and insisted on a return to the primitive law of inequality (that barbarous law that gave all men the right to everything and set them all at one another's throats), that citizen would be a *Hobbist* and would draw upon himself the execration of all his fellow citizens. Similarly, any nation that sought world dominion, playing the same role among societies as the *Hobbist* among his fellow citizens, would merit the general execration of all societies. . . .

. . . We may therefore assert, without danger, that there is no such thing as an innate moral notion and that our knowledge of good and evil arises, like all other forms of knowledge, from the exercise of our corporal faculties. "But how and at what time is that knowledge formed in us?" As for the time, it varies according to the differences in our characters. There are some men who begin to reflect sooner than others, and these will therefore begin to be good or evil, to act virtuously or wickedly, at an earlier age. As for the way in which it is formed, I believe that it is a fairly direct induction from *physical good and evil.* A man cannot be susceptible to pleasant and unpleasant sensations and keep company for any length of time with other beings like himself, beings who think and are able to procure him either of these two kinds of sensation at will, without having experienced them, without having reflected on the *circumstances* in which he experienced them, and without passing fairly rapidly from the examination of those *circumstances* to abstract notions of injury and benefit, notions that may be regarded as the fundamental elements of natural law, of which the first traces are impressed upon the soul at a very early age, grow daily deeper, become ineradicable, bring inner torment to the wicked, console the virtuous, and serve as a model for all legislators.

The Bishop of Auxerre denies that the notion of virtue comes to us from vice, and if we accept a system of thought based upon innate ideas, I believe him to be in the right. But in the contrary system, which is equally Catholic and also truer, it is inconceivable that a man without needs, without passions, without pleasant and painful sensations, and without any notion of physical good or evil could ever attain to a knowledge of moral good or evil. For the rest, I blame no one for thinking otherwise, nor do I believe myself to be blameworthy for thinking as I do.

On the Interpretation of Nature

[1753]

The Pensées sur l'interprétation de la nature *(1753) reflects Diderot's increasing study of the natural sciences. His interest in them grew from his awareness of their importance for the basic philosophical questions—metaphyscial and moral—which were his enduring concern. Diderot usually was provoked to thought, and to self-expression in writing, as a reaction to a book, a person, a conversation. A Latin work by the scientist-philosopher Maupertuis and the spirit of Bacon's* Novum organum *were two of the factors in his thinking. Diderot's plan here is to present a methodology of scientific investigation, followed by conjectures of his own and by sundry articles of advice. The tone of his work, which is occasionally pontifical or obscure, aroused unfavorable, even hostile reactions. (See A-T, Vol. 2.)*

On the Interpretation of Nature

II

One of the truths that have been proclaimed in our time with the greatest courage and force, a truth that no good physicist will ever lose sight of, and one that will certainly have the most profitable results, is that what are taken to be rigorous truths in the purely intellectual sphere of mathematics lose that advantage absolutely when brought down to the world in which we live. It has been concluded from this fact that it is the task of experimental science to rectify the calculations of geometry, and this conclusion has been accepted even by the geometricians. But what good does it do to correct geometrical calculations with experiments? Is it not simpler to content ourselves with the results of the latter? . . .

IV

We are approaching the moment of a great revolution in the sciences. Judging from the inclination that minds seem to have for ethics, literature, natural history, and experimental science, I would almost dare to predict with certainty that in another hundred years there will not be three great geometricians left in the whole of Europe. Geometry will have stopped short at the point where men such as Bernoulli, Euler, Maupertuis, Clairaut, Fontaine, and d'Alembert left it. They will have erected the Pillars of Hercules. No one will go beyond. . . .

VI

When we compare the infinite multiplicity of natural phenomena with the limitations of our understanding and the weakness of our powers of perception and when we consider how slowly our work progresses, forever hampered by long and frequent interruptions and by the scarcity of creative geniuses, can we ever expect anything from it but a few broken and isolated fragments of the great chain that links all things together? . . .

Then what is our goal? The execution of a work that can never be completed and that would be far beyond the comprehension of human intelligence if it ever were completed. Are we not madder than those first inhabitants of the plain of Sennar? We know that the distance separating the earth from the sky is infinite, and yet we do not stop building our tower. But is it to be presumed that a time will never come when our disheartened pride will abandon the operations? . . . Besides, utility sets bounds to everything. It is utility that in a few more centuries will call a halt to experimental science, just as it is on the point of doing with geometry. I grant the former study a few more centuries because its sphere of usefulness is infinitely greater in extent than that of any abstract science and because it is, beyond dispute, the basis of all our genuine knowledge.

VII

As long as things are in our understanding only, they are our opinions, they are notions, which may be true or false, agreed with or contradicted. They can acquire solidity only by being linked to external objects. This can be accomplished either by an uninterrupted chain of experiments or by an uninterrupted chain of reasoning that is supported at one end by observation and at the other by experiment or by a chain of experiments with gaps between them that are bridged by abstract reasoning, like a series of weights strung out along a thread that is supported at both ends. Without these weights, the thread would become a plaything for even the slightest motion of the air.

IX

Men have scarcely begun to be aware as yet how rigorous the rules are for the investigation of truth or how limited the means at our disposal. Everything is reduced to going back from the senses to abstract thought, then from thought back to the senses: a ceaseless going into ourselves and coming out of ourselves. . . .

XII

Nature seems to have taken pleasure in varying a single mechanism in an infinite variety of ways. She never abandons any one kind of production until she has multiplied the individual examples to produce as many different aspects as possible. If we consider the animal kingdom and perceive that there is not a single quadruped whose functions and parts, above all the internal ones, are not entirely similar to those of another quadruped, would it not be easy to believe that in the beginning there was only one animal, a prototype of all animals, certain of whose organs nature has merely lengthened, shortened, changed, multiplied, or obliterated? Imagine the fingers of your hand joined together and the material of which the nails are made becoming suddenly so abundant that they spread and swell, enveloping and covering the whole extremity: instead of a hand you have a horse's hoof.

When we see the successive metamorphoses of the prototype's outward appearance, whatever it may have been in the first place, bring one kingdom gradually and imperceptibly nearer to another kingdom and people the boundaries of those two kingdoms (if one may use the term "boundaries" where there is no real division), and people, I repeat, the boundaries of those two kingdoms with uncertain, ambiguous beings, stripped to a great degree of the forms, the qualities, and the functions of the one and taking on the forms, qualities, and functions of the other, is it not difficult to resist the belief that there was never more than one first being, a prototype of all other beings? But whether we accept this philosophical conjecture, as Dr. Baumann [Maupertuis] does, or reject it as false, as M. de Buffon does, we cannot deny that it must be accepted as a hypothesis essential to the progress of experimental science, to the progress of rational philosophy, and to the discovery and explanation of phenomena dependent upon physical structure. For we can clearly see that nature has been unable to maintain so great a similarity between the parts, while producing so great a variety of different forms, without often making perceptible in one animal's structure what she has contrived to conceal in another's. She is a woman who likes to disguise herself and whose different disguises, now revealing one part of her, now another, permit those who follow her assiduously to hope that one day they will know the whole of her person.

XV

There are three principal means of acquiring knowledge available to us: observation of nature, reflection, and experimentation. Observation collects facts; reflection combines them; experimentation verifies the result of that combination. Our observation of nature must be diligent, our reflection profound, and our experiments exact. We rarely see these three means combined; and for this reason, creative geniuses are not common.

XIX

There is only one way to make philosophy truly desirable in the eyes of the people: to present it to them as something that is useful. The common man always asks, "What's it good for?" and we must never find ourselves in the position of having to reply, "Nothing." He does not know that what enlightens the philosopher and what is useful to the mass of people are two very different things, since the philosopher's understanding is often enlightened by that which is harmful and obscured by that which is useful.

XXX

The habitual practice of making experiments produces even in the most unrefined of workers involved with physical processes an intuition that is akin to inspiration. It depends on the individual whether or not he makes the same mistake as Socrates and calls it a "familiar demon." Socrates was so prodigiously accustomed to observing mankind and evaluating circumstances that even when confronted with the most intricate problems, an immediate and accurate series of combinations took place secretly inside him, followed by a prognostication that was scarcely ever belied by the event. He judged men as people of taste judge works of art: by feeling. The same is true of the instinct shown by our great investigators in the field of experimental science. They have watched the operations of nature so often and so closely that they are able to guess what course she is likely to take, and that with a fair degree of accuracy, even should they take it into their heads to provoke her with the most outlandish of experiments. So that the most important service they can render to those they are initiating into experimental philosophy is not nearly so much to teach them about procedures and results as to pass on to them that spirit of divination by means of which it is possible to *smell out*, so to speak, methods that are still to be discovered, new experiments, unknown results.

XXXIV

In places where electricity is being produced, the electrical matter gives rise to a perceptible sulfurous odor; in view of this property, had the chemists not then a right to seize hold of this phenomenon? Why have they not used every means at their disposal to perform tests on fluids charged with the greatest possible quantity of electrical matter? We do not even know yet whether electrified water dissolves sugar more or less rapidly than ordinary water. The fire in our furnaces causes a considerable increase in the weight of certain substances, such as calcinated lead; if electrical fire, continuously applied to this metal while in the process of calcination, were to increase this effect even further, would this not establish a further analogy between electrical fire and ordinary fire? They did undertake tests to discover whether this extraordinary kind of fire might not increase the potency of certain medical remedies, make a given substance more efficacious, or a local remedy more active; but did they not abandon these tests too soon? Why should electricity not modify the formation and properties of crystals? How many conjectures still remain to be given shape by the imagination and to be confirmed or scrapped by experiment!

XLII

Once we have formed in our heads an abstract line of thought that requires to be checked by experiments, we should neither persist in it stubbornly nor abandon it lightly. Sometimes we think our conjectures are false when we have not taken the correct measures to find them true. Indeed, stubbornness in such a case is less improper than the opposite excess. By dint of multiplying the number of our experiments, we may not find what we are looking for, but we may also find something better. Time spent investigating nature can never be entirely wasted. The extent of our persistence should be determined by the degree of probability. Completely outlandish ideas deserve only one trial. Those that seem a little more likely should be given rather more, and those that hold promise of an important discovery should be abandoned only when we have tried everything. . . .

XLIV

Experiments should always be repeated, firstly in order to avoid uncertainty in matters of detail, secondly in order to establish their exact scope. They must be applied to different objects, permutated and combined in every possible way. While experiments still remain scattered, isolated, unconnected, and irreducible to any other terms, then it is demonstrable, by means of that very irreducibility, that there are further experiments still to be made.

In that case, we must attach ourselves solely to our object and harry it, so to speak, until the phenomena have been so linked that once one of them is given, all the others follow: we must work first at the reduction of effects; there will be time to think about the reduction of causes later. . . . Any experiment that does not extend a law to a new case or that does not restrict it by some exception is meaningless. The shortest way of finding out the value of an experiment is to posit it as the premise of an enthymeme and to examine the consequent. Does it tell us nothing that has not already been proven by another experiment? Then we have discovered nothing; at the most, we have simply confirmed a discovery already made. . . .

XLV

Just as, in mathematics, all the properties of a curve turn out upon examination to be all the same property, but seen from different aspects, so in nature, when experimental science is more advanced, we shall come to see that all phenomena, whether of weight, elasticity, attraction, magnetism, or electricity, are all merely aspects of a single state. But how many intermediary phenomena still remain to be discovered, between the known phenomena already attributed to one of these causes, before we can form the links, fill in the lacunae, and so produce proof of this ultimate identity? That is what we are unable to determine. There perhaps exists a central phenomenon that would throw light not only on the others we already know but also on those that time will reveal in the future, and that would unite them all into a complete system. But without this central point of reference, they will always remain isolated. All the future discoveries of experimental science, though they may decrease the gaps between phenomena, can never unite them into a whole; and even were they to succeed in that task, it would only be by forming them into a closed circle in which we should be unable to distinguish which was the first and which the last. This singular situation, in which experimental science, by dint of sheer hard work, would have created a labyrinth in which the rational investigation of nature, confused and lost, would merely turn in an endless circle, is not impossible in the natural sciences as it is in mathematics. In mathematics, one can always find, either by synthesis or by analysis, the intermediary propositions that separate the fundamental property of a curve from even the remotest subproperty deriving from it.

XLVIII

When we are on the wrong road, the faster we walk, the more lost we become. And when the distance we have already covered is immense, how are we to retrace our steps? Exhaustion renders it impossible; vanity, without our conscious knowledge, is opposed to it; and an obstinate attachment to principles casts a spell on all the things around us that distorts them. We no longer see them as they are, but as we think they ought to be. At this point, we find people who, instead of reshaping their ideas to conform with reality, seem to take it upon themselves to remodel reality in accordance with their notions. Among all the different kinds of philosophers, there are none more evidently dominated by this sort of madness than the classifiers of natural history. As soon as one of these classifiers has placed man in his system at the head of the quadrupeds, he becomes unable to view him as a natural phenomenon other than as an animal with four feet. In vain does man's sublime gift of reason cry out against the label "animal" or his physical structure contradict that of "quadruped"; in vain has nature raised his eyes toward the heavens: this blind insistence on a category bends his body down again to earth. Reason itself, according to this argument, is only a more perfect kind of instinct; and its adherents seriously believe that it is only because he has lost the habit of walking on all fours that man is unable to use his legs properly when he decides to change his hands into two feet.

L

In order to shake a hypothesis, it is sometimes not necessary to do anything more than push it as far as it will go. We are now going to try out this method on the hypothesis put forward by the Doctor of Erlangen [Maupertuis], whose work, filled with singular and new ideas, is going to put our philosophers through a great deal of agony. The object of his study is the highest that the human mind can propose to itself: the universal system of nature. The author begins by giving a brief account of the opinions put forward by his predecessors and of the inadequacy of their principles to provide a general explanation of phenomena. Some had included only *extension* and *motion.* Others had thought it necessary to add *impenetrability* to extension and *inertia* to mobility. Observation of celestial bodies, or, more generally, the physics of large bodies, had proved the need to include also a force causing all parts of the universe to tend or weigh toward one another, in accordance with a specific law; whereupon *attraction* was admitted, acting in simple ratio to the given masses and in inverse ratio to the square of the distance between them. The simplest chemical experiments and the elementary physics of small bodies then forced other philosophers to have recourse to other *attractions* following other laws; and the impossibility of explaining the formation of a plant or an animal by means of these various attractions, inertia, mobility, impenetrability, motion, matter, or extension has now led the philosopher Baumann [Maupertuis] to postulate still other properties in nature. Dissatisfied with those *plastic natures* which have been put forward as the artisans of all the marvels of nature, even though they lack both matter and intelligence; dissatisfied too with *subordinate intelligent substances* acting upon matter in an unintelligible way, with the *simultaneity of the creation and the formation of substances,* which, since they are all contained the one within the other, develop in time through the continuation of an original miracle, and with the *extemporaneity* of their *production,* which is nothing but a chain of miracles repeated at every instant of existence, it then occurred to him that none of these rather unphilosophical systems would ever have been developed were it not for our unfounded fear of attributing extremely well-known modifications to a thing whose essence, since it is unknown to us, may for this very reason, and despite our preconceptions, be perfectly capable of such modifications. But what is this thing? And what are those modifications? Shall I say?

Of course, Dr. Baumann answers. The material universe is the thing; the modifications are desire, aversion, memory, and intelligence—in a word, all those qualities that we recognize in animals, that were included by the Ancients in the term "sensitive soul," and that Dr. Baumann accepts as being present, in due proportion to their forms and masses, in the smallest particle of matter as well as in the very largest animal. If there were any danger, he says, in allowing some degree of intelligence to material molecules, that danger would be no less if we allowed it to an elephant or to a monkey than if we allowed it to a grain of sand. Here the philosopher of the Academy of Erlangen uses every means at his disposal to avoid any suspicion of atheism; and it is evident that he defends his hypothesis, with some heat, only because it seems to him to embrace even the most recalcitrant phenomena without leading to materialism. His work should be read as an example of how to reconcile the boldest of philosophical ideas with the most profound respect for religion. God created the world, Dr. Baumann says, and it is our task to discover, if possible, the laws according to which he willed it to continue in existence and the means he laid down for the reproduction of individuals. We are free to explore as we wish in this direction, and these are the doctor's principal ideas on the subject:

The seminal element, having been drawn from a part of the body similar to that which it must later form in the animal and also possessing powers of feeling and thought, will retain some memory of its place of origin: hence the conservation of species and the resemblance of related creatures.

It may happen that the seminal fluid has either an excess or a deficiency of certain elements, that these elements are unable to combine from some deficiency of memory, or that extraordinary combinations of supernumerary elements may take place. This would explain both sterility and all the possible kinds of monstrous birth.

Certain elements will inevitably have acquired a prodigious facility for combining ceaselessly in exactly the same way. This will result, if the elements are dissimilar, in the formation of an infinite variety of microscopic animals or, if they are identical, in the formation of polyps, which may be compared to a swarm of infinitely small bees that have retained an active memory of only a single place of origin and therefore remain together, clinging to the situation that is most familiar to them.[1]

When the impression of a present situation counterbalances or effaces the memory of a past situation, thereby producing indifference to all situations alike, sterility will ensue. Hence the sterility of hybrids.

What is to prevent elementary, intelligent parts that are capable of sensation from producing endless variations in the pattern that constitutes the species? Nothing: hence the infinite number of animal species that have sprung from the first animal, the infinite number of beings that have emanated from the first being. There was only a single act on the part of nature.

But will each element, as it continues to accumulate and combine, gradually lose the tiny degree of feeling and perception it possesses? Not at all, according to Dr. Baumann. Those qualities are inherent in it. What will happen then? This: from the perceptions of all these elements, when they have been grouped together and combined, there will result a single power of perception, one proportionate to the resulting mass and its arrangement. This system of perceptions, in which each element will have lost all recollection of its *self* and will contribute to creating the awareness of the *whole*, will be the animal's soul.

It is at this point that we are surprised to find either that the author did not realize the terrible consequences of his hypothesis or, if he had realized them, that he did not abandon it. It is here that we must begin to apply our method and examine his principles. I shall ask him, therefore, whether the universe, or the sum total of all molecules endowed with powers of thought and feeling, forms a whole or whether it does not. If he replies that it does not form a whole, then with a single word he is threatening the existence of God by introducing disorder into nature; and he will also be destroying the basis of all philosophy by breaking

[1] Diderot's description does not quite do full justice to Maupertuis' particulate theory of the genetic transmission of traits.

the chain that links all phenomena together. If he agrees that it does form a whole, one in which the elements are no less ordered than the subdivisions (whether they be discrete in fact or only conceivably so) within an element or the elements within an animal, he will have to admit, as a necessary consequence of this universal copulation, that the world, like a vast animal, has a soul. He will also have to admit, since the world may be infinite, that this soul it possesses, I do not say is, but may be an infinite system of perceptions, and that the world may be God.

Let him protest as much as he wishes against these consequences, they will be nonetheless true; and no matter what light his sublime ideas may cast into the deeps of nature, those ideas will be nonetheless frightening. It was necessary only to generalize them in order to become aware of that. The act of generalization is to the metaphysician's hypotheses what the repetition of observations and experiments is to the experimental scientist's conjectures. Are the conjectures valid? Then the more experiments one makes, the more their validity is confirmed. Are the hypotheses true? Then the further one extends their consequences, the more truths they will embrace and the more certainty and force they will acquire. On the other hand, if the conjectures and hypotheses are fragile and ill-founded, one will either discover a fact or run up against an opposing truth, upon which they will founder. Dr. Baumann's hypothesis will explain, if you wish, the most unfathomable of nature's mysteries, the formation of animals or, more generally, that of all organized bodies; but the universal bond that links all phenomena and the existence of God will be the reefs on which it must be wrecked. But though we reject the ideas of the Doctor of Erlangen, we should have formed but a poor conception of how obscure the phenomena were he undertook to explain, of the fecundity of his hypothesis, of the surprising consequences that may be deduced from them, of the merit of new conjectures on a subject that has occupied the greatest men of all ages, and of how difficult it is to combat his conjectures with any success, if we failed to recognize them as the fruit of a profound meditation, a daring attempt to explain the universal organization of nature, and the undertaking of a great philosopher.

LI

On the Impulsion of a Sensation

If Dr. Baumann had restricted his system within just limits and had applied his ideas to the formation of animals only, without extending them to the nature of the soul (for I think I have proved it against him that if they can be carried that far, they can also be extended to the existence of God), he would not have rushed headlong into the most seductive kind of materialism by attributing desire, aversion, feeling, and thought to organic molecules. He ought to have been satisfied with supposing in them a degree of sensitivity a thousand times less than that which the Almighty has granted to those animals closest to nonliving matter. As a result of this muted sensitivity and of the varying configurations of all organic molecules, it would then be clear that there could be only one situation in nature for which each of them was properly fitted. Each molecule would therefore have been impelled, by an automatic and constant feeling of discomfort, to seek out the situation proper to it, just as we see animals move about in their sleep, when the use of almost all their faculties is in abeyance, until they have found the position most suited for repose. The use of this principle, with no further help, would have embraced, quite simply and without any dangerous implications, all the phenomena he was undertaking to explain, as well as all those numberless marvels that keep our observers of insects in such a perpetual state of amazement; and it would have provided him with the following general definition of an animal: *a system of different organic molecules that have combined with one another, under the impulsion of a sensation similar to an obtuse and muffled sense of touch given to them by the creator of matter as a whole, until each one of them has found the most suitable position for its shape and comfort.*

LVI

On Causes

1. If we were to consult only the vain conjectures of philosophy and the weak light of our reason, we should believe that the chain of causes has never had a beginning and that the chain of

effects will never have an end. Imagine a displaced molecule. It has not displaced itself, and the cause of its displacement itself had a cause, that cause another, and so on, without it being possible ever to discover any *natural* limits to those causes in preceding time. Imagine a displaced molecule. That displacement will have an effect, that effect another, and so on, without it being possible ever to discover any *natural* limits to those effects in future time. The mind, panic-stricken at these infinite progressions of even the minutest causes and the most imponderable effects, rejects this supposition, and others of the same kind, only because of a rooted preconception that nothing happens beyond the range of our senses and that everything stops beyond the point at which we can no longer see. But one of the principal differences between the observer of nature and the man who interprets it is that the point at which the former is abandoned by his senses and his instruments is the latter's point of departure; he conjectures from what is what ought also to be; he draws abstract and general conclusions from the order of things, conclusions that for him have all the certainty of particular and observable facts. He raises himself to a level where he can perceive the very essence of order; he sees that the *pure and simple* coexistence of a feeling and thinking being with any given chain of causes and effects does not enable that being to make an absolute judgment about them. He stops there: if he took one step further, he would be breaking the bounds of nature.

On Final Causes

2. Who are we to explain the ends of nature? Shall we never see that whenever we praise her wisdom it is almost always at the expense of her power and that we take away from her resources more than we can ever grant to her purposes? This way of interpreting nature is bad, even in natural theology. It is to substitute human conjecture for the work of God; it is to harness the most important of theological truths to the fate of a hypothesis. But the commonest of phenomena will suffice to demonstrate how contrary the search for such causes is to genuine science. I shall assume that an experimental scientist, having been questioned as to the nature of milk, has replied that it is a form of food pre-

pared inside the female animal after she has conceived and that nature intends this nourishment for the animal that is to be born. What does this definition tell me about the formation of milk? What am I to think of the alleged purpose of this fluid, and of the other physiological ideas that go with it, when I know that there have been men who made milk spurt from their breasts; when the anastomosis of the epigastric and mammary arteries proves to me that it is the presence of milk that causes the swelling of the breasts by which even virgins are sometimes incommoded at the approach of their periods; when there is scarcely a virgin alive who could not become a wet nurse if she allowed herself to be suckled; and when I have seen with my own eyes a female animal so small that no suitable mate had ever been found for her, who had never been covered, who had never been pregnant, and whose teats were so swollen with milk that it was necessary to resort to the usual means in order to relieve her? How ridiculous it is to hear anatomists seriously attributing to nature's modesty a covering that she has also spread over parts of our bodies that it is not immodest to expose. And the purpose that other anatomists attribute to it, though it does rather less honor to nature's modesty, surely does no more to their wisdom. The true experimental scientist, whose profession it is to instruct and not to edify, will therefore abandon the *why* and concern himself only with the *how*. The *how* is deduced from reality; the *why*, from our understanding: it is conditioned by our metaphysical opinions; it depends on the progress of our knowledge. . . .

LVIII

Questions

There is only one possible way of being homogeneous. There are an infinite number of different and possible ways of being heterogeneous. It seems to me as impossible that the entire world of nature should have been fashioned from one perfectly homogeneous material as it would be to represent it as being all the same color. I even think I perceive that the diversity of natural phenomena cannot be the result of just any heterogeneity. I shall therefore call the various heterogeneous kinds of matter necessary for the production of natural phenomena "elements," and I shall give the name "nature" to the existing general result, or to the successive general results, of the combination of those elements. The elements must possess essential differences; otherwise everything could return to a state of homogeneity and could therefore have resulted from it also. There is or has been or will be a natural combination or an artificial combination in which any element is, has been, or will be reduced to its smallest possible components. The molecule of an element in this state of ultimate division is indivisible, absolutely indivisible, since any further division of that molecule, being beyond the laws of nature and beyond the powers of art, can exist only as a purely intellectual concept. Since the state of ultimate possible division, whether natural or artificial, is not the same, according to all appearances, for the various essentially heterogeneous kinds of matter, it follows that there exist molecules essentially different in mass, yet absolutely indivisible in themselves. How many absolutely heterogeneous or elementary kinds of matter are there? We do not know. What are the essential differences between the kinds of matter that we consider as absolutely heterogeneous or elementary? We do not know. How far can the subdivision of an elementary form of matter be carried, either by human artifice or by the action of nature? We do not know, etc., etc., etc. I have not treated artificial combinations separately from natural ones because among the infinite number of facts of which we are ignorant, and always shall be, there is one that still remains hidden from us: to wit, whether the division of an elementary substance has been, is being, or will be carried further by some artificial operation than it has been, is being, or will be carried by any combination in nature if left to herself. And we shall see, from the first of the questions below, why I have introduced the notions of past, present, and future into some of my propositions and why I included the idea of development in the definition of nature that I gave.

1. If phenomena are not all linked, there can be no philosophy. And even supposing that all phenomena are in fact linked, the

state of each individually might not be permanent. But if the state of this world of phenomena is one of perpetual change, if nature is still at work on it, then despite the chain that links all phenomena, there can still be no philosophy. All our natural science becomes as ephemeral as words. What we take to be the history of nature is merely a very incomplete account of a single moment. And this is why I ask: have metals always been, and will they always be, as they are now; have plants always been, and will they always be, as they are now; have animals always been, and will they always be, as they are now, etc.? After a profound contemplation of certain phenomena, there is a doubt that may perhaps be forgiven you, oh, skeptics: not whether the world was created but whether it is now what it was or what it will be.

2. Just as in the vegetable and animal kingdoms an individual begins, so to speak, grows, continues to exist, degenerates, and is no more, so it might well be with species in their entirety. If faith did not teach us that animals sprang from the hands of their Creator just as we now see them and if it were permissible to entertain the slightest doubts about their beginning and their end, might the philosopher not suspect, having given himself up entirely to his own conjectures, that the particular elements needed to constitute animal life had existed from all eternity, scattered and mixed in with the whole mass of matter; that these elements, happening to come together, had combined because it was possible for them to do so; that the embryo formed by these elements passed through an infinite number of structural changes and developments; that it acquired, successively, motion, sensation, ideas, thought, reflection, conscience, feelings, passions, signs, gestures, sounds, articulated sounds, a language, laws, sciences, and arts; that millions of years elapsed between each of these developments; that, unknown to us, it may have further developments still to undergo and further accretions to acquire; that it has experienced, or will experience, a period of stability; that it is moving out of, or will move out of, that period into a long decline, during which it will lose its faculties just as it acquired them; that it will disappear from nature forever or, rather, that it will continue to exist in nature but in another form and

with faculties quite other than those we observe in it at the present moment of its duration? Religion spares us many wanderings and much labor. If it had not enlightened us as to the origin of the world and the universal order that governs phenomena, think how many different hypotheses we should have been tempted to accept as the secret of nature. And those hypotheses, since they are all equally false, would all have seemed to us more or less equally probable. The question *why anything exists* is the most embarrassing that philosophy could ever have asked itself: only revelation can answer it.

Conversations on *The Natural Son*

[1757]

Le Fils naturel *(1757) was Diderot's first play, conceived to illustrate the new genre of "bourgeois tragedy," or "drama," which he suggested to his contemporaries. The play was inept, but the accompanying commentary, written in the form of a dialogue, had considerable influence in both France and Germany. (See A-T, Vol. 7.)*

Conversations on The Natural Son

First Conversation

THAT day, Dorval had been attempting without success to terminate a quarrel that had long been dividing two families in the neighborhood, and one that was capable of ruining them both. He was upset at what had passed, and I saw that his mood was going to cast a tinge of gloom over our discussion. Nevertheless, I said to him, "I have read your play.[1] But either I am quite mistaken or you have not attempted to comply scrupulously with your father's intentions. He had requested you, I think I am right in saying, to depict things exactly as they happened; and I noticed several that bear the stamp of fiction—which is convincing only in the theater, where there exists, one feels, a convention of illusion and applause.

[1] Dorval is here given the role of the author of the play, *Le Fils naturel*, who was really Diderot himself.

"To begin with, you subjected yourself to the law of the unities. Yet it is unbelievable that so many events could have taken place in the same spot, that they could have occupied a period of only twenty-four hours, or that they could have succeeded one another in reality exactly as you linked them together in the play."

DORVAL: You are right. But because the real events took place over a period of two weeks, do you think it was necessary to accord them the same duration on the stage? Or because they were interspersed with other events, that it would have been proper to express this confusion? And because they occurred in different parts of the house, that I too ought to have spread them out over the same area?

The laws of the three unities are difficult to observe, but they are sound.

In everyday life, affairs develop in a series of short incidents. To reproduce such a series of incidents would lend truth to a novel, but it would destroy all interest in a work for the stage. While reading a novel, our attention can be shared by a multitude of different objects, but in the theater, where only selected instants of real life are represented, we must concentrate entirely on one thing at a time.

I prefer a play to be simple rather than overburdened with incidents. Though it is the way in which they are linked together rather than their actual number that I set store by. I am less disposed to credit two events occurring simultaneously or successively by chance than a great number of events that approximate to daily experience—the unvarying rule of dramatic verisimilitude—and appear to be linked together in an inevitable way.

The art of devising plots consists in the linking of events in such a way that the intelligent spectator can always perceive a satisfactory reason for them. The reason should always be stronger in proportion as the events are more unlikely. But the writer must judge of these matters in relation to himself. The actor and the spectator are two very different beings.

I should be sorry if I had taken any liberties that infringed these general principles governing the unities of time and action, and I think we cannot be too rigid in our observance of the unity of place. Without this latter, the movement of a play is almost always cluttered and equivocal. Ah! But if we had theaters in which the scenery could be changed whenever the place of action was supposed to change! . . .

MYSELF: And what great advantage would you expect from that?

DORVAL: The spectator would find it easy to follow the entire action of a play; the spectacle would become more varied, more interesting, and less confused. Since the scenery cannot be changed without the stage remaining empty for a space and since the stage cannot remain empty except at the end of an act, this would mean that whenever two incidents required a change of scenery between them, they would be taking place in two separate acts. In this way, we should never see a senate meeting follow immediately upon the heels of a meeting of conspirators unless the stage was sufficiently large to be divided into clearly separated areas. But as it is, in small theaters such as ours, what is a reasonable man to think when he hears courtiers, men only too well aware that walls have ears, conspiring against their sovereign in the very spot where he has just consulted them about such a very important matter as the possibility of his abdication? Since the characters remain, he apparently assumes that it is the place that goes away.

Here is what I think, in the main, about these theatrical conventions. The writer who is ignorant of poetic reason, and in consequence ignorant of the foundations of these rules as well, will be able neither to abandon them nor to make proper use of them. He will view them either with excessive respect or with excessive scorn—two opposing reefs of equal peril. The latter dismisses all the observations and experience of past centuries as of no importance, thus leading art back to its infancy; the former stops it short where it is and prevents it from making any further progress. . . .

Second Conversation

The next day, I made my way back to the foot of the hill. It was a wild and solitary spot. In the distance, a few hamlets could be seen, scattered across the plain; beyond them, an uneven ridge of jagged mountains, partly shutting off the horizon. There were oak trees providing shade, and the muffled sound of an underground stream flowing nearby. It was that season of the year when the earth is covered with the fruits it grants to men as a reward for all their sweat and toil. Dorval had arrived before me. I drew near without his seeing me. He was absorbed in the natural spectacle before him. His chest was thrown out. He was breathing deeply. He was examining everything in the scene with an attentive gaze. I could follow on his face the various impressions he was receiving, and I was just beginning to share his ecstasy, when I exclaimed, almost without meaning to, "He is under the spell."

He heard me and answered in a voice filled with emotion, "It is true. This is a place where one can truly see nature. This is the sacred haunt of enthusiasm. If a man has been endowed with genius, then he will leave the city and its inhabitants. Following the impulse of his heart, he loves to mingle his tears with the crystal waters of a spring, to place flowers upon a grave, to tread with light feet upon the tender meadow grasses, to move with slow footsteps through fertile fields, to contemplate the toil of men, to escape into the depths of woods. He loves their secret horror; he wanders, he seeks for a cave that will inspire him. Who mingles his voice with the torrent tumbling down the mountainside? Who senses the sublimity in some lonely spot? Who listens to himself in solitude and silence? The man of genius. Our poet lives on the shores of a lake. His eyes wander over the waters, and his genius unfolds. It is there that he is possessed by the spirit, tranquil one moment, violent the next, that agitates his soul or stills it as it lists. . . . O Nature, everything good is unfolded in your heart! You are the fecund spring of every truth! Nothing in this world but truth and virtue are worthy of my concern. . . . Enthusiasm is born of some natural object. If the mind has seen it from various and striking aspects, then the object fills it, agitates it, torments it. The imagination takes fire, the passions are aroused. We are successively astonished, moved, outraged, and angry. Without enthusiasm, either the true idea does not present itself or, if we do encounter it, by chance, then it proves impossible to pursue it. The poet feels the moment of enthusiasm coming upon him; it follows a period of meditation. Its onset is heralded by a quivering that begins in his breast, then flows deliciously and rapidly out to his extremities. Soon it is no longer a quivering, but an intense and lasting fire that sets him aflame, makes him pant, consumes him, kills him—but also endows whatever he touches with a soul and life. If this fire were to flame even higher, then phantoms would multiply before his eyes. His passion would be raised almost to the point of madness. He could experience no relief except by pouring out a torrent of ideas, crowding against one another, thrusting one another aside, driving one another out."

Dorval was himself experiencing this state as he described it. I made no reply. A silence fell between us, during which I saw that he was growing calmer. Soon, like a man emerging from a deep sleep, he asked me, "What have I been saying? What was it I had to tell you? I no longer remember."

MYSELF: You were going to explain some ideas that Clairville's[2] scene of despair had suggested to you concerning the passions: how they should be expressed, what kind of delivery and gestures the actor should use.

DORVAL: The first is that a writer should never make his characters witty, but that he should know how to place them in situations that lend them wit. . . .

Dorval then sensed, from the rapidity with which he had just uttered these words, that his soul was still in a state of some agitation. He broke off; and in order to give himself time to regain his calm or, rather, to counteract this inner disturbance with a more violent but more fleeting emotion, he told me the following story:

DORVAL: A peasant girl who lived in the village whose roofs you can see above the treetops, over there between those two mountains, once sent her husband to visit her relatives, who lived in a neighboring hamlet. While he was there, this unfortunate man was killed by one of his brothers-in-law. The following day, I visited the house where the accident had taken place. I have never forgotten the spectacle I beheld there, nor the words I heard. The dead man was lying on a bed. His bare

[2] A character in Diderot's play.

legs were dangling over the side of it. His wife was lying in distraction on the floor. She was clasping her husband's feet, and she said, breaking into a flood of tears and making a gesture that drew tears from all the others present, "Alas! When I sent you here, I did not think these feet were bearing you to your death." Do you believe that a woman of any higher rank could have expressed herself with greater pathos than that? No. The same situation would have drawn forth the same words, her soul would have existed only in that moment; and what the artist has to discover is what everyone would say in a like case, the emotion that no one will be able to hear without instantly recognizing it in himself.

Great interests, great passions. Those are the wellsprings of noble speech, of true speech. Almost all men speak well when they are dying.

What I like about Clairville's scene is precisely that it contains nothing except what passion does inspire when it is extreme. Passion attaches itself to one principal idea. It falls silent and then it returns to that idea, almost always by means of exclamations.

The scene also employs mime, and though mime is an art that has been badly neglected in this country, you yourself expressed how successful it was in this case.

There is too much talking in our plays; consequently, our actors do not act enough. We have lost an art whose effectiveness was well known to the Ancients. At one time, mime plays depicted all conditions of men—kings, heroes, tyrants, the rich, the poor, city dwellers, and country folk—selecting from every rank the trait that was peculiar to it and from every action its most striking aspect. . . .

What this scene also made me see is that there are moments that should be left almost entirely to the actor. It is his right to use the text of the scene as he sees fit, to repeat certain words, to return to certain ideas, to cut out some, and to add others. In cantabile, the composer will allow a great singer freedom to exercise his own taste and talent; he will be satisfied to provide no more than the principal intervals of a *bel canto*. And the poet should do likewise when he knows his actor well. What is it that moves us when we see a man animated by some great passion? Is it his words? Sometimes. But what never fails to stir us is cries, inarticulate words, a broken voice, a group of monosyllables with pauses in between, a murmur, impossible to describe, deep in the throat or between the teeth. As the violence of the emotion cuts off the breath and fills the mind with perturbation, so the syllables of words become disjunct, and the man jumps from one idea to another; he initiates a great many different lines of thought but does not finish any of them; and though there are a few sentiments he succeeds in expressing during the onset of his passion, and to which he returns again and again, the rest is merely a sequence of confused and feeble noises, of fading sounds, of stifled cries—all things about which the actor knows far more than the poet. The voice, the tone, the gestures, the stage movements—these are what belong to the actor. And these are the things that strike us, especially in the portrayal of great passions. It is the actor who provides the written text with energy. It is he who conveys to our ears the force and the truth of a character's words. . . .

MYSELF: Then you think your play would not be successful on the stage?

DORVAL: There would be difficulties. It would mean either cutting out certain sections of the text or else changing our methods of staging plays.

MYSELF: What do you mean by changing our methods of staging plays?

DORVAL: I mean clearing all those things off the stage itself that are at present making such a small area even smaller still;[3] introducing scenery; being able to present different stage pictures from the ones we've been looking at for the past hundred years; and, in short, transporting Clairville's drawing room to the theater just as it is. . . .

. . . What a moment of terror and pity is that when we hear the prayer and the groans of the unfortunate Orestes as they pierce through the shrieks and frightful gestures of the cruel

[3] Diderot is referring to the seating of privileged spectators on the stage, a custom that was abolished two years later.

beings who are hunting him down![4] Could we execute such a scene on our stages? No, for we can present only single actions, whereas in nature there are almost always several occurring simultaneously, and the concomitant representation of these, each action lending force to the others, would produce terrible effects in us. Then we should tremble indeed at the thought of going to the theater—and yet be unable to prevent ourselves from going. Then at last, instead of all the petty, passing emotions, the lukewarm applause, the scanty tears with which our present-day poets content themselves, they might topple people's minds, bring confusion and fear into their souls, and we should see the prodigies of ancient tragedy, so possible and so little credited, renew themselves in our time. In order to show themselves again, they are only waiting for a man of genius to appear who is able to mingle mime with speech, combine a spoken scene with a silent one, and take advantage of the moment when they come together, especially of that instant, whether it be frightening or comic, when we see, as we always would, that the two scenes are on the point of merging. After the Eumenides have done their savage dance upon the stage, they move on into the sanctuary where the guilty Orestes has taken refuge, and the two scenes become one.

MYSELF: Two scenes at once, alternately mimed and spoken. I understand what you mean. But wouldn't it be confusing?

DORVAL: A mimed scene is a tableau—an animated decor. When we go to the opera, does the pleasure of looking detract from the pleasure of what we hear?

MYSELF: No . . . I meant is that the way we should interpret the information that has come down to us about the ancient drama, the accounts of how they used speech and music and mime, sometimes all together and sometimes separately?

DORVAL: Sometimes, but a discussion of that would take us too far. Let us stick to our subject. Let us consider what might possibly be done today in this respect, and let us take an example from ordinary domestic life.

A father has lost his son in a duel. It is night. A servant who

[4] Dorval is talking about Aeschylus' *Eumenides*.

saw the fight has come to bring the news. He goes into the unhappy father's room, where the latter is asleep. He walks up and down. The noise of his footsteps wakes the father, who then asks who it is in his room. "It's me, sir," the servant answers, in a voice that betrays his emotions. "Well! What's the matter?" "Nothing." "Nothing the matter?" "No, sir." "That's not true. You're trembling, you're turning your head away, you're avoiding my eyes. Now tell me what's the matter. I want to know. Speak! I order you to speak!" "I tell you there's nothing the matter, sir," the servant says again, weeping as he speaks. "Ah, you miserable wretch," the father cries, leaping from the bed where he has been lying, "you are deceiving me. Some great misfortune has occurred. . . . Is my wife dead?" "No, sir." "My daughter?" "No, sir." "It is my son, then?" The servant doesn't reply; the father realizes what this silence means; he throws himself onto the floor, he fills the room with his grief-stricken cries. He does, he says everything that despair would suggest to a father who has lost an only son, his family's sole hope for the future.

The same servant runs to tell the mother. She too is asleep. She is awakened by the sound of her bed curtains being pulled violently aside. "What's the matter?" she asks. "Madame, the greatest possible misfortune. Now is the moment to show yourself a Christian. You no longer have a son." "Oh, God!" the heartbroken mother cries. And then, unhooking the crucifix from above her bed, she folds it in her arms and fastens her lips upon it; her eyes are streaming with tears, and with those tears she sprinkles her God, nailed on his cross.

The tableau of a religious woman. . . .

Meanwhile, the son's body having been carried into the father's room, a scene of despair has been taking place there simultaneously with the mother's mimed expression of piety in hers.

You see how mime and speech move alternately from place to place. That is what we should substitute for our *asides*. But the moment for combining the two scenes is approaching. The mother, led by the servant, moves toward her husband's room. . . . And imagine the feelings of the spectator as she does so. . . .

The eyes of a mother are about to fall upon her husband, her son's father, stretched out upon the young man's corpse! But by now she has crossed the space between the two sets. Agonized laments have reached her ears. She has seen. She recoils violently, then all the strength drains out of her, and she falls senseless into the arms of the servant who is escorting her. Soon her throat will fill with sobs. *Tum verae voces.*[5]

There is very little speech in this action. But a man of genius, when faced with the task of filling up these empty spaces, will scatter no more than a few monosyllables here and there; he will throw in an exclamation in one place, the beginning of a sentence in another, but he will rarely allow himself an entirely coherent speech, no matter how short.

That would be true tragedy; but if we are to create such a genre, we need new authors, new actors, a new theater, and perhaps a new race of spectators.

MYSELF: What! You want to put all those things into a tragedy? A bed, a mother and a father both lying asleep, a crucifix, a corpse, two scenes with speech and mime alternating between them! But what about the conventions?

DORVAL: Ah, those cruel conventions, how decorous, and how petty they make our plays! . . .

"And so," Dorval added, with a composure that amazed me, "you think that what I have suggested is no longer possible?"

MYSELF: No, I don't think we shall ever progress as far as that.

DORVAL: Then all is lost! . . .

At this point Dorval exclaimed, "O you [Voltaire] who still possess all the fire of your genius at an age when others have nothing left but cold reason, why can I not be at your side to scourge you forward like one of the Eumenides? I would give you no peace. You would write it for us, this work. . . . And then, in disappearing from among us, you would not leave us still repining for a genre that you had the power to create."

MYSELF: And what will you call this new genre?

DORVAL: Domestic middle-class tragedy. The English have *The London Merchant* and *The Gamester*,[6] their prose tragedies.

5 "Then the speech is true."

6 Plays by George Lillo and Edward Moore, respectively.

And Shakespeare's tragedies are half in verse, half in prose. The first poet who made us laugh with prose introduced prose into comedy. The first poet who makes us weep with prose will have introduced prose into tragedy.

But in art, as in nature, everything is linked; if we approach nearer to the truth in one way, then we shall find other ways of approach opening up to us as well. Then we shall see those natural situations portrayed upon the stage that propriety, ever the enemy of genius and sublime effects, has outlawed from it. I shall never tire of shouting to our fellow countrymen: Truth! Nature! The Ancients! Sophocles! *Philoctetes!* For Sophocles, in his play about Philoctetes, showed him, lying at the entrance to his cave, dressed in tattered rags. He writhed on the ground, racked by a fit of pain; he gave vent to yells, he made inarticulate noises. The setting was primitive; the action unfurled without the help of machinery. Real clothes, real speech, and a simple and natural plot. Our taste would be quite corrupt if such a spectacle did not affect us more than that of a richly dressed man, tricked out in finery. . . .

Third Conversation

After a few general remarks on the way events occur in real life and the way they are imitated on the stage, he said to me:

DORVAL: We can divide every moral matter into a middle and two extremes. It appears then, since every dramatic action is a moral matter, that there should exist a central genre and two extreme genres. We already have the last two; they are comedy and tragedy. But man is not always in a state of grief or joy. Therefore there must be a point that bisects the distance between the comic genre and the tragic genre. . . .

How would you classify this particular play, then? [Terence's *Hecyra*] Is it comedy? There isn't a funny line in it. Tragedy? There is no point at which it arouses terror or pity or any of the great passions. Yet it holds the interest; and any dramatic composition, even though it contains no laughable absurdity, no perils to make us shudder, will always hold the interest if the poet adopts the tone that we ourselves use in serious matters and if the action evolves through a series of perplexities and hindrances. And since such actions are the ones most commonly met with in real life, it seems to me that the genre taking these as its object will be the most useful and the most comprehensive. I shall term this *the serious genre.*

Once this genre has been established, there will be no rank in society and no important actions in life that we cannot relegate to some part of the dramatic system.

Would you like to enlarge this system to its greatest possible extent? Would you like to see it include truth as well as fantasy, the world of the imagination as well as the world of reality? Then add burlesque below comedy and the supernatural above tragedy.

MYSELF: I understand what you mean: burlesque . . . comedy . . . serious drama . . . tragedy . . . supernatural drama.

DORVAL: It is the advantage of the serious genre, being placed midway between the other two, that it can draw its resources from both above and below itself. This is not true of the tragic and comic genres. All the nuances available to comedy are comprised in the region between itself and the serious genre, and all those available to tragedy between the serious genre and the tragic genre. . . .

If you need to be convinced of the danger that lies in crossing the barrier nature has placed between the genres, then push things to excess: take two widely separated genres, such as tragedy and burlesque, and put them together; the result will be a scene in which a grave senator indulges in the vilest debauchery at the feet of a courtesan being immediately succeeded by another in which a band of conspirators discusses its plans for destroying a republic.[7]

. . . The subject [in the serious genre] should be important, the plot simple, domestic, and close to everyday life.

I want to see no valets in serious drama. Right-thinking people do not admit valets to a knowledge of their affairs, and the scenes will be the more interesting for taking place entirely between masters. If a valet speaks on the stage as he does in

[7] See Otway's *Venice Preserved,* Shakespeare's *Hamlet,* and most plays of the English theater [Diderot's note].

real life, he is tedious; if he speaks in any other way, he is false.

The nuances borrowed from the comic genre must never be too strong. If they are, the work will make us laugh and cry, and it will lack both unity of interest and unity of tone.

The serious genre contains soliloquies. From this, I conclude that it is nearer to tragedy than to comedy; for in comedy, soliloquies are infrequent and always short.

The moral content of a serious drama should be general and strong....

A great deal of attention should be paid to mime. All *coups de théâtre* whose effect is momentary should be eliminated, and tableaux invented in their stead....

But, above all, remember that there is no general principle: there is not one of the rules I have just set forth that could not successfully be infringed by a man of genius. . . .

MYSELF: But what material will it use, this serious kind of comedy that you look upon as a new branch of dramatic literature? There are only a dozen or so clearly defined and truly comic types in the whole of human nature.

DORVAL: I agree.

MYSELF: The minor differences observable in men's characters can never be used to such good effect as clear-cut humors.

DORVAL: Again I agree. But do you know what follows from that? It follows that we should no longer be portraying characters, properly speaking, in our plays, but rank or station. Up till now, character has always been the main object of comedy, and station only accessory. Now the social function must become its principal object, and character merely accessory. The entire plot used to be built from the character. Generally speaking, we tried to find a set of circumstances that would bring it out, then linked those circumstances together. But it is social station—its duties, its advantages, and its difficulties—that should serve as the basis of our plays. In my opinion, this is a more fruitful, more comprehensive, and more useful source of material than mere characters. A character need only be slightly exaggerated for the spectator to be able to say to himself, "I'm not like that." But he cannot deceive himself in this way when it is his social function that is being portrayed before him; he cannot fail to recognize his duties. He is compelled to apply what he hears to himself.

MYSELF: It seems to me that some of these subjects have already been treated.

DORVAL: No, they haven't. Make no mistake about that.

MYSELF: But we have financiers in our plays, don't we?

DORVAL: Certainly we do. But the social role of the financier has never been explored.

MYSELF: It would be difficult to cite a play without a father in it.

DORVAL: True, but the father as a social function has not been done. I would like you to consider, in a word, whether the various social functions, their duties, their disadvantages, and their dangers, have ever been depicted on the stage; whether they have ever formed the basis for the plots and moral arguments of our plays; and whether these same duties, advantages, disadvantages, and dangers do not daily provide us with the spectacle of men enmeshed in the most complicated situations.

MYSELF: So you want us to enact the man of letters, the philosopher, the merchant, the judge, the lawyer, the politician, the citizen, the magistrate, the financier, the great lord, the estate manager.

DORVAL: Yes, all those plus the fundamental family relationships: what it means to be a father, a husband, a sister, or a brother. A father! What a subject that is in an age such as ours, when no one seems to have the slightest idea of what it means to be the father of a family!

Remember that new social roles are coming into being every day. Remember that there is possibly nothing we know less about than social functions, and nothing that should interest us more. We each of us have our own place in society, but we all have to deal with men of every other station.

Social station! Think how many important details such a source will yield! How many public and domestic themes! How many unknown truths! How many fresh situations! Are there not the same contrasts between social roles as between characters? Will the writer have any difficulty in producing conflicts between them?

Though these subjects do not belong to the serious genre alone. They can be made comic or tragic, too, according to the talents of the man who takes possession of them.

Such are the vicissitudes of comic faults and vices that I believe a new *Misanthrope* could be written every fifty years. And isn't the same thing true of many other basic characters? . . .

On Dramatic Poetry

[1758]

Diderot's second play, Le Père de famille, *was published in 1758, accompanied by a* Discours sur la poésie dramatique. *The play was performed at the Comédie Française in 1761, with some success, but it is scarcely better than* Le Fils naturel. *The* Discours sur la poésie dramatique *was a more systematic treatise expounding his dramatic theories. (See A-T, Vol. 7.)*

On Dramatic Poetry

. . . I THEREFORE say again: virtue, virtue. It touches us in a gentler and more intimate way than things that excite our scorn and laughter. Poet, are you sensitive and fastidious? Then pluck that string and you shall hear an answering echo vibrate in every heart.

"Is human nature good, then?"

Yes, my friend, and even very good. Water, air, earth, fire, everything is good in nature: the hurricane rising at the end of autumn, shaking the forest and smashing the trees against one another so that the dead branches break off and fall away; the storm that churns up the waters of the sea and makes them pure; the volcano pouring streams of molten matter down its gaping flank and infusing the air with cleansing vapors.

It is not human nature we should accuse but the despicable conventions that pervert it. For what, after all, affects us more than the narration of a generous deed? Or where is the wretch who can listen unmoved to a good man lamenting his misfortune?

The pit of a theater is the one place where the tears of virtuous and wicked men alike are mingled. There, the wicked man grows angry at injustices that he himself might have committed, sympathizes with misfortunes he might have occasioned, and is filled with indignation by a man whose character is exactly like his own. But the effect has been made, and its impression remains with us despite ourselves: the wicked man leaves his box less disposed to do evil than if he had been reprimanded by some austere and harsh-tongued orator.

The poet, the novelist, and the actor make their way into our hearts by indirect means. They touch our souls all the more strongly and all the more surely because we are relaxed, because we offer ourselves to the blow. The sufferings with which they move me are imaginary, I agree, but they move me all the same. Every line [in the Abbé Prévost's novels] rouses an impulse of concern in me for the misfortunes of virtue and moves me to expend my tears on them. What could be more pernicious than an art that instilled in me a feeling of complicity with an evil man? But, by the same token, what art could be more precious than the one that imperceptibly makes me feel concern for the fate of a good man, that draws me out of the quiet and comfortable situation I myself enjoy in order to accompany him, to plunge with him into the caves where he takes refuge, and to identify myself with all the reverses the writer has been pleased to imagine as trials for his constancy?

Oh, how profitable it would be for men if all the imitative arts were to set themselves a common goal, if they were to cooperate one day with the laws to make us love the virtues and hate vice! It is the philosopher who should urge them to this task. It is for him to appeal to the poet, to the painter, to the musician and to cry out to them with all his strength, "Men of genius, why has heaven given you your gifts?" If his voice is heard, then soon our palace walls will no longer be covered with pictures of debauchery, our voices will no longer be organs of crime, and morality and taste will be the gainers by it. Does anyone really believe that the sight of a blind husband and wife, still reaching out to find each other even now that they are old, pressing each other's hands, and caressing each other, almost, one might say, on the edge of the grave, their eyes moistened with tender tears—does anyone really believe that such a scene would not hold my interest as much, would not demand as much talent, as the spectacle of those violent pleasures that fired their untried senses in adolescence?

I have sometimes thought that the day might come when we would undertake to discuss the most important questions of morality on the stage, and do so, moreover, without any detriment to the violent and rapid progress of dramatic action.

What would this involve, in fact? It would mean constructing the work in such a way that those questions arise naturally out of it, as the Emperor's thoughts on abdication do in Corneille's *Cinna*. In this way, the writer could debate the question of suicide, of honor, of dueling, of wealth, of titles, and a hundred others. Our plays would take on a gravity they lack at present. If such a scene has been made obligatory by the construction, if it arises out of the subject matter, if it has been prepared and the spectator is looking forward to it, then he will give it all his attention and be far more affected by it than by those over-elaborated little maxims with which authors embroider their works today. . . .

What should a poet have? An uncultivated nature or a refined one? A tranquil one or an agitated one? Will he prefer the beauty of a pure and serene day or the horror of a dark night in which the intermittent whistling of the wind is mingled from time to time with the muffled and continuous rumble of distant thunder and in which he can see the lightning flashes lighting up the sky above his head? Will he prefer the spectacle of a calm sea or the sight of turbulent waves? The cold and silent aspect of a palace or a walk through some old ruin? A man-made edifice or the thickets of an ancient forest? A landscaped vista or a hidden hollow among deserted rocks? Pools, ponds, cascades or the prospect of a cataract being shattered into foam as it falls through a gorge of rocks, sending the sound of its thunder to the distant ear of a shepherd who has led his flock up into the mountains and now stands listening in awe?

Poetry must have something in it that is barbaric, vast, and wild.

It is at times when the fury of civil war or fanaticism puts daggers in men's hands, at times when blood is streaming in great floods across the earth, that the laurel of Apollo grows green and flourishes. It needs blood to feed upon. In times of peace and leisure, it withers away. The Golden Age might have produced a song, perhaps, or an elegy. Epic and dramatic poetry require a different way of life.

When shall we see poets born? After a time of disasters and great misfortunes, when harrowed nations begin to breathe again. And then, shaken by the terror of such spectacles, imaginations will paint things entirely strange to those who have not witnessed them. Have we not all, in certain circumstances, felt a kind terror that was foreign to us? Why has it not borne fruit? Have we no genius any more?

Genius is present in every age, but the men carrying it within them remain benumbed unless extraordinary events occur to heat up and melt the mass so that it flows forth. But when they do occur, the emotions build up within our breasts, filling them with torment; and those who possess the voice, urged on by the need to speak, deploy their powers and find relief.

What, then, will the poet do when he finds himself among a people whose way of life is timid, petty, and affected; a people whose conversation, if strictly imitated, would yield nothing but a tissue of false, foolish, and low expressions; among whom there remains not a single vestige of frankness or simplicity; among whom fathers call their sons Sir and mothers call their daughters Miss; whose public ceremonies lack all sense of awe; whose home life is neither affecting nor honest; and whose solemn decrees are insincere? He will try to make them more beautiful; he will chose those circumstances most suited to his art, ignore the others, and some he will even dare to invent. . . .

Do you want your poets to approach nearer to the true, both in the actions they depict and in their dialogue as well? Do you want your actors to act more naturally and speak in a more life-like way? Then raise your voices. You need only insist that the scenery depict the place it is supposed to represent as it should be.

Let nature and truth but introduce themselves onto your stages in even one detail, no matter how small, and you will soon sense ridicule and distaste spreading over everything else that is not in keeping with them.

The dramatic system most difficult to understand would be one that we could accuse of being at once half true and half false. It is but a clumsy lie that contains circumstances within itself indicating the impossibility of the rest. I could more easily tolerate a mixture of incongruities, for at least there is nothing false in such a system. Shakespeare's fault is not the greatest into which a poet may fall. It merely indicates a deficiency of taste.

And when you have decided that your poet's work is worthy of performance, let him send for the designer and read the play out to him. Then let the designer depict the setting exactly as the poet has described it to him, in every detail; and let him remember, above all, that scene painting must be even more exact and true than any other kind. . . .

Eulogy of Richardson

[1761]

The Eulogy of Richardson *(1761) is included as an example of Diderot's literary taste, his moralistic preferences in the arts (which contrast with the ideas in some of his unpublished speculative writings), and his enthusiastic style in literary criticism. (See A-T, Vol. 5.)*

Eulogy of Richardson

By a novel, we have understood up till now a tissue of frivolous and imaginary events the perusal of which was dangerous to both taste and morals. I wish we could find another name for the works of Richardson, works that elevate the mind and move the soul, that breathe a love of good on every side, and are also called novels.

All that Montaigne, Charron, La Rochefoucauld, and Nicole have put into the form of maxims, Richardson has expressed in narrative. But though an intelligent man could reconstruct most of the moralists' maxims from a thoughtful perusal of Richardson's work, he could never make a single page of Richardson out of all the moral maxims ever written.

A maxim is an abstract and general rule of conduct of which the application is left to the reader. It does not itself impress any perceptible image upon our minds. But a character in action is seen; we put ourselves in his place or at his side; we take sides either for or against him; we identify with him if he is virtuous and recoil from him with indignation if he is unjust and vicious. Which of us has not shuddered at the character of a Lovelace or a Tomlinson? Which of us has not been struck with horror by the genuine and pathetic tone, by the air of candor and dignity, by the profound art with which the latter simulates every virtue? Which of us has not said to himself in the depths of his heart that there would be nothing left but to escape from the world, to take refuge in the depths of some forest, if there were many men in existence capable of such dissembling?

Oh, Richardson! Whether we wish to or not, we always identify with the characters in your books, we take part in their conversations, we approve, we blame, we admire, we become angry or indignant. How many times have I not found myself exclaiming, as children sometimes do when they are taken to the theater for the first time, "Don't believe him, he's deceiving you! . . . If you go with him, you're lost!" My soul was kept in a state of perpetual agitation as I read. How good I was! How just! How pleased with myself! And when I laid the book aside, I was like a man at the end of a day spent entirely in doing good. . . .

This writer does not make the woodwork run with blood; he doesn't whisk you away to distant lands; he doesn't expose you to the danger of being devoured by savages; he doesn't lock himself away in establishments intended for clandestine debauchery; he never loses himself in the regions of fantasy. The world we live in is the place where he lays his scene; the backdrop of his drama is reality, and the people he places before it are also as real as possible; their characters are conditioned by their place in society; the events he describes are such as occur in every civilized nation in the world; the passions he depicts are recognizable as the passions I feel myself; they are caused by the same objects and act with a familiar power; the misfortunes and afflictions of his characters are of the same kind as those that constantly threaten me; he depicts the general tenor of the world just as I observe it all about me. Without this art, since my mind can only with difficulty follow the twisting paths of fantasy, the illusion created would be merely momentary, the impression weak and soon erased.

What is virtue? It is, from whatever aspect we consider it, a form of self-sacrifice. And self-sacrifice performed in imagination creates a predisposition to sacrifice ourselves in reality.

Richardson sows seeds of virtue in our hearts that lie there idle and dormant at first; they remain buried until the opportunity arises for them to germinate and throw up shoots. Then they grow; we feel ourselves impelled toward good with an impetuousity we did not know we had. When we see injustice, we feel an inexplicable feeling of revolt rise up inside us. It is because we have become familiar with Richardson, because we have been conversing with a good man at moments when our soul, being disinterested, was open to the truth.

I still remember the first time that Richardson's works came into my hands. I was in the country. And with what delightful emotions his creations then filled my heart! Moment by moment, I saw my joy diminish as I turned each page. Soon I felt the same sensation that men might feel who had lived for a long time together on the best of terms and were now about to part. At the end, I felt that I was suddenly alone.

He is a writer who constantly draws your attention back to the important things in life. The more you read him, the more you enjoy reading him.

He it is who lights up the recesses of the cavern with his torch, who teaches us to discern those subtle and dishonest motives that hide deep inside us, lurking behind other, more honest motives that always rush forward to show themselves first. He breathes on the sublime phantom filling the mouth of the cave and the hideous Moor behind it appears to our view.

He it is who makes the passions speak, now with that violence they have when constraint is no longer possible, now with that moderate and artful tone they affect at other times.

He it is who makes men of all ranks, of all conditions, caught up in all the various circumstances of this life, speak in terms we recognize. If there is some hidden emotion lurking in the depths of a character he is introducing, listen carefully and you will hear a dissonance of tone that reveals it. This is because Richardson knew that a lie can never completely resemble the truth, because truth is truth, and a lie is a lie.

If it is important for men to be persuaded, apart from any considerations beyond this life, that there is no better way of achieving happiness than by being virtuous, then what a service Richardson has rendered to mankind! He has not proved this truth by argument, but he has made us feel it: on every line, he makes the fate of oppressed virtue appear preferable to the fate of vice triumphant. Who would wish to be Lovelace, with all his advantages? Who would not wish to be Clarissa, despite all her misfortunes?

I have often thought to myself as I read: I would gladly give my life to be like her; I would rather be dead than be like him. . . .

Men, come and learn from this author how to reconcile yourselves to life's ills; come, we shall weep together over the unhappy creations of his imagination, and we shall say, "If fate should crush us, at least good people will weep over us too." If ever Richardson attempted to win our sympathy, it was on behalf of those in misfortune. In his works, as in life, men are divided into two classes: those who live a life of pleasure and those who suffer. It is with these latter he makes me identify myself; and without my being conscious of it, my capacity for pity is exercised and strengthened.

His books have left a pleasing strain of melancholy in my character that does not fade; sometimes people become aware of it and ask me, "What's the matter with you? You don't seem in your usual spirits; what has happened?" They question me about my health, my finances, my family, my friends. Oh, my friends! *Pamela*, *Clarissa*, and *Grandison* are three sublime dramas! When torn from their pages by important business, I experienced an invincible feeling of distaste; I left duty to fend for itself and returned to Richardson's books. Take care not to open these spellbinding works when you have important duties to perform.

Which of us has ever read Richardson's works without desiring to know the man himself, to have him for a brother or a friend? Which of us has not wished all sorts of blessings on his head?

Oh, Richardson, Richardson, in my eyes you are unique, and the time will never come when I shall cease to read your books! If ever I am pressed by urgent needs, if my friend should fall into poverty, or if my means should prove insufficient to educate my children, then I shall sell all my books; but you will stay with me, you will stay there on the same shelf with Moses, Homer, Euripides, and Sophocles; and I shall read you all, turn and turn about. . . .

Oh, Richardson! Though you may not have enjoyed the full reputation you deserved during your lifetime, how great you will appear to the eyes of our grandchildren, when they see you from as far off as we see Homer! Who then will dare to expunge a single line from your sublime work? You have even more admirers here in France than you have in your own country, and that gladdens my heart. Flow swiftly, you future ages, and bring in with you all the honors due to Richardson! I call all those now listening to bear witness: I have not waited for the example of others before paying homage to you; this day sees me already kneeling at the feet of your statue; I have worshiped there, searching in the recesses of my soul for words that could express the vastness of the admiration I feel for you and finding none sufficient. And you who glance through these pages that I have penned so incoherently, without plan and without order, just as they were when they flowed from the tumult in my heart, if heaven has given you a soul more sensitive than mine, then blot them out. Whatever genius I had has been crushed by Richardson's. Ghosts of his creation wander ceaselessly through my imagination. If I try to write, I hear Clarissa's laments; Clarissa's shade appears before me; I see Grandison walking toward me; Lovelace comes to disturb my mind, and the pen falls from my fingers. And you, oh, gentler phantoms, Emily, Charlotte, Pamela, and dear Miss Howe, as I talk with you, the years that should be spent in toil, in winning laurels pass me by; I see my end approaching, yet I can attempt no task that might recommend me also to future ages.

Rameau's Nephew

[1 7 6 2]

Le Neveu de Rameau *was written in 1762 and extensively revised at several later dates. It was published in 1821, in an inaccurate French translation of Goethe's German translation, and again in 1823, from an imperfect and bowdlerized copy of the French manuscript. More exact texts came to light during the nineteenth and twentieth centuries. Diderot's autograph manuscript, discovered on the Paris quais in 1891, is presently in the Pierpont Morgan Library in New York.*

Le Neveu de Rameau *is Diderot's outstanding literary achievement, a brilliant dialogue and one of the masterpieces of satire. Its greatness stems from three qualities: style, the creation of character, and intellectual substance. Diderot was truly an experimenter in morals, and this is his most noteworthy experiment, testing the viability of contrasting characters and moral theories. The satire is of the individuals involved, of French society, and of human society in general. (See A-T, Vol. 5.)*

Rameau's Nephew

Vertumnis, quotquot sunt, natus iniquis.[1]

HORACE

In good weather or bad, it is my custom to stroll through the Palais-Royal at about five every evening. I am the person you see, always alone, dreaming on the d'Argenson bench. I talk to

[1] "Born under the capricious malice of the changing gods."

myself about politics, about love, about taste, or about philosophy. I let my mind follow its slightest whim. I leave it free to follow the first wise or madcap idea that presents itself, just as you see our young rakes, in the Allée de Foy on the other side of the garden, stalking some flighty-looking courtesan with a laughing face, a lively eye, a turned-up nose, then leaving that one for another, setting their sights on them all, but settling for none. My thoughts are my whores. If the weather is too cold or too rainy, I take refuge in the Café de la Régence; there, I pass the time watching the customers play chess. Paris is the place in the whole world, and the Café de la Régence is the place in the whole of Paris, where the best chess is played. It is there that the profound Légal, the subtle Philidor, and the solid Mayot confront their opponents; it is there that you see the most amazing gambits and hear the most stupid conversation; for though it is possible to be a man of wit and a great chess player as well, like Légal, it is also possible to be a great chess player and a fool, like Foubert and Mayot.

I was there after dinner one day, observing a great deal, speaking rarely, and listening as little as I could, when I was accosted by one of the oddest characters in France—a country God has not allowed to go short in this respect. He is a mixture of hauteur and obsequiousness, of good sense and utter nonsense. He must have the notions of propriety and impropriety strangely mixed up in his head, for he displays all the good qualities that nature has given him without ostentation, and all the bad ones without shame. For the rest, he is endowed with a powerful physique, an unusually heated imagination, and uncommonly powerful lungs. If you ever meet him and are not put off by his eccentricity, either you will stop up your ears or you will run away. Ye gods, what a pair of lungs!

Nothing can be more unlike him than he himself. Sometimes he is like a man dying of consumption, so skinny and haggard that you could count his teeth through his cheeks. You would say that he either hasn't eaten for two days or else has just come out of a Trappist monastery. Next month he will be fat and plump, as though he'd spent all the intervening time at a banker's dinner table or as though he had been shut up in a

Bernardine monastery. One day he will be walking around in a dirty shirt, torn breeches, clothed entirely in rags, and almost without shoes; he will avoid you, and you will be tempted to call him over and offer him alms. The next day he will be powdered and curled, well shod, well dressed, walking with head held high, proud of himself, and you might almost take him for a gentleman. He lives from hand to mouth, sad or gay according to his circumstances. The first thing he worries about in the morning, as soon as he gets up, is where he is going to dine; after dinner, he thinks about where he can go for supper. The nighttime also brings its anxieties. Either he returns on foot to his little attic lodging—unless the landlady, tired of waiting for her rent, has asked him to return the key—or else he slumps down in some neighborhood tavern and waits for the dawn between a hunk of bread and a pot of beer. When he doesn't even have six sous in his pocket, which does sometimes happen, he is forced to resort either to a cabdriver friend of his or to a great lord's coachman, who lets him stretch out on the straw alongside the horses. In the morning, he still has part of his mattress in his hair. If the weather is mild, he wanders up and down the Cours-la-Reine or the Champs-Élysées all night. When day comes, he reappears in town, dressed from the evening before for the day ahead and sometimes from the day ahead for the rest of the week.

I have no great esteem for this sort of eccentric. Others accept them as close acquaintances, even as friends. I find them interesting once a year, when I happen to run into them, because they provide such a contrast to the normal run of people and because they make a change from the tedious uniformity that our upbringing, our social conventions, and our habitual propriety have imposed on us. If one of them appears at a social gathering, he immediately becomes a grain of yeast that ferments and restores a portion of their natural individuality to all the others. He shakes things up, he creates a stir; he makes people approve or disapprove; he brings out the truth; he makes you see who the decent people are; he unmasks the rogues. It is at such times that the man of good sense keeps his ears open and makes a note of who is who.

I had known this fellow for years. He used to frequent a house where he had been made welcome because of his talent. There was an only daughter; he swore to her father and mother that he would marry her. They used to shrug their shoulders, laugh in his face, tell him he was crazy—and the day came when I saw that he had succeeded. I used to lend him a few crowns when he asked for them. He had wormed his way—I have no idea how—into several respectable homes where he had been given a place at table on condition that he would not speak without being granted permission. He sat in silence and ate in fury. He was a sight worth seeing, restraining himself like that. If he was seized with a desire to break the pact and opened his mouth to speak, at the first word the entire table would cry, "Oh, Rameau!" Whereupon his eyes would glitter with rage and he would fall to eating again, more furiously than ever.

You were curious to know the man's name, and now you know it. He is the nephew of the famous composer who delivered us from all that Lully plainsong we had been chanting for a hundred years and more; who has written so many incomprehensible fantasies and apocalyptic truths on the subject of musical theory—none of which either he or anyone else has ever begun to understand; who has given us a certain number of operas in which there are harmonies, snatches of song, some disconnected ideas, a lot of noise, flights, triumphal processions, lances, triumphs, murmurs, an unending stream of victories, and some dance tunes that will last forever; and who, after having buried his Florentine predecessor, will himself be interred by the Italian virtuosos, as he foresaw, which made him gloomy, sad, and ill-tempered; for no one, not even a woman waking up to find a pimple on her nose, can be as out of humor as an author in danger of outliving his own reputation—as witness Marivaux and Crébillon *fils*.[2]

He accosts me: "Aha! So there you are, mister philosopher! And what may you be doing here amid this heap of layabouts? Do you too waste your time pushing wood?" (That is their contemptuous expression for playing at chess or checkers.)

[2] Marivaux, famous writer of comedies and novels; Crébillon *fils* painted the libertine society of his time in novels.

MYSELF: No, but when I have nothing better to do, I enjoy spending a little time watching those who push it well.

HE: In that case, you must enjoy yourself very seldom. Légal and Philidor excepted, the rest don't know the first thing about it.

MYSELF: And what about M. de Bissy?

HE: He holds exactly the same position among chess players as Mlle Clairon does among actresses. They both of them know all there is to be learned about their respective games.

MYSELF: You are hard to please, and I see that you spare only the great.

HE: Yes, in chess, checkers, poetry, eloquence, music, and other drivel of that sort. What's the good of being a second-rater at such things?

MYSELF: Not much, I agree. But don't forget that a great many men must do these things before the genius can emerge. He's one in a million. But let's not talk about that. It's an age since I've seen you. I don't think about you very often when I don't see you, but I'm always pleased when I do meet you again. What have you been doing?

HE: The things that you and I and all the others normally do: good, bad, sometimes nothing at all. And of course I was hungry, so I ate, when the opportunity presented itself. Then, after eating, I was thirsty, and sometimes I drank. Meanwhile my beard was growing, and when it had grown, I had it shaved off.

MYSELF: That was a mistake. It's the one thing you lack to be a sage.

HE: Yes, indeed. My brow is high and furrowed, my gaze fiery, my nose prominent, my cheeks broad, my eyebrows black and bushy, my mouth wide, and my jaw square. If this great chin were only covered with a long beard, do you know, it would really look very impressive in bronze or marble. . . .

HE: . . . I was once at table with a minister of the king of France, a fellow with wit enough for ten ordinary people. Well, he proved to us, as clearly as one and one make two, that there is nothing more useful to a nation than lies, and nothing more disastrous than the truth. I don't remember his proofs very well, but the inevitable conclusion they led to was that men of genius ought to be hated and that if a child were born with the mark of that dangerous gift of nature on its brow, it ought either to be smothered or thrown into the river.

MYSELF: And yet that kind of person, though they are sworn enemies of genius, all claim to possess it.

HE: I'm sure they all think they do deep down inside, but I don't believe any of them would dare admit as much.

MYSELF: Because they're modest. So that instilled you with a great hatred for genius, did it?

HE: Yes, one that I shall never get over.

MYSELF: But I can recall a time when you were in despair because you were ordinary. You will never be happy if pro and con both distress you equally. You should decide what side you're on, then stick to it. I agree with you that geniuses are generally peculiar, or, as the proverb has it, that there is no great mind without a grain of madness, but there's nothing to be done about it all the same. Any age that has produced no geniuses will always be despised: geniuses will always be the glory of the nations in which they live. Sooner or later, statues are raised to them and they are regarded as benefactors of mankind. With all due respect to the exalted minister you quoted, I believe that while a lie may be useful for a while, it is inevitably harmful in the long run, and that, on the other hand, truth is necessarily useful in the long run, although it may happen to do harm at the moment. From which I should be tempted to conclude that the man of genius who denounces a general error or who persuades us to accept a great truth is always a being worthy of our veneration. It may happen that such a being falls a victim to prejudice and the laws. But there are two kinds of laws: some deriving from absolute equity and capable of absolute and universal application, others, more capricious, that owe their sanction only to blindness or the necessity of circumstances. The latter cast only an ephemeral ignominy upon the guilty man who infringes them, an ignominy that time then turns back upon his judges and on the nation, to whom it remains attached forever. Which of the two, Socrates or the magistrate who made him drink the hemlock, is the dishonored man today?

HE: A lot of good that does for Socrates! Does it change the fact that he was condemned? Does it change the fact that he was put to death? Does it change the fact that he stirred up trouble in the state? Does it change the fact that his contempt for a bad law encouraged the foolish to spurn the good ones? Does it change the fact that he was a rash and eccentric person? A little while ago you were pretty close to saying some pretty uncomplimentary things about men of genius.

MYSELF: Listen to me, my friend. A society ought not to have any bad laws, and if it had none but good ones it would never find itself in the position of persecuting a man of genius. I did not say that genius was necessarily accompanied by a bad character or a bad character by genius. A fool is more likely to be wicked than an intelligent man. And if a man of genius did happen to be habitually difficult to get on with, hard to please, spiky, cantankerous, even if he were downright wicked, what would you conclude from that?

HE: That he ought to be drowned.

MYSELF: Gently, my dear fellow. Now tell me something. I shan't take your uncle as an example: he's a harsh man and a brutal one; he is without any feeling for humanity, miserly, a bad father, a bad husband, and a bad uncle; but we can't yet be sure that he's a genius, that he has carried his art far enough, or that anyone will still be talking about his work in another ten years. But Racine? He certainly had genius, and also the reputation of not being a very nice person. And what about Voltaire?

HE: Don't make me answer that: I can never hedge.

MYSELF: Which would you prefer, that he should have been a good, decent fellow, thinking only of his bookstore, like Briasson, or of his yardstick, like Barbier, giving his wife a legitimate child regularly once a year, a good husband, a good father, a good uncle, a good neighbor, an honest tradesman—but nothing more? Or that he should have been underhanded, treacherous, ambitious, envious, spiteful—but also the author of *Andromaque*, *Britannicus*, *Iphigénie*, *Phèdre*, and *Athalie?*

HE: To be frank, it might perhaps have been better for his own sake if he had been the first of the two.

MYSELF: That is infinitely truer, in fact, than you realize.

HE: Oh, that's just like you people! If we say something worthwhile, it must be the way madmen or visionaries do—by accident. You're the only ones who know what you're saying. But have no fear, mister philosopher, I know what I'm saying just as well as you do.

MYSELF: Very well, then, tell me why you say "for his own sake"?

HE: Because all those sublime works of his didn't bring in as much as twenty thousand francs, whereas if he'd been a good silk merchant on the Rue Saint-Denis or the Rue Saint-Honoré, a good wholesale grocer, or an apothecary with a good clientele, he'd have amassed an immense fortune; and while he was amassing it, there would have been no kind of pleasure he might not have enjoyed. Because once in a while he would have given ten francs to a poor devil of a buffoon like myself, who would have made him laugh and sometimes found him a young girl to relieve him of the eternal and tedious duty of cohabiting with his wife. Because we'd have had excellent meals at his house, played for high stakes, drunk the very best wines, the very best liqueurs, the very best coffee, and gone on picnics. So you see, I did know what I was talking about. You find that funny. But let me finish: because it would have been better for everyone around him.

MYSELF: There can be no doubt about the last point. Provided he didn't use the wealth he acquired in an honest trade for dishonorable purposes; provided he drove away all those gamblers, all those parasites, all those distasteful sycophants, all those idlers, all those immoral hangers-on—and provided he gave his shopboys sticks to thrash that too obliging man who makes it his job to relieve a husband, with a little variety, of the eternal and tedious duty of cohabiting with his wife.

HE: Thrash, my dear sir, thrash! No one is thrashed in a well-governed city! It's an honest profession you're attacking! A great many people, even titled ones, have a hand in it. And what the devil do you want a fellow to use his money for if it's not to keep a good table, good company, a good cellar, beautiful women and to enjoy every kind of pleasure, every kind of fun? I'd as soon be a beggar as own a great fortune without any of those enjoyments. But let's get back to Racine. There was a fellow good only for people he didn't know and ages he would never see.

MYSELF: Agreed. But weigh the good against the bad. In a thousand years from now, he will still be making people weep. He will be admired by men in every country on this earth. . . .

HE: But if nature is as powerful as she is wise, why has she not made men as good as they are great?

MYSELF: Don't you see that with an argument like that you are upsetting the whole scheme of things and that if everything on this earth were excellent, then nothing would be excellent?

HE: You're quite right. The important thing is that you and I should exist and that we should be you and me. As for all the rest, let it get along as best it can. The best scheme of things, as I see it, is the one I was meant to be a part of, and a fig for even the most perfect of worlds if I'm not in it. I had rather be—and even be an unwanted argufier—than not be.

[*Rameau describes his life as parasite and buffoon in the house of a wealthy financier and how he was ejected once he refused to crawl.*]

MYSELF: Agreed. But all the same, if I were you I would go back there right away, with your downcast face, your wild gaze, your unbuttoned shirt, your uncombed hair, just as you are now, in that truly tragic state. I would throw myself at the goddess's feet. I would press my face to the ground, and I would whisper, without getting up, in a voice broken with sobs, "Forgive me, madame, forgive me! I am a wretch and a scoundrel. It was but the unfortunate impulse of a moment. You know that I don't usually suffer from common sense, and I promise not to do so again as long as I live."

The amusing part of it was, that as I made this speech to him, he was miming it. He had sunk to the ground, pressed his face against it, and appeared to be holding the toe of a slipper between his two hands. He wept, he sobbed, he said, "Yes, my little queen, yes, I promise. I'll never suffer from it again as long as I live, as long as I live." Then, suddenly rising to his feet, he added in a serious and thoughtful tone:

HE: Yes, you're right. I think that's the best thing to do. She's kindhearted. M. Viellard says she is—very kindhearted! And I have reason to know she is myself. But all the same, having to go and humble myself in front of a frump like that! Begging for pity at the feet of a little ham actress who's hissed by the pit every time she sets foot on a stage! I, Rameau, son of M. Rameau, apothecary of Dijon, a man of substance, an honest citizen who has never bowed the knee to any man alive! I, Rameau, nephew of the man of the same name, referred to as the great Rameau, who is always to be seen walking so upright through the Palais-Royal, with his arms swinging, ever since M. Carmontelle[3] painted him bent over, with his hands tucked under his coattails! I who have composed pieces for the harpsichord, which nobody plays, but which may be the only ones that will go down to posterity—and then they will be played. I! Me! I should go! . . . Listen, my good sir, it just can't be done. *(And placing his right hand on his breast, he continued)* I feel something in there that is rising up and saying: Rameau, you will do nothing of the kind. There must be a certain dignity inherent in man's nature that nothing can stifle. And it is awakened sometimes for no discernible reason, yes, for no reason at all that I can see; for there are other days when I'd have no trouble at all in being as base as you could wish. On days like that, for half a farthing I'd get down and kiss little Miss Hus's bottom.

MYSELF: Ah, but my friend, she is so fair, so pretty, so young, so sweet, so dimpled! And that act of humility is one to which even someone more fastidious than yourself might sometimes stoop.

HE: Let's be clear on this point: there is a difference between kissing a bottom literally and kissing one figuratively. . . .

MYSELF: Then if the expedient I have suggested doesn't suit you, you must have the courage to be a beggar.

[3] Carmontelle (1717–1806), French painter, engraver, and playwright.

HE: But a beggar's life is such a hard one, and there are so many rich fools it's possible to live off. And then there is one's self-contempt: that makes it unbearable.

MYSELF: Are you familiar with that feeling?

HE: Am I familiar with it! Oh, the times I've said to myself: What's this, Rameau? There are ten thousand good tables being kept in Paris, each one with fifteen or twenty covers, and out of all those covers, not a single one for you! There are purses full of gold, pouring out their contents left and right, and never a single coin that falls on you! When a thousand untalented, undeserving, inferior wits, a thousand little hussies without a trace of charm, a thousand uninspired intriguers are all well dressed, ought you to go around naked? Can you be that much of an imbecile? Can't you flatter like the rest? Can't you lie, swear, perjure yourself, make promises, then keep them or break them, the way the others do? Can't you get down on all fours and crawl, like anyone else? Can't you give a hand with Madame's love affairs and deliver Monsieur's billet-doux, just like the next fellow? Couldn't you encourage that young man to speak to Mademoiselle and encourage Mademoiselle to listen, the way the others do? Couldn't you intimate to that bourgeois magnate's daughter that she is not very well dressed? That a beautiful pair of earrings, a little rouge, some lace, and a dress *à la polonaise* would suit her no end? That those little feet were not meant for walking in the streets? That there is a handsome gentleman, young and rich, who has a coat laced with gold, who keeps superb horses, a carriage, six tall footmen, and who saw her as he was passing by, who finds her charming, who hasn't eaten or drunk since that day, who can no longer sleep, and is dying because of her? "But my papa!" "Yes, yes, your papa! He'll be a little cross at first." "And Mama, who is always so anxious that I should be a good girl, who says that our honor is the only thing we have in the world?" "That's old-fashioned stuff; it doesn't mean a thing." "And my confessor?" "You won't be seeing him any more; or if you do persist in being so whimsical as to go on telling him how you pass your time, it won't cost you more than a few pounds of sugar and coffee." "He's a very strict man—he's already refused me absolution once because I sang that song 'Come into My Cell with Me.' " "That's because you hadn't anything to give him. . . . But when you appear before him all in lace . . ." "Shall I have lots of lace then?" "Of course, all kinds . . . and wearing your beautiful diamond earrings." "Shall I have beautiful diamond earrings then?" "Certainly." "Like the ones that Marquise wears who comes and buys gloves in our shop sometimes?" "Exactly like them. And a fine carriage, with dapple-gray horses, two tall footmen, a little Negro page, and a runner to go in front. Rouge, patches, and your train carried behind you." "At balls?" "At balls, at the opera, at the theater." Already her heart is trembling with joy. You play with a piece of paper between your fingers. . . . "What's that?" "Oh, nothing." "I think it is." "It's just a little note." "Who for?" "For you, if you are curious enough." "Curious? Oh, I'm very curious. Let me see it." She reads. "A meeting, that's not possible." "Not on your way to church?" "Mama always goes with me. But if he were to come here quite early in the morning . . . I'm always the first up, and down behind the counter before the others are even out of bed." He comes; she finds him attractive; one fine day, at twilight, the pretty little thing vanishes—and I get my two thousand crowns. . . . What, Rameau! You have a talent like that and yet you're going hungry? Aren't you ashamed of yourself, you pitiful wretch? I would recall a whole crowd of rogues who couldn't hold a candle to me and whose pockets were bulging with money nevertheless. There I was in my fustian, and they were dripping with velvet. Yes, they were walking with gold-topped canes and flashing rings carved into portraits of Aristotle and Plato on their fingers. And what were they? Fifth-rate musicians is what most of them had been, and now they were all behaving like lords. Well, thoughts like that used to give me fresh heart. I would feel self-confident again, quick-witted, capable of anything. But that happy frame of mind apparently doesn't last very long with me, because up till now I really haven't gotten very far. But however that may be, you now have the text of my frequent soliloquies, which you are free to paraphrase as you please, provided that you draw the conclusion from them that I am no stranger to self-contempt or to that agony of conscience that comes from not using the gifts with which heaven has endowed us. For that is the sharpest pang of all. It would almost be better for a man who feels it never to have been born.

I listened to this speech, and as he acted out the scene of the pander and the young girl he was seducing, feeling myself besieged by two contrary impulses, I didn't know whether I was about to succumb to my desire to laugh or to the flood of indignation rising inside me. The conflict was painful. Twenty times, a burst of laughter choked back my anger; twenty times, the anger welling up inside me broke forth as a peal of laughter. I was completely bewildered by this alliance of so much cleverness and so much baseness, by this torrent of alternately true and false ideas, by such a total perversion of right feeling, by such utter turpitude and so rare a candor.

He noticed the conflict going on inside me. "What's the matter?" he asked.

MYSELF: Nothing.

HE: You seem upset.

MYSELF: And so I am.

HE: But tell me what you think I should do.

MYSELF: Change the subject. Ah, you poor wretch! To have been born or to have fallen into a state so abject!

HE: Oh, I agree. But you mustn't let it upset you. I had no intention of making you unhappy when I confided in you. I did manage to save a little while I was with those people. Remember, I didn't have to find anything for myself there, absolutely nothing, and then they gave me quite a lot of pocket money too.

Whereupon he began banging his forehead with his fist again, biting his lips, and rolling his eyes wildly at the ceiling, adding meanwhile, "But that's all over and done with. I've got a little put away. The time I spent there has passed, and that's always something saved."

MYSELF: You mean wasted, don't you?

HE: No, no, saved. Every moment enriches us. A day less to live or a crown more in the pocket—they both amount to the same thing. The important thing is to move the bowels freely, easily, pleasantly, copiously, every evening: *O stercus pretiosum!* That's the chief end of life no matter what your rank. When the last moment comes, we are all equally rich: Samuel Bernard, who by dint of stealing from people, fleecing them, and bankrupting them, leaves twenty-seven million in gold, and Rameau, who will leave nothing, Rameau, who will have to depend on charity even for his burlap shroud. The dead man does not hear the bells. In vain do a hundred priests bawl themselves hoarse for him, in vain do those long files of burning torches follow and precede him to his tomb: his soul is no part of the procession. You may rot under marble or you may rot under earth, but you still rot. What difference does it make whether you have the Redcoat Orphans or the Bluecoat Orphans round your coffin, or nobody at all? And then just look at this wrist of mine; it used to be as stiff as a poker. These ten fingers here were like so many sticks jammed into a metacarpus carved out of solid oak. And these tendons! Like old, shriveled catgut, drier, stiffer, more inflexible than if they'd been used to work a woodturner's wheel. But I've worked at them, you see; yes, I've broken them in, I've put them through it. So you don't want to go, eh? Well, damn you, I say you shall! And that means you will.

And as he spoke, seizing the wrist and fingers of his left hand with his right one, he began bending them up and down. The tips of the fingers were touching his arm, the joints were making great cracking noises; I was afraid that the bones would be completely dislocated.

MYSELF: Be careful, I said, you'll cripple yourself.

HE: Don't worry. They're used to it. I've given them worse than this in the past ten years. They may not have liked it, but the damned things had to get used to it, else how would they learn how to find the right keys and touch the right strings? In any case, they're fine now. Yes, that's it.

Whereupon he assumed the pose of a man playing a violin; he hummed a Locatelli allegro; his right hand mimed the bowing, while the fingers of his left hand appeared to move up and down the strings. If he played a bad note, he stopped, tightened or loosened the string, then plucked it with his nail to check that he'd tuned it properly. He resumed the piece exactly where he left off, beating time with one foot. His head, his feet, his hands, his arms, his whole body seemed to have gone mad. You may have been to the Tuileries concerts sometimes and seen Ferrari or Chiabran or some other virtuoso going through exactly the same convulsions, creating the same image of a creature being tortured to death, and producing the same distressing effect. For it is distressing, is it not, to see someone who is trying to give us pleasure suffering agony? Let there be a curtain drawn between that man and me, let him be hidden from my eyes if it is absolutely necessary that he should perform like a man on the rack. But if an ostinato passage occurred, one of those harmonious passages where the bow moves slowly across several strings at once, then the cries and the fidgeting stopped, his face took on a look of ecstasy, his voice grew soft, he listened to himself enraptured. There is no doubt that those chords were really sounding in his ears and in mine. Then, tucking his instrument under his left arm with his left hand and letting his right hand fall to his side with the bow still in it, "Well," he said to me, "how did you like it?"

MYSELF: I was thinking that all you've just been telling me is more specious than solid. But enough of that. You say you've taught accompaniment and composition?

HE: Yes.

MYSELF: And yet you knew nothing whatever about them?

HE: Nothing whatever. And that's why there were a lot worse teachers than I was—the ones who thought they did know something. At least I didn't spoil the children's judgment or their hands. Since they hadn't learned anything, at least when they went on to a good teacher they had nothing to unlearn. That was always so much time and money saved.

MYSELF: How did you go about it?

HE: Just like all the others. I arrived. I collapsed into a chair. "What terrible weather we're having! How those cobbles wear me out!" Then I produced a few scraps of gossip. "Mlle Lemierre was to play the role of a vestal virgin in the new opera, but she's pregnant for the second time. They don't know who'll take over. Mlle Arnould has just left her little count; they say she's opened up negotiations with Bertin. However, the little count seems to be consoling himself with M. de Montamy's porcelain. There was an Italian girl at the last Concert des Amateurs who sang like an angel. That Préville fellow is really something on a stage. You should go and see him in *Le Mercure galant;* the riddle scene is priceless. That poor Dumesnil creature is no longer responsible for anything she says or does. Come now, mademoiselle, take your book." While Mademoiselle, in no great hurry, looks for her book, which she has misplaced, while a chambermaid is called, while the mother scolds, I continue. "Clairon is really quite incomprehensible. They're talking about the oddest marriage—Mlle . . . what's her name? That little tart he was keeping, the one who's had two or three children by him and was kept by so many others before." "Come now, Rameau, that can't be true. You're talking nonsense." "I'm not talking nonsense. I've even heard the thing's already done. There's a rumor Voltaire's dead too—which is all to the good." "Why all to the good?" "It means he's got something really amusing coming out. He always dies a fortnight before."

What more do you want to know? I would tell a few scabrous rumors I'd picked up in the other houses I'd visited, because of course we're all great scandalmongers. I'd clown around; they would listen, laugh, exclaim, "He's always so charming." Meanwhile Mademoiselle's book had finally been found under an armchair, where it had been dragged, then chewed and torn, by some young puppy or kitten. Mademoiselle would seat herself at the harpsichord. To begin with, I'd leave her there making a noise all by herself, then, after a gesture to the mother expressing my approbation, I would go over to her. *The mother:* "It's really not at all bad, is it? If only we'd make more of an effort, but we won't; we prefer to waste our time chattering, fussing with clothes, running hither and thither, and I don't know what. You're no sooner out of the door than the book's banged shut and stays that way till your next visit. But of course you never scold her."

Meanwhile, since I had to do something. I would take her hands and place them differently. I'd get tetchy and cry, "G, G, G, mademoiselle, it's a G!" *The mother:* "Have you no ears, miss? I, who am not at the keyboard and cannot see your book, even I can sense that it must be a G. You give Monsieur such a deal of trouble. I don't know how he can be so patient. You don't remember anything he tells you. You're not making any progress."

Then I would soften my criticisms a little, nod my head, and say, "Forgive me, madame, forgive me. It could be better if only Mademoiselle would really try, if she would practice a little; but even so, it's not bad at all." *The mother:* "If I were in your place, I'd keep her on the same piece for a whole year." "Oh, as far as that goes, she'll be staying on this one until she's mastered all the difficulties. And it won't take as long as Madame thinks." "Monsieur Rameau, you are flattering her. You're too kind. That's the only thing she'll remember of the whole lesson, and she'll remind me of it whenever she gets a chance."

The hour would draw to an end; my pupil would hand me my tiny fee with a curtsy and a graceful gesture of the arm learned from her dancing master. As I put it in my pocket, the mother would say, "Excellent, mademoiselle. If Javillier were here he'd compliment you on that." I would chat with them a moment longer, just to be polite, then I would disappear. And that's what used to be called an accompaniment lesson.

MYSELF: It's different now, then?

HE: Different! I should say it is! I arrive, I look serious. I make haste to take off my muff. I open the harpsichord. I play a few notes to make sure it's in tune. I'm always in a hurry. If I'm kept waiting a single moment, I start yelling as though I've been robbed. In an hour's time I have to be in such and such a place, in two hours' time at the Duchess of Thingummy's. I'm expected for dinner at the home of a beautiful marquise, and then, when I leave her, I have to go to a concert at Baron de Bagge's in the Rue Neuve-des-Petits-Champs.

MYSELF: And of course you're not expected anywhere?

HE: Correct.

MYSELF: But why do you employ such despicable tricks?

HE: Despicable? Why despicable, if you please? Everyone in my situation uses them. There's nothing despicable in doing what everyone else does. After all, I didn't invent them. And it would be very eccentric and stupid of me if I refused to conform. Oh, I know perfectly well that if you go and apply certain general principles to these things, dragged in from this morality they all talk about and never practice, well of course everything that's black turns out to be white and everything white becomes black. But, mister philosopher, there are general principles of morality just as there are general principles of grammar, and then, in every language, the exceptions to those principles, which I believe you scholars call, er . . . help me, can't you, er . . .

MYSELF: Idioms.

HE: Exactly. Well, every occupation has its exceptions to the general principles of morality, which I am tempted to refer to as professional idioms.

MYSELF: I see what you mean. Fontenelle speaks well, writes well, and yet his style teems with French idioms.

HE: And the sovereign, the minister, the financier, the magistrate, the soldier, the writer, the lawyer, the attorney, the merchant, the banker, the artisan, the singing master, the dancing master —they are all extremely honest people, yet there is not one of them whose conduct does not depart in some particulars from the general principles of morality and is not full of moral idioms. The longer things have been established, the greater the number of idioms. The worse the times are, the more the idioms increase. A trade is as good as the man who practices it. And the converse of that is: in the long run, a man is no better than his trade. So a man has to make the most out of his trade.

MYSELF: The only thing I understand clearly from all that rigmarole is that there are either few trades that are practiced honestly or few honest people who extend their honesty to their trades.

HE: You've hit it! But in fact there are none. Though on the other hand, there aren't many people who are rogues outside their trade. Everything would really go quite well if it weren't for a certain number of people who are referred to as industrious, trustworthy, rigorous in carrying out their duties, strict, or, which amounts to the same thing, are always in their shops from morning till night, practicing their trades, and doing nothing but that. As a result, they are the only ones who become rich and respected.

MYSELF: By using a great many idioms.

HE: Precisely. I see you've caught on. Now one idiom in almost all trades—because certain idioms, like certain idiocies, are common to all ages and climes—one common idiom is to get the largest clientele you can. Because, you see, one of the common idiocies is to believe that the man with the largest clientele is necessarily the best at his trade. Those are two exceptions to the general principles of morality you just have to accept. It's a kind of credit. It's nothing in itself, but public opinion makes it valuable. "A good name is worth more than a golden belt," so the saying goes. Though having a good name doesn't guarantee you the golden belt, and these days, I notice, no one who has a golden belt ever seems to lack a good name. As far as possible, you should try to have the good name and the belt as well. And that is what I'm aiming at when I try to increase my value in people's eyes with what you call my despicable ruses and my unworthy little tricks. I give my lesson, and I give it well: that's the general principle. I also pretend that I have more lessons to give than there are hours in the day: that's the idiom.

MYSELF: And you say you give the lesson well?

HE: Yes, pretty well, quite passably. My dear uncle's fundamental bass has made all that much simpler now. There was a time when I was stealing my pupils' money, yes, stealing it, there's no doubt about that. Today I earn it—as much as the others do, anyway.

MYSELF: And you stole it without remorse?

HE: Without remorse! What do you think? There's a saying, "When one thief steals from another, the devil laughs." The parents were all bursting with money that God alone knows how they came by. They were all courtiers, financiers, big merchants, bankers, promoters, and so on. I was helping them to make restitution—me and a whole crowd of others they were employing in exactly the same way. In nature, all the species devour each other. And all the different classes devour each other in society. It's a way of squaring accounts without having to drag the law into it. The dancer at the Opéra, for instance—once it was La Deschamps, nowadays it's La Guimard—avenges the sovereign by fleecing the financier; then the purveyor of fashions, the jeweler, the interior decorator, the dressmaker, and the swindler avenge the financier by fleecing La Deschamps. And the only ones who do no harm to anyone and still come out of the whole thing any the worse off are the fools and the layabouts—which is just as it should be. So you see that these exceptions to the general principles of morality, or these moral idioms, which everyone makes such a fuss about and refers to as swindler's tricks, don't amount to a thing, and the main thing, as always, is to keep a sense of perspective.

MYSELF: Yours is certainly astonishing.

HE: And, then, there's poverty. The voice of conscience and the claims of honor are difficult to hear when your insides are yelling for food. But that's all right, because if ever I become rich I shall be obliged to make restitution, and I am quite reconciled to making restitution in every possible way, with good food, with gambling, with wine, and with women.

MYSELF: But I'm afraid you're never going to become rich.

HE: Yes, I rather suspect that too.

MYSELF: But supposing you did, what would you do?

HE: I'd do the same as all the other beggars who suddenly get rich: I'd turn into the most insolent rogue you've ever seen. I'd remember everything they made me go through, and I'd repay every humiliation I've been made to suffer with a vengeance. I see it all. I love to give orders, and give orders I shall. I love to be praised, and praise me they shall. I shall have all those hangers-on of Vilmorin's on my payroll, and I shall say to them what people used to say to me: "Get to it, you rogues—amuse me!" And they will amuse me. "Tear all the respectable people I know to ribbons!" And they'll tear them to ribbons, if there are any left. And then we'll have some girls in, and I'll treat them all as equals when we've gotten drunk—and we shall get drunk. And then we'll tell lies about people—oh, and we'll be wicked and vicious in all sorts of ways. It will be delightful. We'll prove that Voltaire hasn't a scrap of genius and that Buffon is just an old windbag, always stuck up there on his high horse, and that Montesquieu is nothing but a clever-clever social butterfly; we'll dump d'Alembert back where he belongs, with all that mathematics of his; and we'll make pulp of all those petty upstart Catos, like you, who despise us out of envy, whose modesty is just a cloak for their pride, and whose respectability is merely a result of their poverty. And as for music—ah, such music we'll make then!

MYSELF: From the praiseworthy use to which you would put your riches, I now perceive what a great pity it is that you're a beggar. The way of life you have described would assuredly bring great honor to the human race, great benefits to your fellow citizens, and glorious renown upon yourself.

HE: I have a feeling you're making fun of me. You don't know who it is you're dealing with, mister philosopher. You don't seem to realize that as things stand, I represent the most influential section of both the city and the court. All our rich men, whatever their rank may be, may have admitted to themselves or may not have admitted to themselves all those things I've just confided to you; but the fact is that the life I said I would lead in their place is the life they are actually leading. That's how much you know, you fellows. You think the same sort of happiness is right for everybody. What a bizarre way of seeing things! Your sort of happiness presupposes a certain romantic turn of mind that we just don't have, an exceptional mental outlook, unusual tastes. You dignify this eccentricity with the name of virtue, you call it philosophical. But are virtue and philosophy suited to everyone? They're things you acquire if you get the chance and hang on to if you can. Just imagine what the world would be like if everyone were wise and philosophical—damnably dull, you will agree. Long live philosophy, say I! Long live the wisdom of Solomon: good wine to drink, good food to stuff yourself with, pretty women to tumble, soft beds to lie on. Take all that away and the rest is mere vanity.

MYSELF: What! Fighting for one's country?

HE: Vanity. No one has a country any more. I can see nothing but tyrants and slaves from one pole to the other.

MYSELF: Being of use to one's friends?

HE: Vanity. Who has friends? And even supposing we did, ought we to turn them into ingrates? Because, if you think about it, that's almost always what happens when you help people. Gratitude is a burden, and all burdens are things to be gotten rid of.

MYSELF: To fill a position in society and carry out its duties?

HE: Vanity. The only reason anyone ever wants a position is to become rich. So what does it matter if you have a position or not if you're rich already? And what does doing your duty lead to? Jealousy, anxiety, persecution. Is that any way to get ahead? Bowing and scraping, dammit, that's the way, bowing and scraping. You have to keep your eyes on the people at the top, study their tastes, fall in with their whims, pander to their vices, praise the rotten things they do—that's the secret.

MYSELF: What about supervising your children's education?

HE: Vanity. There are tutors paid to do that.

MYSELF: But suppose the tutor shares your own principles and neglects his duties. Who is going to suffer?

HE: Certainly not me. Perhaps my daughter's husband, one day. Or my son's wife.

MYSELF: But suppose they both rush headlong into debauchery and vice?

HE: With their social position, it's to be expected.

MYSELF: What if they dishonor themselves?

HE: You can't dishonor yourself if you're rich, whatever you do.

MYSELF: Then what if they ruin themselves?

HE: That's their hard luck. . . .

MYSELF: [Rich people in search of pleasure] wear everything out in the end. Their spirits become dulled. They sink into the clutches of boredom. They lie there suffocating in their own affluence, and if someone were to end their lives for them then and there, he would be doing them a favor. Why? Because the only kind of happiness they know is the kind most quickly blunted. I don't despise the pleasures of the senses: I have a palate too, and one that enjoys delicate foods or a fine wine. I have a heart and eyes: I enjoy looking at a pretty woman. I like to feel the firm curves of her breast beneath my hand, to press my lips against hers, to drink deep of pleasure in her eyes, and die of it in her arms. Occasionally, I quite enjoy an evening spent drinking with my friends, even if it gets a little rowdy. But I cannot pretend to you that I don't find it infinitely more pleasant still to have helped the needy, to have settled some particularly thorny problem, to have given a piece of useful advice, to have read an enjoyable book, to have gone for a walk with a man or woman dear to my heart, to have spent a few instructive hours with my children, to have written a good page, to have carried out the duties of my station in society, to have said a few sweet and tender words to the woman I love and felt her answering arms cling mutely around my neck. I can think of some actions that I would give everything I possess to have performed myself. [Voltaire's] *Mahomet* is a sublime work. But I would rather have rehabilitated the memory of the Calas family. A man I know once went away to live in Cartagena. He was a younger son in a country where custom transmits all family wealth to the eldest. While still abroad, he learned that his elder brother, always spoiled by the family, had stripped his too indulgent parents of everything they possessed and thrown them out of their home, so that the good old couple were now dragging out a miserable existence in a small provincial town. So what did he do, this younger son who had been harshly treated by his parents and forced to seek his fortune far from home? He sent them help; he hastily wound up his affairs, returned to his own country a rich man, restored his father and mother to their own home, and saw to it that his sisters married well.

Yes, my dear Rameau, and that man still thinks of that period as the happiest in his life. There were tears in his eyes as he told me about it; and I myself, even as I am telling you his story, feel my heart stirring with joy and my tongue faltering with happiness.

HE: What an odd lot of creatures you philosophers are!

MYSELF: And what an unfortunate lot of creatures you and your kind are if you are unable to apprehend that man can rise above his fate, that it is impossible to be unhappy when you are protected by such nobility as I have described.

HE: It's a kind of happiness I would have found rather difficult to study closely; it's not very often you meet it. So according to you, we ought all to behave like decent people?

MYSELF: If you want to be happy? Without a doubt.

HE: Yet I see an infinite number of decent people who are not happy and an infinite number of people who are happy without being decent.

MYSELF: No, you only think you do.

HE: And isn't it precisely because I had one moment of common sense and honesty that I have no place to go for supper tonight?

MYSELF: No, Rameau, no! It's because you haven't had them the rest of the time. It's because you didn't realize early enough that the most important thing in this world is to find a way of life that will free you from slavish dependence on others.

HE: Well, slavishly dependent or not, the way I found is at least the easiest.

MYSELF: And the least reliable, as well as the least honest.

HE: But the most in keeping with my character, since I am an idler, a fool, and a good-for-nothing.

MYSELF: Agreed.

HE: And, then, since I can achieve the happiness I want by using my natural defects—which I acquired without effort and am able to preserve without effort, which fit in nicely with the customs of the country I live in, which suit the taste of my protectors and satisfy their private needs better than a lot of virtues that would simply point an accusing finger at them from morning till night—it would be very odd in me to go around tormenting myself like a damned soul in order to twist myself into some other shape, make myself into someone quite different from what I am, and give myself a new character nothing at all like my own. I'll agree that all the new qualities I'd acquire would be very admirable, because I don't want to argue with you, but acquiring them and using them would be a terrible effort, and they would get me exactly nowhere. They might even get me worse than nowhere—by implying a constant criticism of the wealthy people that beggars like myself have to depend on for a living.

People praise virtue, but they hate it, they run away from it. It freezes you to death, and in this world you've got to keep your feet warm. Apart from which, it would make me bad-tempered, inevitably. Why is it that the pious people we see are so often hard and irritable, so difficult to get on with? It's because they're forcing themselves to do something that isn't natural to them. They're unhappy; and when you're unhappy, you make others unhappy too. That's not what I'm looking for, and that's not what my protectors are looking for. I've got to be gay, quick-witted, entertaining, full of buffoonery, funny. Virtue demands respect, and respect makes people uncomfortable. Virtue demands admiration, and admiration doesn't amuse people. I have to deal with people who are bored, and my job is to make them laugh. Therefore, since absurdity and folly are what make people laugh, I have to be absurd and foolish. And even if nature hadn't made me that way, the easiest thing would be to pretend she had. Happily, I have no need to be a hypocrite. . . .

But suppose your friend Rameau should one day start to display contempt for money, for women, for good food, and for an idle life of pleasure, suppose he should ever start to play the stoic, what would he be then? A hypocrite. Rameau must be what he is: a happy robber among wealthy robbers, not a fellow who goes round trumpeting about virtue or even a simple virtuous man gnawing his crust of bread alone or in company with other beggars. To put it bluntly, I have no use for your idea of happiness or that of the handful of visionaries like you.

MYSELF: I can see, my dear fellow, that you have no idea what it is like and, indeed, that you are not even capable of learning.

HE: And thank heaven for that, say I! Thank heaven for that. I should simply end up dying of hunger, boredom, and perhaps regret.

MYSELF: If that's the case, then the only advice I can give you is to hurry back as fast as you can to the house you so imprudently got yourself kicked out of.

HE: And to do that thing you don't object to in its literal sense and I find rather distasteful in its metaphorical sense?

MYSELF: That's my advice.

HE: Well—apart from this metaphor that I find so unattractive at the moment but may find quite attractive again later on . . .

MYSELF: What a bizarre attitude!

HE: There's nothing bizarre about it at all. I'm quite willing to be abject, but I don't wish to be forced into it. I'm quite willing to lower my dignity . . . Are you laughing?

MYSELF: Yes, your dignity strikes me as rather funny.

HE: Every man has his dignity. I'm willing to forget mine, but at my own discretion and not when someone else tells me to. When people feel like saying, "Crawl!" to me, must I be obliged to crawl? That's the way a worm gets about. And the way I do too. Left to ourselves, we're quite happy that way; but we both rear up when someone treads on our tail. . . .

HE: If it is important to attain the sublime in any field, then it is in doing evil. People spit on a petty pickpocket, but they can never refuse a kind of admiration to a great criminal. We are amazed by his courage, we shudder at his savagery. Consistency of character is a matter for admiration in every walk of life.

MYSELF: But this admirable consistency of character is something you don't have yet. I find you vacillate in your principles from time to time. I'm not certain whether the badness of your character is natural to you or acquired, and if the latter, whether it might not be possible for you to cultivate it even further.

HE: You're right there, but I've done my best. Have I not at least had the modesty to recognize the existence of beings more perfect in their badness than myself? . . .

HE: . . . I want my son to be happy, or, what amounts to the same thing, respected, rich, and powerful. I know something about the easiest ways of reaching that goal, and I shall teach them to him early. And though all you wise people may blame me, I shall be absolved by the crowd and by his success. He will have money, I guarantee that. If he has a lot of it, then he will lack for nothing, not even your esteem and respect.

MYSELF: You might be mistaken.

HE: Or he'll do without it, like a lot of other people.

In all that he told me, there were a great many of those things that people think, that they allow to determine their actions, but that they never admit in words. And that, truth to tell, is the only really noticeable difference between this fellow of mine and most of the people we see all around us. He was admitting all his vices—and everyone else's vices—but he was not a hypocrite. He was being neither more nor less despicable than they. He was merely being more honest, more willing to face facts, and occasionally profound in his depravity. . . .

MYSELF: . . . True, a man who is prepared to stop at nothing in order to be rich must be pretty ineffectual if he fails. But it so happens that there are people, like myself, who do not look upon wealth as the most desirable thing in the world: eccentrics.

HE: Very eccentric. No one is born thinking that way. It's something you have to acquire; it doesn't exist in nature.

MYSELF: Not in human nature?

HE: Not in human nature either. Everything living, man not excepted, seeks its own good at the expense of whoever is at hand. And I am sure that if I let my little savage grow up without ever mentioning such things to him, he would still want to be finely dressed, magnificently fed, made much of by men, adored by women, and showered with all the things that make for happiness in life.

MYSELF: If your little savage were left entirely to himself, if his childish ignorance were left intact, if he were allowed to acquire all the violent passions of a grown man while still remaining as deficient in reason as he had been in his cradle, then he would end up strangling his father and going to bed with his mother.

HE: That proves the necessity of a good upbringing, and who denies that? But what is a good upbringing if it is not one that teaches us how to enjoy all sorts of pleasures without danger and without inconvenience?

MYSELF: I am in almost complete agreement there, but we'd better not go into it any further.

HE: Why not?

MYSELF: Because I'm afraid we only appear to be in agreement. If we enter into a discussion of what the dangers and inconveniences to be avoided are, there is a risk that our opinions might diverge. . . .

MYSELF: Whatever the task a man applies himself to, that is the one that nature intended him for.

HE: Then she makes some odd blunders. I'm not one of those people who look down from such a height that differences disappear, so that a man pruning a tree with a pair of shears and a caterpillar nibbling one of the tree's leaves just look like two different insects, each performing its appointed task. But there's nothing to stop you perching up there on the epicycle of Mercury if you want to. You can look down at us like another Réaumur. Just as he classified flies into the sewing kind, the measuring kind, and the clipping kind, so you can classify men as carpenters, cabinetmakers, runners, dancers, singers, and so on. That's your business; I don't want any part of it. I'm down here in this world, and I'm staying here. But if it's natural to be hungry—and if I always come back to hunger, that's because it's a sensation that's always with me—then I don't see how a society in which a person doesn't always have enough to eat can be a good one. What a hell of a system if there are some men with too much of everything while others, with the same demands being made on them by their stomachs, the same ever-returning hunger, can't get as much as one little bite to eat. And the worst part of all is the unnatural posture that our poverty forces on us. The needy man doesn't even walk like anyone else—he hops, he crawls, he wriggles, he drags himself along. His whole life is spent in taking up attitudes.

MYSELF: What do you mean by "attitudes"?

HE: Go and ask Noverre [the choreographer] that. But there are a lot more to be seen in real life than his art can ever imitate.

MYSELF: So now you're up there too, if I may use your own expression—or, rather, Montaigne's—"perched on the epicycle of Mercury" and contemplating the varied pantomime of humankind.

HE: Not at all. You are wrong, I assure you. I am too heavy to rise so high. I leave those cloudy regions to the cranes. I stick close to earth. I keep watch on all that's going on around me, and I perform my attitudes—or else amuse myself by watching the others performing theirs. I am an excellent mime, as you shall see.

Whereupon, with a smile, he proceeded to give an imitation of a man expressing admiration, a man begging, a man fawning. Right foot forward, left foot back, spine bent, head tilted up and back, eyes apparently hanging on the expression of another pair of eyes, mouth half open, arms stretched out toward some object in front of him, he seemed to be waiting for a command. The command was given; he darted away like an arrow; he came back; the task had been performed; he expressed as much. His eyes were missing nothing; if anything fell to the floor, he picked it up; he slipped a footstool or a pillow under someone's feet; he held out a saucer; he pulled up a chair; he opened a door; he closed a window; he drew the curtains; he watched his master and mistress, motionless, arms hanging at his sides, legs together, listening, straining to interpret the expressions on their faces and saying: Now you've seen my attitudes. Most people's are the same; flatterers, courtiers, lackeys, beggars—they're all like that. . . .

MYSELF: But according to you, there are a great many beggars in this world of ours; and I can't think of anyone who doesn't know a few steps of that ballet of yours.

HE: You are right. There is only one man in the whole of any kingdom who walks: that's the king. All the others just go through a series of attitudes.

MYSELF: The king? I'm not so sure about that. Don't you think there may occasionally be a little foot by his side, a little curly head, a little nose that makes him join the dance from time to time? Anyone who needs someone else is a beggar, and a beggar must have an attitude. The king performs his attitudes to his mistress and to God; he dances his ballet for them. The minister, in his turn, dances the role of the courtier, the flatterer, the valet, or the beggar before the king. Then there is the crowd of ambitious climbers, all dancing the steps you've just shown me, all doing their variations, each more despicable than the last, in front of the minister. The wellborn *abbé*, in his Geneva collar and his long cloak, humbles himself once every week, at least, in front of the official who hands out the livings. Believe me, what you call the beggar's pantomime is the whole world's ring-around-the-rosy. Everyone has his Bertin and his little Hus.

HE: That's a consoling thought.

But while I was talking he had been mimicking the attitudes of the characters as I named them, in the most hilarious way. For example, when it came to the little *abbé*, he held his hat under one arm and his missal in his left hand. With the right, he lifted up the tail of his coat, then he stepped forward, head tipped slightly toward one shoulder, eyes lowered, imitating the hypocrite so perfectly that I thought I was actually seeing the author of the *Refutations*[4] at his audience with the Bishop of Orléans. When it came to the flatterers and the climbers, he went

[4] Refers to the Abbé Gauchat (1709–1774), enemy of the philosophes, author of a *Refutation* of their writings.

down on his belly. It was the very image of Bouret pleading with the comptroller general.[5]

After telling him what a superb performance I thought he had given, I added, "Nevertheless, there is one being who is exempt from this pantomime. I mean the philosopher, who has nothing and asks for nothing."

HE: And where is that animal to be found? If he has nothing, then he is suffering; if he begs for nothing, then he'll get nothing, so he'll always continue to suffer.

MYSELF: No. Diogenes laughed at his needs.

HE: But a man has to have clothes.

MYSELF: No. He went naked.

HE: It must have been cold in Athens sometimes.

MYSELF: Less so than here.

HE: But people used to eat there.

MYSELF: Of course.

HE: At whose expense?

MYSELF: Nature's. To whom does a savage turn? To the earth, the animals, the fish, the trees, the plants, the roots, the streams.

HE: Nature keeps a pretty poor table.

MYSELF: The fare is abundant.

HE: And very badly served.

MYSELF: Yet all the food we pile onto our tables is only the leavings from hers.

HE: But you won't deny that the art of our chefs, our pastry-cooks, our confectioners, our caterers improves it somewhat. If he managed to keep up that ascetic diet, this Diogenes of yours can't have been bothered very much by the demands of his body.

MYSELF: You're wrong there. But the dress of the Cynics then was like the dress of our monks today and had the same virtuous effect. The Cynics were the Carmelites and Franciscans of Athens.

HE: Then I've caught you out. Diogenes must have danced in the pantomime too—if not in front of Pericles, then at least in front of Lais or Phryne.

[5] Refers to the financier Bouret's attempt to avoid bankruptcy.

MYSELF: Wrong again. The courtesans all the others had to pay such a high price for gave themselves to Diogenes for their own pleasure.

HE: But suppose the courtesans were busy and the Cynic in a hurry?

MYSELF: Then he went back into his barrel and managed without them.

HE: And you would advise me to imitate him?

MYSELF: I'll be hanged if it wouldn't be better than crawling all the time, debasing and prostituting yourself.

HE: But I need a good bed, good food, warm clothes in winter, cool clothes in summer, rest, money, and a great many other things, all of which I prefer to owe to someone else's kindness than to my own hard work.

MYSELF: That's because you're a loafer, a glutton, a coward, and rotten through and through.

HE: I thought I'd made that clear.

MYSELF: Worldly things have their value, I know; but you overlook the value of what you are sacrificing to attain them. And so you dance, you have danced, and you will continue to dance that despicable pantomime.

HE: It's true. But it never took much effort to do that, and now it doesn't take any at all. That's why it's better for me not to try to change my way of life, because I should only find the new one too difficult and have to give it up. But I can see from what you say that my poor little wife was something of a philosopher. She had the courage of a lion. Sometimes we hadn't a crust of bread to eat or so much as a sou to buy any with. We'd already sold most of our clothes. I used to throw myself across the bed and lie there racking my brains to think of someone who would lend me a crown or two—which I would never have paid back. But she—as gay as a lark she'd sit down at the harpsichord and accompany herself as she sang. She had the voice of a nightingale. I'm sorry you never heard her. When I was playing at a musical evening, I used to take her along with me. On the way there, I'd say to her, "Now, then, my dear, you must make sure they admire you. Let them see all your talents and charms. Carry them away, overwhelm them." We arrived, she sang, she carried them away and overwhelmed them. Alas! I lost her, poor darling. Apart from her talent, she had a mouth you could hardly have put your little finger in; teeth like two rows of pearls; eyes, feet, skin, cheeks, breasts, legs like a gazelle; thighs and buttocks that were a sculptor's dream. Sooner or later she would have landed the head of a Treasury department at the very least. What a walk! What a rump! Oh, God, what a rump!

At which he began giving an imitation of his wife's walk. He took tiny little steps, tipped his nose up in the air, fluttered a fan, threw his bottom from side to side. It was the funniest, the most devastating caricature of all our little coquettes.

Then, taking up the thread of his speech again, he added, "I took her out walking everywhere. The Tuileries, the Palais-Royal, the Boulevards. I could never have kept her. If you'd caught sight of her in the morning, crossing the street in her little short jacket and without her hat, you'd have stopped to look at her; and you could have put your hands right around her waist without having to squeeze her. The men who followed her, watching her trip along on those tiny feet, gauging the exact curves of that sumptuous rump beneath the clinging petticoats, they all used to quicken their pace. She'd let them catch up with her; then she'd quickly turn and look at them, all wide-eyed, with those dark, glowing eyes of hers. That used to stop them in their tracks, all right. For the front of the medal was no less attractive than the back. But, alas, I have lost her, and my hopes of making a fortune all went with her! That was the only reason I married her. I had explained all my plans to her. She was too intelligent not to see that they were certain of success and too sensible not to approve of them."

At which he began to weep and sob, saying, "No, no, I'll never get over it. After that, as you see from this skullcap, I took holy orders."

MYSELF: From grief?

HE: If you like. But more in order to have my soup bowl handy on my head, really. . . . But do look and see what time it is! I have to go to the Opéra.

MYSELF: What are they giving tonight?

HE: The Dauvergne thing. There are some fine things in his music—it's a pity he wasn't the first to write them. There are always one or two out of all those dead people to make trouble for the living. But there it is. *Quisque suos patimur manes.*[6] But it's half-past five. I can hear the bell ringing for the Abbé Canaye and for me. Good-bye, mister philosopher. I'm the same as ever, don't you think?

MYSELF: Alas! Yes, unfortunately.

HE: I only hope I can go on being just as unfortunate for another forty years. He laughs best who laughs last.

[6] "Each of us suffers from his own antecedents."

The Salons

Diderot was a regular contributor to La Correspondance littéraire, *the private newsletter of his closest friend, Melchior von Grimm. It was sent to a select group of highly placed foreign subscribers, eager to keep up with current goings-on in Paris. Diderot was also a frequent visitor at the biennial art exposition known as the Salon. As his interest grew, he thought of writing a critical description of the expositions for* La Correspondance littéraire. *His contribution became a regular one, from 1759 to 1781, with the exception of 1773, when he was in Russia. In the Salons, one can follow Diderot's increasing familiarity with the arts, their techniques and problems, and also his increasing mastery of art criticism. He was a creative critic, able to make what he saw come to life on the printed page and sometimes even re-creating the work of art by expounding his ideas about how it should have been done. He frequented painters in their studios and tried conscientiously to understand their processes and problems, as we can see in the* Essay on Painting *(1765). The great Salons of 1763, 1765, and 1767 are charming reading, highlighted by piquant digressions on aesthetic theory and a variety of other subjects. None of these works was published until after Diderot's death. (See A-T, Vols. 10–13.)*

The Salons

Salon of 1763

Deshays: *La Chasteté de Joseph*

Here we have a piece of work that may be smaller than the preceding one but need not yield to it on the point of merit, while also reinforcing the argument of my digression:[1] it is *La Chasteté de Joseph.*

I don't know whether this painting was intended for a church, but it is enough to damn a priest's soul to hell in the middle of a mass and send the entire congregation to the devil. Have you ever seen anything more sensual? And I'm not even excepting the Correggio in the Dresden museum, that *Magdalene* of which you are so careful always to keep an engraving handy—for the mortification of your senses.

Potiphar's wife has thrown herself from the head of the bed toward the foot; she is lying on her stomach and clinging, with one arm, to the arm of the simple and handsome slave with whom she is infatuated. You can see her bosom and her shoulders. How beautiful that bosom is! And how beautiful those shoulders! A look of love and angry disappointment, though the anger is stronger than the love, is depicted on her face; the artist has endowed it with an expression that reveals her brazenness and her wickedness without marring her beauty: when you have looked at her closely, you are not surprised either by her present posture or by the rest of her story. Meanwhile, Joseph is inexpressibly troubled: he does not know whether he should run or stay; his eyes are turned toward heaven; he is calling upon it to help him; he is an image of the most violent agony. Deshays has not been foolish enough to lend him that outraged, angry look so inappropriate in a man of the world who is being gazed at enticingly by a charming woman. He is perhaps a little less chaste than in

[1] Diderot had just written, in discussing another painting by Deshays: "There has never been any religion as fertile in crimes as Christianity; from the murder of Abel to the torture of Calas, there is not a line of its history not covered in blood."

the Holy Bible, but he is infinitely more interesting. Don't you prefer him like this too: hesitating and perplexed? Isn't it easier to put yourself in his place? Whenever I go back to the Salon, I am always hoping to find him in his mistress's arms. For there is that naked leg of hers, hanging over the edge of the bed. Oh, those wonderful, muted flesh tints! For, to be precise, her thigh is not actually uncovered; but there is such magic in the light veil that is covering it—or rather uncovering it—that there is no woman who would not blush at the sight, and no man whose heart would not palpitate. If Joseph had been standing on that side, his chastity would not have stood a chance: either the grace he is invoking would not have come or it would have arrived only in time to arouse his remorse. There is a heavy, flowered cloth with a green background, rich and velvety, falling in wide, straight folds and covering the head of the bed.

If you ask me to choose one picture from the whole Salon, then I pick this one; you must look for your own. You will find others more expert, more perfect, perhaps; but I defy you to find a more seductive one. You will say that the woman's head is not quite correct, perhaps; that Joseph's isn't young enough; that the red cloth covering a portion of the commode is too harsh; that the yellow drapery the woman has placed her hand on to support herself is coarsely executed: it looks like bark and hurts your delicate eyes. I laugh at all these criticisms, and I stick to my choice.

Chardin

Here is the real painter; here is the true colorist.

There are several small paintings by Chardin in the Salon. Almost all of them depict various fruits surrounded by the accessories of a meal. They are nature itself; the objects all stand out from the canvas in such a way that the eye is ready to take them for reality itself.

The one you see as you walk up the stairs is worth particular attention. On top of a table, the artist has placed an old Chinese porcelain vase, two biscuits, a jar of olives, a basket of fruit, two glasses half-filled with wine, a Seville orange, and a meat pie.

I feel I need to make myself another pair of eyes when I look at other artists' paintings; to see Chardin's I need only keep those that nature gave me and use them well.

If I wanted my child to be a painter, this is the painting I should buy. "Copy this," I should say to the child. "Copy it again." But perhaps nature itself is not more difficult to copy.

The fact is, that porcelain vase is made of porcelain; those olives really are separated from the eye by the water they are immersed in; you have only to put out your hand and you can pick up those biscuits and eat them, that orange and cut it and squeeze it, that glass of wine and drink it, those fruits and peel them, that meat pie and slice it.

Here is the man who truly understands the harmony of colors and their reflections. Oh, Chardin! It is not white or red or black you mix on your palette, it is the very substance of things themselves, it is air and light that you take on the point of your brush and apply to your canvas.

After my child had copied and recopied this piece of work, I should set him to work on the same master's *La Raie dépouillée* [*The Gutted Skate*]. The object itself is disgusting, but that is the fish's very flesh, its skin, its blood: the real thing would not affect you otherwise. Monsieur Pierre, [you are a famous painter], but when next you go to the Academy, look carefully at this canvas and learn, if you can, the secret of using your talent to redeem the distastefulness that is present in certain natural objects.

This magic is beyond our understanding. There are thick layers of paint in some places, laid one on top of the other, that make their effect by glowing through, from the bottom upward. In other places, it is as though a vapor had been breathed onto the canvas; in others still, a light foam has been thrown across it. Rubens, Berchem, Greuze, Loutherbourg could all explain this technique to you better than I, for all of them can also make your eyes experience its effects. If you move close, everything becomes confused, flattens out, and vanishes. Then as you move back, everything takes shape and re-creates itself again.

I have been told that Greuze, upon coming into the Salon and noticing the Chardin painting I have just described, looked at it, then heaved a profound sigh as he walked on: a eulogy both briefer and more valuable that mine. . . .

Greuze

Now here is the man for my money, this Greuze fellow. Ignoring for the moment his smaller compositions, which will provide me with some very pleasant things to say to him later, I come at once to his picture *Piété filiale*, which might better have been entitled *The Reward for Providing a Good Upbringing*.

To begin with, I like this genre: it is a painting with a moral. Come, now, you must agree! Don't you think the painter's brush has been employed long enough, and too long, in the portrayal of debauchery and vice? Ought we not to be glad to see it competing at last with dramatic poetry in moving us, instructing us, correcting us, and encouraging us to virtue? Courage, Greuze, my friend: you must go on teaching morality in your paintings, and you must go on painting pictures like this one! When the moment comes for you to say farewell to life, there will be not one of your compositions you cannot recall without pleasure. Why were you not there beside that girl who looked at the head of your *Paralytic* and then exclaimed, with charming spontaneity, "Oh, heavens! How touching it is! But if I look at it any more, I'm sure I shall cry"? How I wish that she had been my daughter! I would have recognized our kinship in those impulsive words. Like her, as I looked at that eloquent and pathetic old man, I felt my heart melting and the tears springing to my eyes. . . .

Salon of 1765

Boucher

I don't know what to say about this painter. The degradation of his taste, his colors, his composition, his figures, his expression, and his drawing has kept exact pace with the increasing depravity of his morals. What do you expect an artist to put on his canvases? Whatever is in his imagination. And what must any man have in his imagination who spends his whole time with the lowest kind of prostitute? . . . I defy you to go into any stretch of countryside and find a blade of grass anything like the ones in his pictures. And, then, the confusion of objects piled one on top of the other, so out of place, so ill-assorted, that the painting as a whole is less the product of a well-ordered mind than a madman's fantasy. . . .

I must dare to speak the truth: this man does not know what true grace is; he has never been acquainted with truth; the ideas of delicacy, decency, innocence, and simplicity have become almost total strangers to him; he has never for an instant really looked at nature—not, at least, at that nature capable of stirring an interest in my heart or yours or that of a wellborn child or a sensitive woman. And he has no taste. Among the infinity of proofs that I could give of this fact, one alone will suffice: in all the multitude of figures, male and female, that he has painted, I defy you to find four that would be suitable for a bas-relief or statue. There is too much grimacing, too much simpering, too much artificiality of manner and affectation there for an art of any rigor. It is no good his painting the women nude for me: I still see them wearing their rouge, their patches, their pompons, and all their other boudoir frills. Can you believe that anything has ever passed through his mind resembling in any way that charming and yet decorous picture we find in Petrarch?

E'l riso, e'l canto, e'l parlar dolce umano.[2]

Those delicate and subtle analogies that demand the presence of certain objects on a canvas and link them one to another with secret and imperceptible threads—I swear by all that's holy, he doesn't even know they exist. All his compositions are filled with an unbearable visual uproar. He is the deadliest enemy of silence that I know; he has now reached the stage of painting the prettiest little puppets in the world; he will end up a mere illustrator. And yet, my friend, it is at the very moment when Boucher has ceased to be an artist that he has been named chief painter to the king. And don't go believing that he is the equivalent in his genre of Crébillon *fils* in his. The morals are about the same, but the writer has far more talent than the painter. The only ad-

[2] "Her laughter, her singing, and her sweet, kindly voice."

vantage the latter has is an inexhaustible fecundity, an unbelievable facility, especially in the accessory elements of his pastorals. When he paints children, he groups them well; but he may as well have left them frolicking up in the clouds. In the whole of that numberless brood, you will not find one engaged in any activity related to real life: studying lessons, reading, writing, beating flax. They are fanciful, imaginary creatures: little bastards sired by Bacchus or Silenus. They are the sort of children that would be in place gamboling around a Greek or Roman vase. They are fat, chubby, dimpled. If the artist knows anything about working in marble, we shall see if I'm not right. In short, take all this man's paintings and there is scarcely one to which you could not say—as Fontenelle said to the sonata, "Sonata, what is it you want of me?"—"Painting, what is it you want of me?" Do you remember how at one time he had that passion for painting virgins? Well, what were they, his virgins? A lot of pretty little hussies. And his angels? Licentious little satyrs. And, then, he uses such grayish colors in his landscapes, such uniform tones, that from a distance of two feet, you might easily mistake his canvas for a piece of well-mowed lawn or a neatly squared-off parsley bed. And yet he's not a fool. He is a fake good painter, in the same way that there are fake wits. He has no concept of art, only its conceits.

BOUCHER: *Autre pastorale*

Well, my good friend, perhaps you think my cruel taste is going to be more indulgent toward this one? You are wrong. I can already hear that voice inside me crying, "Out of the Salon, out of the Salon!" Try as I may, I simply cannot teach it Chardin's lesson: "Be gentle, be gentle"; it simply flies into a worse rage still and shouts, "Out of the Salon with it!"

It is an image from some delirious fantasy. On the right, in the foreground, the usual shepherdess, Catinon or Favart, lying asleep with a nice big sty on her left eye. Which makes one wonder why she's gone to sleep like that, in such a damp place, with that little cat on her lap. Behind the woman, starting from the edge of the canvas and receding through several successive planes, we see turnips, cabbages, leeks, an earthenware pot and a syringa in that pot, a large block of stone, a large vase garlanded with flowers on top of the large block of stone, trees, foliage, and some landscape. Facing the sleeper stands a shepherd, looking down at her. He is separated from her by a little rustic fence; in one hand he holds a basket of flowers, in the other a rose. Now, my friend, just tell me what a kitten is doing in the lap of a peasant girl when she isn't sleeping at the door of her cottage. And that rose the peasant is holding—isn't that an inconceivable platitude? And why isn't the stupid bumpkin bending down toward her? Why isn't he kissing, or preparing to kiss, that mouth being offered to him? Why isn't he moving quietly toward her? But do you think that's the end of what the painter has chosen to throw onto his canvas? Oh, by no means! Didn't you realize that there was yet another landscape in the distance? That we can see rising behind the trees what appears to be the smoke from a neighboring hamlet?

Chardin

Oh, Chardin, you are just in time to restore the use of my eyes to me after the mortal injuries inflicted on them by your colleague Challe. So there you are again, great magician, with your mute symphonies! How eloquently they speak to the artist! What lessons he learns from them about the imitation of nature, the science of color, and the creation of harmony! How the air moves around those objects! Even sunlight cannot blend the disparate objects it illumines better. For one who can paint like this, the distinction between compatible and incompatible colors seems almost unnecessary.

If it is true, as the philosophers say, that there is nothing real but our sensations, that neither the emptiness of space nor even the solidity of bodies possesses anything in itself of what we experience from it, then let them tell me, those philosophers, what difference they can find, four feet away from your paintings, between the Creator and you.

Chardin is so true, so harmonious, that even when there is nothing to be seen on his canvas but inanimate objects—vases, bottles, bread, wine, water, grapes, fruit, pastries—he can still hold his own and even draw you away perhaps from two of the most beautiful Vernets, beside which he has not hesitated to place himself. And that is just the way it is in the world we live in, my friend, where the presence of a man, a horse, or an animal never destroys the effect of a piece of rock, a tree, or a brook. The brook, the tree, and the piece of rock undoubtedly interest us less than the man, the woman, the horse, or the animal, but they are equally true.

I must tell you an idea that has just occurred to me, my friend, one that may not come back to me later. It is this: that what we call "genre" painting ought only to be practiced by older painters or by those who were born old. It demands only study and patience. No fire, little genius, scarcely any poetry, a great deal of technique and truth—and nothing else. It is also true that the time of life at which we devote ourselves to what is called—according to usage rather than experience—the quest for truth, or philosophy, is precisely that at which our temples are becoming grizzled and at which we should cut a somewhat ludicrous figure trying to write a love letter. Reflect upon this resemblance between philosophers and genre painters. But speaking of gray hairs, my friend, I noticed this morning that my head was quite silver with them; and I exclaimed, as Sophocles did when Socrates questioned him about his love affairs, "I am escaping from that wild and furious master."

Vernet

Twenty-five paintings, my friend! Twenty-five paintings. And what paintings! He is like the creator himself for celerity and like nature herself for truth. There is scarcely one of these compositions on which another painter, working hard all the time, would not have spent the entire two years in which Vernet was able to do them all. What unbelievable effects of light! What beautiful skies! What water! What composition! What a prodigious variety of scenes! Here, a child rescued from a shipwreck is being carried on his father's shoulders; there, a woman stretched out on the shore, dead, while her husband grieves beside her. The sea roars, the winds whistle, the thunder rolls, while the darkling flashes of the pale lightning rend the clouds, revealing yet also obscuring the scene. You can hear the noise of a ship as it breaks up; its masts are tilted, its sails torn; some of the crew are on the deck, stretching their arms up to the heavens; others have thrown themselves into the sea. The waves are dashing them against the nearby rocks, where their blood mingles with the white foam of the breakers. I can see some who are floating, some about to be engulfed, and others hastening to reach the shore on which they will be broken. There is the same variety of character, of action and expression among the spectators: some are shuddering and averting their eyes; others are trying to help; others, motionless, are simply watching. Some have lighted a fire under a rock; they are trying to revive a dying woman; I hope they will succeed. Turn your eyes to another sea and there you behold calm weather with all its charms. The placid waters, smooth and welcoming, stretch into the distance, their transparency fading by imperceptible gradations, their surface by imperceptible gradations growing brighter, out to the line of the horizon where they meet the sky. The ships are motionless; the sailors and passengers are engaged in every kind of diversion that will help to beguile their impatience. If it is morning, look at those light mists rising! How that mist, spread over all the natural features of the scenes, has enlivened and refreshed them! If it is evening, how golden the crests of those mountains are! With what delicate tints the skies are washed! See how the clouds are moving up there, wafting across the sky and dyeing the sea below with their reflected colors! Go out into the countryside, turn your eyes upward to the vaulted heavens, observe exactly what is to be seen there at that moment, and you will swear that a piece of the great, glowing canvas that is lighted by the sun has been cut out and carried back to the artist's easel. Or close your hand so that it makes a tube, then observe the limited area of that great canvas you can perceive through it, and you will swear that it is a Vernet painting, taken from his easel and hung up in the sky. . . . It is impossible to describe his compositions: they must be seen. His nights are as touching as his days are beautiful; his ports are as beautiful as his imaginary pieces are piquant. He is equally wonderful whether his captive brush is humbling itself to depict a scene already provided by nature or whether his muse, all her fetters struck off, is left free to create what she pleases; equally incomprehensible whether he uses the star of the day or the star of the night, natural light or artificial lights to illumine his pictures; always harmonious, vigorous, and wise, like those great poets, those rare men whose natural fire is so well balanced by their judgment that they are never either exaggerated or cold. His factories, his buildings, the clothing, the actions, the men, the animals—everything is true. Close to, his works are striking; from a distance, they are more striking still. Chardin and Vernet, my friend, are two great magicians.

Greuze

Here is your painter and mine, the first among us to conceive the notion of endowing art with moral content, of linking events in such a way that it would be easy to make a novel from them.

La Jeune Fille qui pleure son oiseau mort:[3] What a pretty elegy! What a charming poem! A delicious painting, possibly the most pleasing and interesting in the whole Salon. The poor little girl is facing us; her head is resting on her left hand; the dead bird is lying up near the top of the cage, its head hanging down, its wings drooping, its feet in the air.

What a pretty catafalque the cage makes! How gracefully that green garland winds around it! Poor little girl! Oh, how upset she is! How naturally she is placed! How beautiful her head is! How elegantly her hair is dressed! Her sorrow is profound; she is completely immersed in her grief. Oh, what a beautiful hand! What a beautiful hand! What a beautiful arm! Look how true the detail in those fingers is—and those dimples, and that softness, and that rosy glow the pressure of her head has brought to the tips of those delicate fingers, and the charm of it all. We would undoubtedly go over and kiss that hand if it were not for the respect we feel for the child and her grief. Everything about her

[3] *Girl Weeping for Her Dead Bird.*

is enchanting, even her attire. That kerchief around her neck is so natural! It is so fine and light! When you first look at this work, you say, "Delightful!" If you stay in front of it or come back to it, you cry "Delightful! delightful!" Soon you catch yourself talking to the little girl, consoling her. And to show how true this is, here are some of the things I remember having said to her at different times:

"Your sorrow is very profound, very thoughtful, little girl. What does that dreamy, melancholy air mean? What! For a bird! . . . Come, now, open your heart to me; tell me the truth. Is it really the death of your bird that is making you withdraw so sadly into yourself? You lower your eyes; you do not answer me. You are about to start crying. . . . Well, I understand: he loves you, he swore he did, and he'd been swearing as much for a long time. He was suffering so much, and how could you bear to watch someone you love suffering?

"No, let me go on. Why do you stop my mouth with your hand? That morning, unhappily, your mother was out of the house. He came; you were alone; and he was so handsome, so passionate, so tender, so charming! He had so much love in his eyes, so much truth in his words! He spoke the sort of words that go straight to your heart! He held one of your hands; from time to time, you felt the warmth of a few tears as they fell from his eyes and trickled down your arm. And still your mother did not come. It wasn't your fault; it was your mother's. But there you are crying harder than ever now. I'm not saying all this to make you cry. And why should you? You have his promise; I'm sure he'll do all the things he promised to do. . . ."

"But my bird? . . . Why are you smiling?"

Ah, my friend, how beautiful she was! If you could have seen how she smiled and wept! I continued, "Ah, yes, your bird! Alas, when one has forgotten oneself, how can one remember a bird? When the hour for your mother's return approached, your beloved left. How happy, how content, how enraptured he was! How hard it was to tear himself away from you. . . ."

"And my mother?"

"Your mother? She returned right after he had left; she found you dreaming, just as you were a little while ago. Your mother spoke to you, but you didn't hear what she said; she told you to do one thing, and you did another. A few tears welled up in your eyes; you held them back or turned away your head so that you could wipe them away without being seen. You were so preoccupied that your mother lost her patience; she scolded you—which gave you an opportunity to weep without constraint, to ease the tumult in your heart. . . . Shall I go on, my little one? I'm afraid that what I'm about to say may renew your pain. You want me to go on? Well, then your good mother reproached herself for having made you unhappy; she came over to you, she took your hands, she kissed you on the forehead and on the cheeks, and you only wept all the more. Your head bent down toward her, and your face, which was beginning to blush —yes, just as it's doing now—hid itself in her bosom. What sweet, kind things that good mother of yours said to you! And how miserable those sweet, kind things made you feel!

"Meanwhile, your canary was singing away for all it was worth, warning you, calling to you, beating its wings, complaining about your neglect, but all in vain. . . . It was given neither fresh water nor fresh seed; and this morning, the bird was dead. . . . You're still looking at me. Is there something I still haven't said? Ah, I understand! The bird, it was he who gave it to you. Never mind, he'll find you another just as pretty. . . . But I can see that's still not all. You are staring at me, and your eyes are filling with tears again. What else can there be? Tell me, I cannot guess."

"What if my bird's death were only a forewarning of something else? What would I do? What would I become? If he were ungrateful . . ."

"What foolishness! You have nothing to be afraid of, little girl. It is impossible; it cannot happen!"

Well, my friend, you can laugh in my face if you want. You can be amused at the thought of a serious-minded person spending his time trying to console a little girl in a painting for the loss of her bird—or for the loss of whatever you like. But don't you see how beautiful she is! How interesting she is! I don't enjoy making people sad; and yet, in spite of that, I should not at all mind being the cause of her sorrow.

Le Fils ingrat (La Malédiction paternelle):[4] I don't know how I'm going to manage with this one, and still less with the one that comes next. This Greuze fellow is going to be the ruin of you, my friend.

Imagine a room into which scarcely any light can penetrate except through the door, when it is open, or, when the door is closed, through a square opening above it. Let your eyes wander around this dismal room: they will perceive nothing but poverty. In one corner, however, to the right, there is a bed that does not seem too bad; it has been carefully made. In the foreground, on the same side, is a large, black leather confessional that looks fairly comfortable to sit on: seat the ungrateful son's father upon that. Close to the door, place a low cupboard, and beside the failing old man a small table, on top of which is a bowl of soup that has just been brought to him.

Despite the assistance that the eldest son of this family might have been to his old father, to his mother, and his brothers, he has enlisted. Yet even so, he refuses to leave without having extracted further financial assistance from these wretched and unhappy folk. He has come in with an old soldier; he has made his demands. His father is outraged by this request; he does not scruple to use harsh words to this unnatural child who no longer acknowledges his father, his mother, or his responsibilities and who is returning insults for his father's reproaches. We see the son in the center of the picture; he has a violent, insolent, angry air; his right arm is raised in the direction of his father, over the head of one of his sisters; he is standing very upright, his raised hand expressing a threat; he has his hat on; his gesture and his expression are equally insolent. The good old man, who has loved his children but never permitted any of them to show him disrespect, is making an effort to rise from his chair; but one of his daughters, kneeling in front of him, is clutching the bottom of his coat in an attempt to restrain him. Surrounding the young rake are his eldest sister, his mother, and one of his little brothers. His mother has her arms around his body; he is making a brutal attempt to free himself and spurn her away from him. The mother looks crushed and grief-stricken; the eldest sister has also

[4] *The Ungrateful Son* (*A Father's Curse*).

come between her brother and her father; judging by their attitudes, both mother and sister seem to be trying to conceal the two men from each other. The sister has seized her brother by his coat; the way in which she is pulling at it speaks for itself: "Wretched man, what are you doing? You are spurning your mother, you are threatening your father. Get down on your knees and beg forgiveness." Meanwhile, with one hand covering his eyes, the little brother is weeping; with his other hand, he is hanging on to his elder brother's arm and trying to drag him out of the house. Behind the old man's chair, the youngest brother of all is standing with a frightened, bewildered look. At the opposite end of the room, near the door, the old soldier who enlisted the son and then came back with him to his parents' home is leaving, his back turned to what is happening, his saber under his arm, his head lowered. And I almost forgot to add that in the foreground, in the midst of all this tumult, there is a dog whose barks are making the uproar even more unbearable.

Everything in this sketch is skillful, well ordered, properly characterized, clear: the grief, even the weakness, of the mother for a child she has spoiled; the violence of the old man; the various actions of the sisters and young children; the insolence of the ungrateful son; and the tact of the old soldier, who cannot help but be shocked at what is going on. And the barking dog is an example of the particular and unrivaled talent that Greuze has for imagining meaningful details.

Essay on Painting

[1 7 6 5]

CHAPTER I: *My Strange Thoughts on Drawing*

Nature never makes a mistake. Every form, beautiful or ugly, has its cause: there is not one natural object in existence that is not as it ought to be.

Look at that woman who lost her eyes as a child. The eyeballs have failed to continue their growth and distend her eyelids; they have sunk back into the cavities created by the absence of the two organs; they have shrunk. The upper lids have pulled down the eyebrows; the lower ones have pulled the cheeks up slightly, and even the upper lip, affected by this movement, has turned up; the change has affected all the different parts of the face in varying degrees, according to their relative distances from the seat of the accident. But do you think that this process of deformation was limited to the face? Do you think that the neck has been completely unaffected by it? And the shoulders, or the bosom? Yes, certainly, to your eyes and mine. But call nature in; present her with that neck, those shoulders, that bosom, and nature will say, "This is the neck, these are the shoulders, this is the bosom of a woman who lost her eyes as a child."

Now turn your eyes upon this man; his back and chest both jut out to form extreme convexities. As the anterior cartilages of the neck lengthened, so the backs of the vertebrae were forced together; the head tilted back, the hands were pulled back and upward from the wrists, the elbows were forced backward, and all the limbs have sought to accommodate themselves to the common center of gravity most suitable to this anomalous structure; the face has a constant look of constraint and effort as a result. Now cover that face; allow nature to see nothing but the feet, and nature, without hesitation, will say, "Those feet are the feet of a hunchback."

If we possessed a clear knowledge of all these causes and effects, we could do no better than simply to represent natural objects as they are. The more perfect the imitation, the greater its conformity with the underlying physical causes, the more satisfactory we should find it.

Despite our ignorance of causes and effects, and the artistic conventions that have resulted from it, I can hardly believe that any artist who preferred to subject himself to a rigorous imitation of nature, and was bold enough to neglect those conventions, would not often find his oversized feet, his shortened legs, his swollen knees, and his heavy and unwieldy heads justified in our eyes by that subtle instinct we all acquire from a continual observation of natural phenomena and which would make us divine a hidden network of causes, an inevitable series of connections, linking all those deformities. . . .

If I were an initiate in the mysteries of art, perhaps I should know up to what point an artist ought to submit to the accepted proportions, and then I could tell you. But what I do know is that they cannot resist the absolute power of nature and that the age and occupation of the subject demand that those proportions be sacrificed in a hundred different ways. I have never heard any figure accused of being badly drawn that gave a clear indication, by its external structure, of its age and habits or of the ease with which it carried out its everyday functions. It is these latter that determine both the size of the figure as a whole and the correct proportion of each limb and their ensemble; these are the things that tell me whether I am looking at a child, an adult man, an old man, a primitive man, a civilized man, a magistrate, a soldier, or a porter. If there were any figure difficult to find, it would be that of a man of twenty-five who had been created instantaneously from a handful of earth and who has never done anything; but that man is a myth. . . .

CHAPTER V: *A Paragraph on Composition, in Which I Hope I Shall Treat of It*

. . . Although no one ever seems to have noticed it as yet, there is one thing that painting and poetry have in common: they should both be moral. Boucher has no idea of this; he is always depraved and never holds our attention. Greuze is always moral, and the crowds never fail to throng around his paintings. I would not scruple to say to Boucher, "If your work is never intended for anyone but smutty-minded eighteen-year-olds, then you're quite right, my friend; go on painting your breasts and bottoms; but for decent people, and for me, the fact that you are hung in the best and brightest place in the Salon will avail you nothing; we shall still leave you hanging there and go looking in some dark corner for that charming Russian by Le Prince [*Le Baptême russe*] and that young, virtuous, innocent godmother standing beside him. Make no mistake: that face of hers has more power to lead me into sin one morning than all your strumpets. I don't know where you find them, but no one who has any regard for his health would even stop to look at them.

I am not prudish. I sometimes read my Petronius. Horace's satire *Ambubaiarum* pleases me at least as much as the others. As for Catullus's infamous little madrigals, I know three-quarters of them by heart. . . . I forgive the poet, the painter, the sculptor, even the philosopher an instant of gaiety and madness, but I don't like it when an artist never dips his brush in anything else and perverts the aims of art. One of the most beautiful lines in all Virgil, and one of the most admirable principles of imitative arts, reads as follows:

Sunt lacrimae rerum et mentem mortalia tangunt.
Virgil, *Aeneid,* I, 462

On the door of the painter's studio, there should be an inscription: "Here the wretched find eyes that weep for them."

To make virtue desirable, vice odious, and absurdities evident, that is the aim of every honest man who takes up the pen, the brush, or the chisel. Suppose there is a wicked man among us, carrying the awareness of some infamy deep inside him, here is where he will meet his punishment. All the decent people, without their knowing it, are thrusting him into the dock. They judge him, they arraign him. And it is in vain that he turns pale and stammers out confused excuses: he must subscribe to his own sentence. If his steps should lead him to the Salon, let him beware lest his eyes light upon the severe and righteous canvas! And it is the artist's task also to celebrate great and noble actions so that they are always remembered, to honor blasted and unhappy virtue, to blast honored and happy vice, to strike terror into tyrants. Show me Commodus hurled to the lions; let me see him on your canvas being torn to pieces by their fangs. Make me hear the mingled cries of wrath and joy around his corpse. Avenge the good man on the wicked, on the gods, and on fate. Anticipate, if you dare, the judgments of posterity; or if you are not bold enough for that, then at least portray the judgments it has already made. Hurl back upon fanatical nations that ignominy with which they wished to cover the men who were instructing them and telling them the truth. Unfurl before me the bloody scenes created by religious bigotry. Teach sovereigns and their peoples what they must expect from such sanctified preachers of lies. Why should you refuse to take your place among the mentors of mankind, the consolers of life's ills, the avengers of crime, the remunerators of virtue? . . .

. . . Composition is ordinarily divided into the picturesque and the expressive. For my part, I care not a jot how well the artist has disposed his figures in order to achieve striking light effects if the work as a whole does not speak to my heart, if the characters in the painting are simply standing about like people ignoring one another in a public park or like animals at the foot of a landscape painter's mountains. . . .

. . . Most of our paintings are so feeble in conception and so deficient in ideas that it is impossible for them to produce any violent disturbance or profound sensation in us. You look at them, you turn your head away—and it is impossible to remember anything you saw. No phantom obsesses you and follows you. I shall make so bold as to suggest to the most intrepid of our artists that he strike as much terror into our hearts with his brush as a recent newspaper article did with an account of how a group of English people were suffocated to death in a black pit of a dungeon on the orders of an Indian nabob. What is the use of mixing all your colors, taking up your brush, exhausting all the resources of your art if the result moves me less than a newspaper can? The fact is, these men are without imagination, without fire; any bold or great idea is quite beyond their reach. . . .

CHAPTER VII: *A Little Corollary to the Preceding*

But what do all these principles signify if taste is a matter of caprice and if there is no eternal, immutable principle of beauty?

If taste is a matter of caprice, if there is no principle of beauty, then what is the cause of those delightful emotions that spring so suddenly, so involuntarily, so tumultuously from the depths of our souls, that dilate or constrict them and force tears of joy, of sorrow, of wonderment to our eyes at the sight of some noble physical phenomenon or at the narration of some great and moral action? *Apage, Sophista!*[5] You will never persuade my

[5] "Be off with you, Sophist!"

heart that it is wrong to tremble or my viscera that they are wrong in being moved.

The true, the good, and the beautiful are closely linked. Add to one of the first two qualities some rare, some striking circumstance and the true will be beautiful, the good will be beautiful. If the problem of the attraction among three bodies[6] is conceived as merely the movement of three arbitrary points on a scrap of paper, then it is nothing, a purely speculative truth. But if one of those three bodies is the star that gives us light in the daytime, another the star that shines upon us in the night, and the third this globe that we inhabit, then suddenly the truth becomes great and beautiful.

A poet once said of another poet, "He will not go far; he hasn't the secret." What secret? That of presenting us with subjects of great interest: fathers, mothers, husbands and wives, women and children.

I see a high mountain covered by a dark, deep, and immemorial forest. I see and hear a torrent cascading thunderously down the mountain, its waters crashing against the sharp ridges of a great rock. The sun is sinking in the west; it is transforming the drops of water hanging from the jagged edges of the rock into so many diamonds. But the scattered waters of the torrent, having found their way through the obstacles that were holding them back, have met again in a vast, wide channel that leads them toward a machine some distance away. There, between massy stones, the food that man relies on more than any other for his sustenance is being crushed and prepared. I glimpse the machine, I glimpse its wheels as they are whitened by the foaming waters, I glimpse, through some willows, the roof of the owner's cottage; I withdraw into myself, and I muse on all this.

Yes, the forest, which takes me back to the beginnings of the world, is a beautiful thing; yes, that rock, an image of constancy and duration, is a beautiful thing; of course those drops of water, transformed by the sun's rays, scattered and broken up into so many sparkling and liquid diamonds, are a beautiful thing; of

[6] The three-body problem is one of the classical unsolved problems of mechanics, relating to the motions and velocities of three bodies owing to the forces they exert on one another.

course the noise, the thunder of a torrent breaking the vast silence of the mountain and its solitude and bringing a violent shock, a secret terror to my soul, is a beautiful thing!

But those willows, that cottage, those animals grazing nearby—does the sight of all these useful things not add something to my pleasure too? And, then, think of the difference between the reactions of an ordinary man and those of a philosopher! For the philosopher reflects; in the forest tree, he sees the proud-topped mast that will one day front the tempest and the winds; in the bowels of the mountain, he glimpses the unmined metal that will one day boil at the bottom of roaring furnaces, then take upon itself the forms not only of machines to make the earth more fruitful but also of others intended to visit destruction upon its inhabitants. . . .

Such are the processes by which imagination, sensibility, and knowledge can increase our pleasure. Nature and the art that copies her have nothing to say to a man who is stupid or cold, and very little to an ignorant one.

What, then, is taste? A facility, acquired by repeated experiences, for grasping the true or the good, as well as those circumstances that render either of them beautiful, and for being promptly and keenly affected by them. If the experiences that determine the judgment are still present in the memory, then we have enlightened taste; if the memory of them has disappeared and only the impression they made on us remains, then we have flair, instinct.

Michelangelo gave the dome of St. Peter's in Rome the most beautiful form possible. When the geometrician La Hire, struck by this form, made a sectional drawing of it, he discovered that its section was the curve of greatest resistance. What inspired Michelangelo to use that particular curve rather than any of the numberless others he could have chosen? Everyday experience of life. It is this that suggests to the master carpenter, as surely as it suggests it to the sublime Euler himself,[7] the angle of the support he is making for a collapsing wall. . . .

Experience and study—those are the preliminary requirements, both for the man who creates and for the man who judges those

[7] A renowned eighteenth-century mathematician.

creations. For my own part, I also require that they possess sensibility. But just as we see men who are habitually just, beneficent, and virtuous solely out of enlightened self-interest, out of a spirit and love of order, without experiencing any delight or pleasure from their actions, so there may also be taste without sensibility, in the same way that sensibility may exist without taste. When a man is in the grip of an excessive sensibility, he loses the power of discernment: everything excites him indiscriminately. He will begin to stammer; he will be unable to find words to express what he is feeling.

There can be no doubt that the man of extreme sensibility will be a happier person than the cold-natured man. But the best judge? That is another matter. Cold men, severe and tranquil observers of nature, often know better what delicate strings to pluck: they make enthusiasts, but they are not enthusiasts themselves. It is the difference between man and animals.

Reason will sometimes modify the hasty judgments of our sensibilities: it appeals against them. This is why there are so many works of art that are forgotten almost as soon as they have been acclaimed, and so many others, whether passed by or openly disdained when they appear, that receive from time, from the progress in our understanding of the art, from a more collected appraisal, those just tributes they deserve.

This explains the uncertainty that attends the success of any work of genius. It is alone. It can be appreciated only by relating it directly back to nature herself. And who can go back that far? Another man of genius.

Salon of 1767

. . . That you[8] are aware of the difference between a general idea and a particular object, individual even down to its smallest parts, is indisputable, since you would not dare to assure me that you have at any time, from the first moment you took up your brush until today, subjected yourself to the rigorous imitation of a single hair. You have added and you have taken away,

[8] Diderot is talking to an *abbé,* with whom he has taken a long walk in the country.

otherwise you could not have made a direct image, a first copy of truth, but only a portrait, or copy of a copy, "the phantom and not the thing"; and you would only have been in the third rank, since between truth itself and your work there would have been the truth of the prototype, its persistent phantom serving you as a model, and the copy you were making of the ill-defined shadow of that phantom. Your line would not have been the true line, the line of beauty itself, the ideal line, but a given, diluted, deformed, portraitistic, individual line; and Phidias would have said of you, "You are only in the third rank: below the beautiful woman and beauty itself." And he would have been right: between the truth and its image stands the individual beautiful woman who was used as a model.

"But where, then," the artist who thinks before he contradicts me will reply, "is the true model, if it exists neither wholly nor in part in nature? . . ."

To which I reply: And if I were unable to tell you, would you not have felt the truth of what I have been saying nevertheless? Would it be any the less true that for a microscopic eye even the strict imitation of a fingernail or of a hair would constitute a portrait? Very well then, I shall prove to you that you possess such an eye and that you make use of it constantly. Do you not agree that everything in nature, especially a living being, has its fixed functions and passions in life and that, with constant use and time, those functions necessarily impose a change on its whole structure, a change so marked that it sometimes permits us to guess those functions? Do you not agree not only that this change affects the general mass, but that it is impossible for it to affect the general mass without also affecting each part taken separately? Do you not agree that when you have faithfully rendered both the change in the mass and the resulting change in each of the parts, then you have made a portrait? If so, then there is something that is not the thing you have painted, and there is also something you have painted that stands between the first model and your copy. . . . You must agree, then, that there is not and cannot be any entire animal actually in existence, or any part of such an animal, that you can, if we are to be strict in this matter, take as a first model. You must admit that this model is purely ideal and that it is not borrowed directly from any individual image in Nature of which you have retained a copy in your imagination—a copy so exact that you can recall it at will, hold it steady before your eyes, and recopy it slavishly—unless you wish to become a portraitist. You must admit that when you create beauty, you are not creating anything that is or even anything that can be. And you must also agree, in consequence, that the difference between the portraitist and you, the man of genius, consists essentially in the fact that he, the portraitist, renders Nature faithfully as she is and places himself according to the canons of taste in the third rank, whereas you, because you seek the truth, the first model, are raised by this continuous effort to the second rank. . . .

. . . the true line, the ideal model of beauty, which exists nowhere except in the heads of artists like Agasias, Raphael, Poussin, Puget, Pigalle, Falconet; the ideal model of beauty, the true line, of which lesser artists can derive their incorrect, more or less approximate notions only from the works of the Ancients or from the imperfect works of nature; the ideal model of beauty, the true line, which these great masters are unable to inspire in their pupils in as pure a form as that in which they themselves apprehend it; the ideal model of beauty, the true line, beyond which they themselves can allow their inspiration to soar into fantasy—depicting the Sphinx, the Centaur, the Hippogriff, the Faun, and all the mixed varieties of nature—or below which they can descend in order to produce the various portraits of life—the distortion, the monster, the grotesque—adding to their work exactly that amount of falsehood required by the particular composition or the particular effect they are trying to produce, so that the question of how near one should stay to the ideal model, the true line, or how far one should stray from it is almost a meaningless one; the ideal model of beauty, the true line, untrammeled by convention, which almost disappears with the man of genius himself, which can form for a certain time the spirit, the character, the taste of a whole nation, a century, a school; the ideal model of beauty, the true line, of which the genius himself will have a more or less rigorous notion according to the climate, the government, the laws, the circumstances to which he is born; the ideal model of beauty, the true line, which is corrupted, which is lost, and which no nation could ever regain, perhaps, other than by returning to a state of primitivism, for that is the only state in which men, accepting their own ignorance, can resign themselves to the slowness of their groping progress. More civilized ages remain mediocre precisely because they are born, so to speak, already knowing everything. Servile and almost stupid in their imitation of those who have gone before them, they approach nature as something already perfect, instead of something perfectible. . . .

. . . Chardin, La Grenée, Greuze, and others have assured me (and painters aren't given to flattering writers) that I am almost the only one among these latter whose images could be transferred onto a canvas almost exactly as I arrange them in my head.

La Grenée said to me, "Give me a subject for Peace," and I answered, "Show me Mars wearing his breastplate, his sword girt about his loins, his head very beautiful, noble, proud, disheveled. Standing beside him, paint me a Venus, but a nude Venus, tall, divine, voluptuous; let one of her arms be thrown softly around her lover's shoulders, and let her be pointing out to him with a bewitching smile the one piece of his armor he still lacks, his helmet—in which her doves have made their nest." "I see what you mean," the painter said. "We can see a few pieces of straw sticking out from under the female; the male is standing guard on the visor; and there's my picture."

Greuze said to me, "I should like to paint a completely naked woman without offending modesty." I replied, "Paint *The Virtuous Model.* Let there be a naked girl sitting in front of you; her ragged clothes are all on the floor beside her, indicating how poor she is; her head is resting on one of her hands; two tears are running from her lowered eyes down her beautiful cheeks; her expression is one of innocence, modesty, and reticence; and let her mother be beside her; she is covering her face with one of her hands and one of her daughter's hands, or else she is hiding her face in her own two hands and her daughter's is resting on her shoulder; let the mother's clothes also betray extreme poverty, and let the artist, moved and touched by the scene before him, be letting his palette or his pencil fall from his hand." And Greuze said, "I see my picture."[9]

This seems to be the result of my imagination having subjected itself for so long a period to the true rules of art, simply by dint of observing their results; of my habit of arranging my own figures in my head as though they were on a canvas; perhaps of my actually transferring them to one, since I am always gazing at a large wall as I write; of my long-established practice of judging whether a woman who passes me in the street is well or badly dressed by imagining her in a painting—so that I have gradually come to see everything in terms of attitudes, groupings, passions, expressions, movements, perspectives, and arrangements suitable for use in works of painting. In short, the definition of a well-ordered imagination ought to rest upon the facility with which a painter could produce a beautiful painting from whatever it is that the writer has conceived. . . .

". . . The imitator of nature will always relate his work to some important end. I do not mean that he will necessarily do so deliberately, methodically, consciously, but that he will do so instinctively, under the influence of his secret inclinations, his natural sensibility, and an exquisite and noble taste. When Voltaire was shown a copy of *Denis le Tyran,* Marmontel's first and last tragedy, the old poet said, 'He will never do anything; he doesn't know the secret. . . .' "

"You mean genius, perhaps?"

"Yes, Abbé, genius, and also how to choose his subjects: natural man shown in opposition to civilized man, man beneath the sway of despotism, man crushed beneath the yoke of tyranny, fathers, mothers, husbands, and wives, the most sacred, sweet, violent, and universal bonds that link mankind, the ills of society, the inexorable law of fate, the consequences of great passions; for it is difficult to be greatly moved by any peril that we may never feel ourselves. The smaller the distance between the person

[9] Baudouin (not Greuze) used this idea for his gouache *Le Modèle honnête,* exhibited in 1769.

represented and myself, the more violent the work's attraction and the stronger its power of holding me. Horace said, 'If you wish to see me weep, you must first suffer yourself.' But you will weep alone, without my being tempted to mingle a single tear with yours, if I am unable to put myself in your place: I too must be able to cling to the end of the rope that is suspending you over the abyss, otherwise I shall not tremble."

... "That is a very surprising mystery; for, after all, without recalling any ideas, without conjuring up any images inside me, I have nevertheless experienced in my own person the whole impression created by this sublime and terrifying description.[10] That is the mystery of everyday conversation."

"Will you explain it to me?"

"If I can. We have both been children, my dear Abbé, even though it was a long time ago, unfortunately. When we were children, we heard people say words to us; those words became fixed in our memories, and their meanings in our understanding, whether by means of an idea or an image; those ideas or those images were accompanied by feelings of aversion, hatred, pleasure, terror, desire, indignation, contempt; for some years, each time a word was pronounced, the idea or the image came back to us, together with the sensation with which it had been associated; but in the course of time, we have come to deal with words as we do with coins: we no longer look at what is stamped on them in order to ascertain their value; we hand them out or accept them solely according to their size and weight—and so it is with words, in my opinion. We have come to ignore the image or the idea and are satisfied merely with its sounds and the sensations it produces. A speech is no longer anything but a long sequence of sounds accompanied by the sensations they originally produced. The heart and the ears are engaged, but the mind no longer plays any part; it is by the successive effect of those sensations, by their violence, their accumulation, that we understand and judge. Without this ellipsis in our method of apprehension, we could not converse: to speak or to understand a sentence of even moderate length would take us an entire day. And the philosopher, who weighs, pauses, analyzes, decomposes

[10] Diderot has quoted a description of Hades from Homer.

every word, what is he doing? He is returning, under the impulsion of his doubts and suspicions, to the state of childhood. Why is it that it is easy to excite a child's imagination and so difficult to excite an adult's? It is because every time the child hears a word, it looks for the idea or image to fit it; it searches about inside its head. But the same words to the adult are merely so much small change; a long sentence is nothing to him but a series of worn impressions, a simple sum of addition or subtraction, a piece of unconscious calculation. . . ."

Everything that astonishes the soul, everything that impresses it with a sensation of terror, leads to the sublime. A vast plain does not have the same power to astonish as the ocean has, nor the ocean when it is calm the same power as the ocean when lashed by a storm.

Darkness adds to terror. Scenes of darkness are rare in tragedy. Their technical difficulty makes them rarer still in painting, in which, moreover, they are unfruitful, producing an effect that only the masters can truly judge. . . .

Night conceals shapes and lends horror to sounds; it can set the imagination to work on even the slightest noise, on the sound of a leaf falling in a forest; our imagination makes our bowels shudder within us; everything becomes exaggerated. The cautious man becomes wary; the coward halts his steps, trembles, or flees; even the brave man puts his hand on the hilt of his sword.

Temples are filled with darkness. Tyrants do not often walk abroad; they are never seen; and because of their cruel deeds, they are thought to be larger than life. . . . Priests, raise your altars, erect your temples in the hearts of forests. Let the cries of your victims pierce their shadows. Let your arcane, theurgic, bloody scenes be lit only by the fateful glare of torches. Light is useful when you wish to persuade; it is worthless for emotional effect. Clarity of any kind is antipathetic to frenzy. Poets, speak ceaselessly of eternity, infinity, immensity, time, space, divinity, tombs, ghosts, hell, black skies, deep seas, dark forests, thunder, cloud-searing lightning. Be somber and mysterious. Great noises heard from afar, waterfalls heard but not seen, silence, solitude, deserted places, ruins, caves; the sound of muffled drums with long pauses between each beat; the tolling of a bell, so slow that we wait in awed expectancy for every stroke; the screech of night birds, the howls of wild beasts in winter, in the night, above all when mingled with the murmur of the winds; the moan of a woman giving birth; any lament that breaks off, then begins again, that bursts on our ears once more with a sudden clamor, then slowly sinks into a dying moan—for in all these things there is something inexplicably terrible, huge, and tinged with darkness.

It is these accessory ideas, inevitably linked with the night and darkness, that complete the task of filling a young girl's heart with terror as she walks toward the dark thicket where someone is expecting her. Her heart is beating violently; she stops. The turbulence of her passions is increased by her terror; she grows weak, her knees begin to fail beneath her. Her happiness is almost excessive as she reaches her lover's arms, as they receive her, as they support her; and her first words are: "Is it you?" It is with poetry as it is with painting. How many times that has been said! But neither he who said it first nor any of the multitude that repeated it after him has ever fully grasped the whole purport of this maxim. The poet has his palette, just as the painter has his shadings, his transitions, his tones. He has his brush and his manner; he can be dry, harsh, rough, anguished, strong, vigorous, gentle, harmonious, or smooth. The language he is using provides him with every imaginable color and shade: it is for him to choose them well. And he has his own chiaroscuro—the source and rules of which lie in the depths of his own soul. Do you write poetry? You think you do, because you have learned from Richelet how to arrange words and syllables in a certain order and in accordance with certain prescribed rules and because you have acquired the facility to round off these sets of words and syllables with rhymes. You are not painting: you scarcely know how to make a tracing. You do not have, you may even be completely incapable of acquiring, the first notion of rhythm. Horace has said: "Who dares to imitate Pindar? He is a torrent hurling his waters in thunder from the summit of a cliff. He swells, he boils, he overturns and rushes past the obstacle impeding him. He spreads out. He is a sea plunging into a deep abyss."

You have felt the beauty of the image, but that is nothing: in the original, the rhythm is everything; it is the same magical prosody that is to be found in such and such a passage of a painting but that you perhaps may never feel. "What, then, is rhythm?" you will ask me. It is a particular choice of expressions; it is a certain distribution of syllables, long or short, harsh or sweet, dull or sharp, light or heavy, slow or rapid, plaintive or gay; a sequence of little onomatopoeias that reflect the ideas one is deeply concerned with, the sensations one is feeling and wishes to arouse, the phenomena whose individual details one is trying to express, the passions one is experiencing and the animal cry they tear from the throat, the nature, character, and movement of the actions one is intending to depict. And such an art is no more a product of conventions and rules than the effects of a rainbow: it is not acquired, it cannot be communicated, it can only be perfected. It is inspired by natural taste, by a certain mobility of the soul, by sensibility. It is the very image of the soul expressed by inflections of the voice, by progressions of shading, by transitions, by all the hundred different ways in which the tones of speech may be accelerated or slowed down, made muffled, violent, or calm. Listen to the brief and energetic challenge with which that child is defying its companion. Listen to that sick man dragging his words out into long and painful syllables. Both of them have found the appropriate rhythm without having to think about it. Boileau searched for it and often found it. Racine never had to search: it was as though it came looking for him. Without this quality, a poet is scarcely worth reading: his work is colorless. There is something artificial and wearisome in rhythm that has been arrived at by reflection. That is one of the chief differences between Homer and Virgil. . . . It is Nature, and Nature alone, that dictates the true harmony in an entire period or in any verse sequence of any length.

Oh, my friend! What a wonderful opportunity to digress and ask the Italian poets whether, with all their ebony eyebrows, their blue and tender eyes, their lily-white cheeks, their alabaster bosoms, their coral lips, their dazzling and enameled teeth, and all those cupids nestling in every little dimple, they could ever give us so great an idea of beauty? True taste attaches itself to one or two features and leaves the rest to the imagination. Detail is petty, puerile, and pedantic. . . . When Helen walks past the aged Trojans and they cry out, then Helen is beautiful. When Ariosto describes Angelica (I think) from the top of her head to the tips of her toes, then despite the grace, the facility, and the sensuous elegance of his poetry, Angelica is not beautiful. He shows me everything: he leaves nothing for me to do. He wears me out, he makes me impatient. If a figure is walking, then depict its carriage and its lightness: I shall take care of the rest. If it is bending, tell me only about its arms and shoulders: I shall take care of the rest. If you do anything more, then you are confusing the genres: you cease being a poet and you are trying to be a painter or a sculptor. I see all your details, and I lose the whole—which a single trait, such as Virgil's *vera incessu,*[11] would have shown me instantly. . . .

You may attempt these detailed descriptions in a gallant, playful, or burlesque poem; that, I shall accept. Elsewhere, they are puerile and in bad taste.

I shall suppose that when he begins any long and detailed description of a figure, the poet already has the ensemble fixed in his mind. How is he to convey this ensemble to me? If he tells me about the hair, then I see it. If he then tells me about the brow, I see that too, but the brow doesn't go with the image I already have of the hair. If he goes on to tell me about the eyebrows, the nose, the mouth, the cheeks, the chin, the neck, and the bosom, I see them all; but since none of these parts he has successively described fits in with the ensemble I have built up from the preceding ones, he is forcing me either to accept that the figure I am creating in my imagination is incorrect or to retouch the whole figure every time he provides me with a new feature for it.

A single trait, one all-important trait—and leave the rest to my imagination. That is true taste, that is the highest taste. . . .

I shall therefore say to the poets: my head and my imagination can encompass only a certain degree of size, beyond which the object loses all shape and escapes me. Therefore concentrate all

11 "*Et vera incessu dea patuit.*" ("And she appeared a true goddess by her step.")

the powers of imagination and thought I do possess onto one aspect of those objects, while defining it in enormous terms, and you may be sure that the whole will then become immeasurable, infinite. Who can imagine the size of Apollo as he strides from mountaintop to mountaintop? Or the strength of Neptune, shaking Etna, opening the earth to its center with his trident, and uncovering the desolate shore of Styx? Or the power of Jupiter, shaking Olympus with a single movement of his black brow? An enormous action of the entire figure will produce the same effect as the enormity of one of its parts.

D'Alembert's Dream

[1769]

Le Rêve de d'Alembert *is Diderot's major philosophical effort. It brings together his materialistic speculations in the realms of cosmology, biology, psychology, and morals. The three sections, progressively more daring, are in the form of a scintillating dialogue, infused with wit and flights of the imagination, brought to life by characters who were real and who are made to seem real. D'Alembert had regained Diderot's friendship after a serious illness. Théophile de Bordeu was a distinguished doctor, investigator, and theorist who had considerable influence on Diderot. Julie de Lespinasse was d'Alembert's passionate and unfaithful mistress. By putting a large part of the dialogue in the form of a dream, Diderot emphasized the speculative character of his thinking.*

Le Rêve de d'Alembert *was written in 1769; it was first published in 1830. (See A-T, Vol. 2.)*

D'Alembert's Dream

Conversation Between D'Alembert and Diderot

D'ALEMBERT: A being existing somewhere, yet corresponding to no one point in space; a being that lacks extension, yet occupies space; that is present in its entirety in every part of that space; that is essentially different from matter, yet is at one with it; that follows the motions of matter and gives it motion, yet is not moved itself; that acts on matter, yet suffers all its vicissitudes; a being that I can form no idea of; a being, in short, whose nature is so wholly contradictory is, I admit, difficult to accept. But there are other difficulties in wait for the man who refuses to do so; for, after all, if this universal sentience that you wish to substitute for it is a general and essential quality of all matter, then stone must be sentient.

DIDEROT: And why should it not be?

D'ALEMBERT: It's hard to believe.

DIDEROT: Agreed, for the man who quarries it, carves it, crushes it, and doesn't hear it cry out in pain.

D'ALEMBERT: I'd very much like you to tell me what difference there is, according to you, between a man and a statue, between marble and flesh.

DIDEROT: Not a great deal. Flesh can be made into marble, and marble into flesh.

D'ALEMBERT: But they are not the same.

DIDEROT: In the sense that what you call vital energy is not the same as what you call inanimate energy.

D'ALEMBERT: I don't understand.

DIDEROT: I'll make it clearer. The displacement of a body from one place to another cannot in itself be termed motion; it is merely the effect of motion. Motion exists equally both in a moving body and in a stationary body.

D'ALEMBERT: That's a new way of looking at things.

DIDEROT: But true, for all that. Remove the obstacle that is opposing the displacement of a stationary body and it will be displaced. Remove the air surrounding the trunk of that huge oak by some instantaneous process of rarefaction and the water contained in the trunk will immediately expand, bursting it into countless pieces. And the same, I should like to add, is true of your own body.

D'ALEMBERT: Very well. But what relation is there between motion and the capacity for sensation? Do you mean, by any chance, that you recognize two different kinds of sentience, analogous to animate force and inanimate force? So that there is an animate force that expresses itself in the movement of bodies, an inanimate force that manifests itself as pressure, an active sentience that is characterized by certain observable behavior in animals, and perhaps also in plants, and an inactive sentience whose existence would be revealed to us only when it became active?

DIDEROT: Precisely. You've expressed it beautifully.

D'ALEMBERT: The statue, then, possesses only an inactive kind of sentience; whereas man, animals, perhaps even plants are endowed with active sentience.

DIDEROT: That difference between the block of marble and living tissue does undoubtedly exist; but, as you are of course aware, it is not the only one.

D'ALEMBERT: Of course. Whatever the resemblance between the external forms of the man and the statue, there is no resemblance whatever between their internal structures. The chisel of even the most gifted sculptor cannot even create skin. But there is a very simple means of transforming an inanimate force into an animate one; it is an experiment we see repeated before our eyes a hundred times a day; whereas, on the other hand, I'm not at all sure I see how a body can be made to pass from a state of inactive sentience to a state of active sentience.

DIDEROT: That's because you're not looking hard enough. It's just as common a phenomenon.

D'ALEMBERT: Then what is it, this common phenomenon, if you please?

DIDEROT: Very well, since you seem to want me to put you to shame, I'll tell you. It occurs every time you eat.

D'ALEMBERT: Every time I eat!

DIDEROT: Yes. For what are you doing when you eat? You are removing the obstacles that were preventing the food from exercising an active capacity for sensation. You are assimilating it into yourself, turning it into flesh, making it animal, making it actively sentient. And what you do to your food, I can do any time I choose to marble.

D'ALEMBERT: And how will you do it?

DIDEROT: How? By making it edible.

D'ALEMBERT: Making marble edible? That doesn't sound too easy a task to me.

DIDEROT: Then it's up to me to show you how it's done. I take this statue here. I put it in a mortar. And then I have at it with my pestle. . . . When the block of marble has been reduced to the finest of powder, then I mix that powder with humus or leaf mold; I knead them well together; I sprinkle water on the mixture, then I leave it to decompose for a year, two years, a century—time means nothing to me. When the whole mass has finally been transformed into a more or less homogeneous substance, into humus, do you know what I do with it?

D'ALEMBERT: I'm sure you don't eat the humus.

DIDEROT: No, but there does exist a means of uniting myself with, of appropriating, the humus. A *latus*, as the chemists would say.

D'ALEMBERT: And that *latus*, is it plant life?

DIDEROT: Well done. I sow beans, peas, cabbages, and other vegetables in the humus. The plants feed on the soil, and I feed on the plants.

D'ALEMBERT: Well, whether it's true or false, I must say I like this idea of marble changing into humus, humus into plant life, and then plant life into animal life, into flesh in fact.

DIDEROT: So you see, I've made flesh—or soul, as my daughter puts it: a form of matter with an active capacity for sensation. And though I may not have solved the problem you set me, I have at least got very near to doing so; for you will admit that there is a much greater difference between a piece of marble and a sentient being than between a sentient being and one that can think.

D'ALEMBERT: Yes, I agree there. But the fact remains that the sentient being is still not a thinking being.

DIDEROT: Before we go on to the next step, let me tell you the life story of one of Europe's greatest geometricians. Now, what was this marvelous being to begin with? Nothing.

D'ALEMBERT: Nothing! What do you mean? Nothing can be made from nothing.

DIDEROT: You are taking my words too literally. My meaning is this, that before his mother, the beautiful and wicked canoness Mme de Tencin, had reached the age of puberty and before the soldier La Touche had reached his adolescence, the molecules that were destined to form the first rudiments of my geometrician were still scattered here and there throughout the delicate bodies of both these young people. They then filtered through those bodies with their lymph and circulated in their blood until they finally reached the organs of storage from which they were destined to emerge and unite: the ovaries of the mother and the testicles of the father. So our precious seed has been formed. And now, according to widely held opinion, it is brought down through one of the Fallopian tubes into the womb, to which it is attached by a long cord; and there it stays, continually growing and finally developing into a fetus. Now comes the moment for it to emerge from its dark prison; it is born, then abandoned on the steps of Saint-Jean-le-Rond, which was to provide it with its name; rescued from the foundlings' home; put to the breast of Mme Rousseau, the glazier's good wife; suckled; and finally, after having grown in body and mind, we behold it a man of letters, an engineer, and a geometrician.[1] How was all this made to happen? Merely by eating and by other purely mechanical operations. The general formula is, put as briefly as possible: Eat, digest, and distill *in vasi licito, et fiat homo secundum artem.*[2] And anyone expounding to the Academy the process by which a man or an animal is formed need concern himself with none but material agents, whose successive results would be: an inert being, a sentient being, a thinking being, a being solving the problem of the precession of the equinoxes, a sublime being, a marvelous being, a being aging, degenerating, dying, passing through dissolution, and returning finally to humus.

D'ALEMBERT: So you don't believe in preexisting germs?

DIDEROT: No.

D'ALEMBERT: Ah, I'm glad to hear it.

DIDEROT: Such an idea is contrary to both experience and reason: contrary to experience because no amount of experiment would ever discover those germs in an egg or in most animals before a certain age; against reason because, although there may be no limit to the divisibility of matter in the mind, there

[1] The foundling geometrician is d'Alembert himself.

[2] ". . . into the appropriate vessel, and in this way let man be made."

is such a limit in nature; and the mind rejects the notion of an elephant already completely formed inside an atom, with another elephant completely formed inside that one, and so on to infinity.

D'ALEMBERT: But without these preexisting germs, there is no way of explaining how the very first generation of animals was produced.

DIDEROT: If you're bothered by the "Which came first, the chicken or the egg?" problem, then that means you're supposing that animals have always been as they are now. What folly! We know no more about what they were like originally than we know about what they are to become in the future. The worm wriggling in the mud, so tiny that we cannot see it, may be on the way to becoming a huge animal; the enormous animal that now strikes terror into us because of its size may be on the way to becoming a tiny worm; it may be only a particular and ephemeral production of this planet.

D'ALEMBERT: I didn't quite follow that.

DIDEROT: I said . . . But it would only lead us away from the subject of our discussion.

D'ALEMBERT: What does that matter? We can get back to it later—or not, as we please.

DIDEROT: Will you allow me to anticipate time by a few thousand years?

D'ALEMBERT: Why not? Time means nothing to nature.

DIDEROT: Have you any objections to my snuffing out our sun?

D'ALEMBERT: None at all. After all, we know it won't be the first to have been snuffed out.

DIDEROT: The sun once extinguished, then, what will happen? The plants will perish, the animals will perish, and the earth will become a silent and unpeopled planet. Relume that star: immediately, you have reestablished the cause that will necessarily produce an infinity of new forms of life, among which, as the centuries passed, I should not dare to guarantee that our plants and our animals, as we see them today, would either recur or not recur.

D'ALEMBERT: But why should the same scattered elements, when they came together, not yield the same results?

DIDEROT: Because in nature everything is indissolubly linked, and anyone who supposes the creation of a new phenomenon or brings back a moment of the past is creating a new and different world.

D'ALEMBERT: No one who thinks at all deeply could deny that. But to return to man—since the general order of things decided that he should exist. If you remember, you left me where the sentient being is about to become a thinking one.

DIDEROT: Yes, I remember.

D'ALEMBERT: Frankly, I'd be most obliged if we could get the transformation over with: I'm anxious to start thinking.

DIDEROT: And if I fail, what weight would my attempt carry against an opposing array of linked and incontrovertible facts?

D'ALEMBERT: None. We should be unable to go any further.

DIDEROT: And in order to go on, would it be permissible to invent an agent with contradictory attributes? A meaningless, unintelligible word?

D'ALEMBERT: No.

DIDEROT: Can you tell me what the existence of a sentient being is for that being itself?

D'ALEMBERT: A consciousness of having been itself from the first moment when it became capable of reflection until the present time.

DIDEROT: And on what is that consciousness based?

D'ALEMBERT: On the memory it has of its actions.

DIDEROT: And without that memory?

D'ALEMBERT: Without that memory, it would have no self, since if it was aware of its existence only at the instant it received any given impression, it would have no life story. Its life would be an interrupted series of sensations with nothing to link them together.

DIDEROT: Excellent. And what is this memory? Where does it originate?

D'ALEMBERT: In a certain organization, which develops, grows weaker, and is sometimes lost entirely.

DIDEROT: And, therefore, if a sentient being that possesses this memory-producing organization links the impressions it receives together, forms them, by means of this connecting power, into a sequence that constitutes the story of its life, and thus acquires self-consciousness, then it must be able to deny, to affirm, to draw conclusions, and to think.

D'ALEMBERT: So it seems to me; there is only one remaining difficulty.

DIDEROT: You're wrong there: there are a great many more than one.

D'ALEMBERT: But one principal one. And it is this: it seems to me that we are able to think of only one thing at a time and that, in order to formulate even a simple proposition, to say nothing of much vaster logical sequences that must embrace thousands of individual ideas in the course of their development, it would seem that we must have at least two objects present in our minds at the same time: the object, which seems to remain in the mind's eye, and also the quality that the mind is considering whether or not to attribute to that object.

DIDEROT: I think as you do here, and it has sometimes led me to compare the fibers of our organs to vibrating and sensitive strings that continue to vibrate and produce sound long after they have been plucked. It is this vibration, this inevitable resonance, as it were, that keeps us constantly aware of the object's presence, while the mind occupies itself with deciding what qualities that object possesses. But vibrating cords also have another property: that of making other strings vibrate; and it is in this way that a first idea summons up a second, those two a third, those three together a fourth, and so on, without our being able to set a limit to the number of ideas awakened, then linked together in the mind of the philosopher as he meditates or listens to his own thoughts in silence and darkness. The mind is an instrument capable of astonishing leaps, and an awakened idea will sometimes set another string vibrating whose harmonic will produce a wholly incomprehensible interval between itself and the first. But if this phenomenon can be observed between resonating strings that are inanimate and disjunct, why should it not take place between points that are animate and linked together, between continuous and sentient fibers?

D'ALEMBERT: Well, it's certainly a very ingenious idea—even

if it isn't in fact true. But I am now rather inclined to think that you are slipping, by imperceptible degrees, into the difficulty that you set out to avoid.

DIDEROT: What is that?

D'ALEMBERT: You are opposed to the notion that we are composed of two different substances, are you not?

DIDEROT: I make no secret of that.

D'ALEMBERT: Well, if you look into the matter closely, you will see that you are making the philosopher's understanding distinct from the instrument. You are making it into a sort of musician who listens to the sounds emanating from the cords and then decides whether they are producing concords or discords.

DIDEROT: Possibly I did lay myself open to this objection, but you might not have made it if you had considered the difference between the philosopher-instrument and the harpsichord-instrument. The philosopher-instrument is sentient: he is, simultaneously, both the musician and the instrument. As a sentient being, he has a moment-by-moment awareness of the sounds he is producing. As an animal, he retains a memory of them. It is this faculty of the physical organism that, by linking the sounds together, produces and stores up the melody. Imagine a harpsichord with the faculties of sensation and memory. Will it not be able to repeat the tunes that you have played upon it all by itself? We are all instruments endowed with feeling and memory. Our senses are so many strings that are struck by surrounding objects and that also frequently strike themselves. That, as I see the matter, is all that happens in a harpsichord constructed like you or me. First, an impression is created by some cause either inside or outside the instrument; this impression gives rise to a sensation, a sensation that has duration, for it is impossible to conceive that it could be caused and then fade away again all in one indivisible moment; another impression then follows, similarly created by a cause either inside or outside the animal; then a second sensation; then voices, which express the sensations in either natural or conventionally formulated sounds.

D'ALEMBERT: I understand. So, therefore, if this sentient and animate harpsichord were also endowed with the capacity to feed and reproduce itself, it would be a living creature and would engender, either by itself or with its female counterpart, young harpsichords, also living and capable of vibration.

DIDEROT: Undoubtedly. What else, in your opinion, is a chaffinch, a nightingale, a musician, or a man? And what other difference do you find there to be between a bird and a bird-organ?[3] Do you see this egg? With this you can topple every theological theory, every church or temple in the world. What is it, this egg, before the seed is introduced into it? An insentient mass. And after the seed has been introduced into it? What is it then? An insentient mass. For what is that seed itself other than a crude and inanimate fluid? How is this mass to make the transition to a different structure, to sentience, to life? Through heat. And what will produce that heat in it? Motion. What will the successive effects of that motion be? Instead of answering that, sit down, and let us follow them with our eyes, moment by moment. First, there is a dot that quivers; then a little thread that grows longer and takes on color; flesh is being formed; a beak, rudimentary wings, eyes, and feet appear; a yellowish substance empties out and produces intestines: it is an animal. The animal is moving about, struggling, emitting cries; I can hear its cries through the shell; it becomes covered in down; it can see. The weight of its head, as it moves it about, brings its beak into repeated contact with the inner surface of its prison wall; the wall breaks; the bird emerges, it walks, it flies, it becomes angry, it flies away, it comes back again, it complains, it suffers, it loves, it desires, it feels pleasure; it has all the same affections as you yourself; it performs the same actions. Are you going to claim, as Descartes did, that it is nothing but an imitative machine? Little children will laugh at you if you do, and philosophers will tell you that if this bird is a machine, then you are one too. If you admit that the only difference between you and the bird is one of structure, then you will be showing good sense, for the admission will be both reasonable and honest. But your opponents will then point out that what you are saying is this: that from a piece of inanimate

[3] Mechanical music box used to teach a canary tunes.

matter, arranged in a certain way, impregnated with a further quantity of inanimate matter, then with heat and motion, there can result sentience, life, memory, consciousness, passion, and thought. You therefore have only one of two courses left open to you: either you suppose an element hidden in the inanimate mass of the egg that waited for that mass to develop further before manifesting its presence or you suppose that this invisible element crept in through the shell at some fixed point during that development. But what is this element? Did it occupy space or not? How did it come or how did it escape without moving? Where was it before? What was it doing there? Or anywhere? Was it created at the very instant that the need for it arose? Was it already in existence? Was it waiting for a host? Was it of the same substance as that host? Or of a different substance? If it was of the same substance, then it was material. If it was of a different substance, then it is impossible for us to conceive either its inert state before the development of the egg or its present activity in the finished animal. You will only have to listen to yourself to pity yourself. You will realize that in order to avoid admitting one simple supposition that explains everything—to wit, that sentience is a general property of matter or a product of physical structure—you are renouncing all common sense and plunging headlong into an abyss of mysteries, contradictions, and absurdities.

D'ALEMBERT: A supposition! That's what you're pleased to call it. But what if this quality is essentially incompatible with matter?

DIDEROT: But how can you tell whether sentience is essentially incompatible with matter, when you have no knowledge of the essence of anything at all and certainly not of matter or sentience? And do you know any more about the nature of motion? How it exists in a body or how it is communicated from one body to another?

D'ALEMBERT: Without being able to conceive the nature of sentience or of matter, I can see that sentience is a simple quality, entire, indivisible, and incompatible with any divisible subject or suppositum.

DIDEROT: Metaphysico-theological mumbo jumbo! What? Can't you see that all the qualities, all the perceivable forms that nature takes are essentially indivisible? There can be no greater or lesser degree of impenetrability. There is such a thing as a half of a sphere, but there is no such thing as a half of sphericity. You can have a greater or lesser degree of motion, but there is no halfway house between motion and non-motion. You can no more have a half, a third, or a quarter of a head, an ear, or a finger than you can have a half, a third, or a quarter of a thought. If there is no molecule in the universe that is exactly like another, and no particle within any molecule that is exactly like any other particle, then you must admit that even the atom is endowed with an indivisible quality or form; you must admit that division is incompatible with the essences of forms, since it destroys them. Be an experimental scientist: when you see an effect produced, accept that it is produced. Don't reject it simply because you cannot explain the cause that led to that effect. Be logical: don't replace a cause that explains everything with another cause that is inconceivable, whose link with the effect is even less capable of apprehension, and that engenders an infinite multiplicity of difficulties without removing a single one.

D'ALEMBERT: Very well, say I abandon this inconceivable cause?

DIDEROT: Then the universe, animals, and men are all made of a single substance. The bird-organ is made of wood, the man is made of flesh. The bird is made of flesh, the musician is made of flesh differently organized; but they both of them share the same origin, the same process of formation, the same functions, and the same end. . . .

D'Alembert's Dream

The speakers are: d'Alembert himself, Mlle de Lespinasse and Dr. Bordeu.

BORDEU: Well! What's been happening here? Is he sick?

MLLE DE LESPINASSE: I'm afraid he is. He's had a very restless night.

BORDEU: Is he awake?

MLLE DE LESPINASSE: No, not yet.

BORDEU (*after going over to d'Alembert's bed and taking his pulse*): There's nothing to worry about.

MLLE DE LESPINASSE: Are you sure? . . . After he'd gone to bed, instead of sleeping quietly as he usually does, just like a child, he began tossing and turning, throwing his arms about, pushing off the bedclothes, and talking out loud.

BORDEU: And what did he talk about? Geometry?

MLLE DE LESPINASSE: No, it really sounded as though he were delirious. Listen. [*She reads out the notes she has taken of what d'Alembert said in his sleep.*] "A living speck. . . . No, I'm wrong there. First of all, nothing, then a living speck. . . . Then to this living speck, another living speck is added, then another; and from these successive additions, there results a unified being, for I am a unit, I can't doubt that." . . . As he said that, he felt himself all over. "But how was this unity made?" "Oh, really, my friend," I said to him, "what does it matter? Do go to sleep." . . . He quieted down. After remaining silent for a moment, he began speaking again. But this time it was as though he were addressing another person. "The fact is, philosopher, I can see how it could turn into an aggregation, a tissue made up of tiny sentient beings—but an animal . . . a whole, a unified system, a self, with a consciousness of its own unity! That I can't see. No, I really can't see that at all. . . ." Can you understand all that, Doctor?

BORDEU: Perfectly.

MLLE DE LESPINASSE: Then you're very lucky. . . . "But perhaps my difficulty arises from a misconception."

BORDEU: Is that you talking?

MLLE DE LESPINASSE: No, it's our dreamer. I'll continue. He then began addressing himself: "Be careful, d'Alembert, my friend, you are positing contiguity alone, when in fact there is also continuity. . . . Yes, he's clever enough to tell me that. . . . And how did this continuity come to be there? He won't find that particularly difficult to answer. . . . Just as one drop of mercury melts into another drop of mercury, so one animate and sentient molecule can melt into another. . . . There were the two drops; they touched—and there is only one. . . . Before the assimilation there were two molecules, after the assimilation there is only one . . . and their capacity for sensation becomes the common property of the common mass. And, indeed, why not? . . . I can imagine the animal fiber to be divided along its length into as many parts as I please, but the fiber will still be continuous, it will still form a whole . . . yes, a whole. . . . The continuity is formed by the contact of two homogeneous molecules. . . . No more complete form of union, of cohesion, of combination, of identity, can be imagined. . . . Yes, philosopher, I agree—if those molecules are elementary and simple ones. But what if they are aggregates, what if they are composite? . . . They will still combine with one another; and, in consequence, they will still create a unity, a continuous whole. . . . But then there is perpetual action and reaction. . . . It is quite certain that the contact of two animate molecules is an entirely different thing from the contiguity of two inanimate masses. . . . Yes, yes, we'll let that pass. It might be possible to quibble there, but I don't care to; I hate carping. . . . Let's pick up the argument again. A thread of extremely pure gold; that was one comparison he suggested, I remember; a homogeneous network first of all; then other molecules pushing in between the molecules of that first network and forming another network, also homogeneous: a tissue of sentient matter; assimilation of the molecules in contact with one another, active sentience in one place, inactive sentience in another, transmitted just as motion is, not to mention, as he so clearly expressed it, that there must be a difference in kind between the contact of two sentient molecules and the contact of nonsentient ones. And what can it be, that difference? . . . A perpetual state of action and reaction . . . and this perpetual action and reaction having a particular character. . . . So that everything occurs to produce a sort of unity—the sort of unity that exists only in animal life. . . . Well, I must confess, if all that isn't the truth, it bears a very strong resemblance to it. . . ." You're laughing, Doctor. Can you see any meaning in all this?

BORDEU: A great deal.

MLLE DE LESPINASSE: Then he's not mad?

BORDEU: Not in the slightest.

MLLE DE LESPINASSE: After that preamble, he began to cry out:

"Mademoiselle de Lespinasse! Mademoiselle de Lespinasse!" "What is it?" "Have you ever seen a swarm of bees leaving a hive? . . . The world, or the general mass of matter, is our great hive. . . . Have you ever seen them settle on the end of a branch and form a long cluster of tiny, winged animals, all hanging onto one another with their feet? . . . That cluster is a being, an individual, any given animal. . . . But all those clusters ought to be exactly like one another. . . . Yes, exactly, since he recognized the existence of only a single, homogeneous kind of matter. . . . Have you ever seen them?" "Yes, I've seen them." "You have seen them?" "Yes, my friend, I told you I have." "Then, if one of those bees took it into its head to pinch or bite in some way the bee it's hanging on to, what do you think will happen? Tell me what you think." "I've no idea." "Try all the same. . . . All right, then, you don't know. But the philosopher, he knows. If you ever meet him—and you may meet him or you may not, because that's what he promised—he will tell you that the bee that was pinched will pinch the next one; that there will be as many sensations aroused in the whole cluster as there are little animals composing it; that the whole swarm will be disturbed, will shift, will change its position and its shape; that it will make a noise composed of thousands of tiny cries; and that anyone who had never seen such a cluster settling before would be very likely to take it for an animal with five or six hundred heads and double that number of wings. . . ." Well, Doctor?

BORDEU: Well, I really must say that that was a fine dream. And you were quite right to take it down as you did.

MLLE DE LESPINASSE: Are you dreaming too?

BORDEU: I am so far from dreaming that I would almost undertake to tell you the rest of our patient's dream.

MLLE DE LESPINASSE: I challenge you to try.

BORDEU: You challenge me?

MLLE DE LESPINASSE: Yes.

BORDEU: And if I'm right?

MLLE DE LESPINASSE: If you're right, I promise . . . I promise to take you for the greatest madman in the world.

BORDEU: Keep your eyes on your notes, then, and listen to what

I say: The man who took this cluster for an animal would be in error (though I presume, mademoiselle, that he continued to address himself to you). Would you like to make his opinion less mistaken? Would you like to change the swarm of bees into a single and unified animal? Then soften the feet with which they are clinging to one another. Make them continuous instead of merely contiguous. There will certainly be a very marked difference between this new cluster and its former state; and what can that difference be, if not that it is now a whole, an individual animal, as opposed to being a group of separate animals, as it was before? . . . All our organs . . .

MLLE DE LESPINASSE: All our organs!

BORDEU: . . . to one who has practiced medicine and made a few observations . . .

MLLE DE LESPINASSE: And then?

BORDEU: And then? . . . are merely separate animals held together in a sympathetic union, a unity, an enveloping identity, by the law of continuity.

MILLE DE LESPINASSE: I'm speechless! What can I say? It's exactly the same. Almost word for word. So that I am now in a position to proclaim to all the world that there is no difference whatever between a doctor who's awake and a philosopher in a dream.

BORDEU: That was already suspected. Is there any more? . . .

MLLE DE LESPINASSE: Then he went on to say: "In Needham's drop of water, everything happens in the twinkling of an eye. In the world we know, the same phenomenon takes a little more time. But what is our duration compared with the eternity of time? Less than the drop I can pick up on the end of a needle compared with the limitless space all around me. An indefinite sequence of minute animals in the fermenting atom, the same indefinite sequence of minute animals in this other atom that we call Earth. Who knows what races of animals have preceded us here? Who knows what races of animals will succeed us? Everything changes, everything passes away: only the whole endures. The world is beginning and ending ceaselessly; its beginnings and its end are both present in every instant of time; it has never had any other kind of beginning or end, and it never will have.

"In this immense ocean of matter, there is not one molecule exactly like another; there is not one molecule exactly like itself for even an instant. *Rerum novus nascitur ordo*,[4] that is its inscription, eternally true. . . ." Then he added with a sigh: "Oh, the vanity of all our thought! Oh, the poverty of our fame and all our works! Oh, wretchedness! Oh, the smallness of our understanding! There is nothing solid in this life but eating, drinking, existing, loving, sleeping. . . . Mademoiselle de Lespinasse, where are you?" "I'm here." Then his face became flushed. I went to take his pulse, but I couldn't find his hand. He seemed to go into a convulsion. His mouth was half open, and he was breathing very quickly; he gave a deep sigh, then a weaker but even deeper sigh; he turned his head over on his pillow and fell asleep. I looked at him closely, and I felt very much disturbed, without knowing why; my heart was pounding, and it wasn't from fear. After a few moments, I saw a slight smile hovering around his lips; in a very low voice, he said: "If there were a planet where men reproduced themselves after the fashion of fishes, where the man's milt was brought into contact with the woman's spawn . . . then I'd regret it less. . . . We should never waste anything that could be useful. Mademoiselle, if it could be collected, kept in a flask, and sent to Needham tomorrow morning . . ." Doesn't that sound like madness to you, Doctor?

BORDEU: In your presence, yes, assuredly!

MLLE DE LESPINASSE: In my presence, not in my presence, it makes no difference at all; you don't know what you're talking about. I had hoped that he would be quiet the rest of the night.

BORDEU: That is the normal result.

MLLE DE LESPINASSE: Not in this case. At about two in the morning, he was back with his drop of water again. Calling it a mi . . . cro . . .

BORDEU: A microcosm.

MLLE DE LESPINASSE: Yes, that was the word he used. He was admiring the wisdom of the ancient philosophers. He said, or

4 "A new order of things is being born."

his philosopher said—I don't know which of them was supposed to be talking: "If when Epicurus announced that the earth contained the seeds of everything and that the animal kingdom was a product of fermentation, he had offered to show his listeners a small-scale illustration of what had happened on a large scale at the beginning of time, what would their answer have been? . . . And you have such an illustration right in front of your eyes, yet it teaches you nothing. . . . Who can tell whether that process of fermentation and its products are now exhausted? Who knows what exact stage in the succession of animal generations we have reached at the moment? Who can say whether that malformed biped, no more than four feet high, that is still, in the neighborhood of the North Pole, referred to as a man, but would very quickly lose the name if it were to become even slightly more malformed, who knows whether it is not an example of a vanishing species? Who can say that such is not the case with every other species of animal? Who can say that everything is not tending toward a gradual reduction into one vast, inanimate, and motionless sediment? Who knows how long that inanimate state would last? Who knows what new race might spring anew from so vast a mass of animate and sentient specks? Why not one single animal? What was the elephant in the first place? Perhaps the enormous animal we see today, perhaps only an atom, for both are equally possible; both require no other suppositions than motion and the various properties of matter. . . . The elephant, that vast, structured mass, a product of fermentation! Why not? It is less difficult to relate that huge quadruped back to its original matrix than to relate the tiny worm to the molecule of flour that gave rise to it, but the tiny worm is only a tiny worm. . . . By which you mean that its smallness, by concealing its structure from you, also removes the element of wonder. . . . But the miracle is life, sentience itself; and that miracle is a miracle no longer. . . . Once I have seen inanimate matter actually become sentient, then nothing should ever be able to astonish me again. . . . What a comparison! On one side a small number of elements fermenting in the hollow of my hand; on the other, that immense reservoir of various elements scattered through the bowels of the earth, on its surface, in the depths of the seas, in the thin air itself! . . . And yet, since the same causes still persist, why have their effects ceased? Why do we no longer see the bull piercing the earth with its horns, pressing its feet against the earth, and straining to wrench its heavy body free? . . . Let the races of animals still in existence at present pass away; leave the great inanimate sediment to work for several million centuries. Perhaps the time required for the renewal of the species is ten times that allotted for their life-span. Wait, don't be in a hurry to make a judgment on the work of nature. You already have two great phenomena before you: the transition from the inanimate state to the state of sentience and spontaneous generation; be content with these. Draw the correct conclusions from them; and in an order of things in which there is no absolute greatness or smallness, permanence or transience, take care you do not fall into the mayfly's fallacy. . . ." Doctor, what is the mayfly's fallacy?

BORDEU: The erroneous belief an ephemeral creature has in the immutability of nature.

MLLE DE LESPINASSE: Like Fontenelle's rose, that said no rose could ever remember a gardener having died?

BORDEU: Exactly—that is very profound and very gracefully put. . . .

[*Mlle de Lespinasse challenges the usefulness of philosophical inquiry into such subjects.*]

BORDEU: Very well, you find some of these questions so self-evident that any inquiry into them seems to you superfluous. But may I ask which ones?

MLLE DE LESPINASSE: Well, the question of my individual identity, of whether I have a self or not, for example. Heavens, it seems to me that there's no need of all that talk just to tell me that I am me, that I've always been me, and that I shall never be anybody else.

BORDEU: The fact itself is self-evident enough, no doubt; but the reason for the fact is by no means so, especially if we accept the hypothesis of those who say that there is only one substance and who explain the formation of men, or of animals in general, by successive accretions of sentient molecules. Each sentient molecule had its own self before it merged with the whole; but how did it lose it, and how did all those losses result in the consciousness present in the whole?

MLLE DE LESPINASSE: It seems to me that contact is quite sufficient in itself. For instance, here's something I've experienced a hundred times. . . . But wait . . . I must just go and see what's going on behind those curtains. . . . He's asleep. . . . Now, when I put my hand on my thigh, at first I can feel that my hand and my thigh are separate, but after a while, when they're both just as warm as each other, then I can't tell which is which: the boundaries of the two different parts of me melt away and the two parts become one.

BORDEU: Yes, unless someone sticks a pin in one or the other; then the distinction would reappear. There is therefore something inside of you that knows whether it was your hand or your thigh that was pricked. And that something is not your foot; it is not even the hand that was pricked: the hand felt the pain, but the something else knew what had happened even though it felt no pain.

MLLE DE LESPINASSE: Well, I suppose it's my head.

BORDEU: Your whole head?

MLLE DE LESPINASSE: No, but I'll tell you what, Doctor: I'll explain myself by using a comparison. Women and poets think almost entirely in comparisons, you know. Imagine a spider. . . .

D'ALEMBERT: Who's there? . . . Is that you, Mademoiselle de Lespinasse?

MLLE DE LESPINASSE: Hush, hush. . . . (*Mlle de Lespinasse and the doctor remain silent for a while, then Mlle de Lespinasse says softly*) I think he's gone to sleep again.

BORDEU: No, I think I can still hear something.

MLLE DE LESPINASSE: Yes, you're right. I wonder if he's beginning to dream again.

BORDEU: Let's listen.

D'ALEMBERT: Why am I as I am? Because it was inevitable. . . . Yes, here, but what if I had lived elsewhere? At the North Pole? In the Southern Hemisphere? Or on Saturn? . . . If a distance of a few thousand miles can change my species, what might a distance equal to many thousands of times the earth's diameter not do? . . . And if everything is in universal flux, as the spectacle of the universe proves to me on all sides that it is, then what may the passing and the vicissitudes of several million centuries not produce? Who knows what a thinking and feeling being is like on Saturn? . . . But do feeling and thought exist on Saturn? . . . Why not? . . . Would the thinking and feeling being on Saturn have more senses than I have? . . . If he has, ah! What an unfortunate creature that inhabitant of Saturn is! . . . The more senses, the more needs.

BORDEU: He is right there: organs produce needs, and needs produce organs.

MLLE DE LESPINASSE: Doctor, are you delirious too?

BORDEU: Why? Is what I have said so impossible? I have seen two stumps gradually turn into arms.

MLLE DE LESPINASSE: You're lying.

BORDEU: True, but where arms were lacking, I have seen two shoulder blades lengthen, form a pair of pincers, and become two stumps.

MLLE DE LESPINASSE: Don't be silly.

BORDEU: It's a fact. Imagine a long succession of generations born without arms; imagine their continual efforts and you will slowly see the two ends of this pair of pincers grow longer, longer still, cross over at the back, grow forward again, perhaps develop fingers at their ends, and create arms and hands once more. The original conformation of animals degenerates or is perfected by necessity and by the constant fulfillment of their normal functions. We walk so little, do so little manual labor, and think so much that I have not yet given up hope of man ending up as nothing but a head.

MLLE DE LESPINASSE: A head! A head! But that's not particularly worrying. I wonder, though, if excessive lovemaking . . . You're putting some very silly ideas into my head.

BORDEU: Hush.

D'ALEMBERT: I am what I am, therefore, because it was inevitable that I should be so. Change the whole and you necessarily change me too, and yet the whole is changing constantly. . . . Man is merely a common effect, and the monster an uncommon one; both are equally natural, both equally inevitable, both equally part of the universal and general order. . . . And what is there astonishing in that? . . . All parts of created nature are constantly circulating through one another, and therefore all species are doing likewise . . . everything is in perpetual flux. . . . Every animal is more or less human; every mineral is more or less part of plant life; every plant is more or less animal. There are no clear-cut boundaries in nature. . . . And you talk of individuals, poor philosophers! Forget about your individuals and answer me this: Is there one atom in nature exactly like one other atom? . . . No. . . . Don't you agree that everything in nature is linked together and that it is impossible for there to be a break in the chain? What do you mean, then, when you talk about individuals? There are none, no, none whatsoever. . . . There is only one great individual: the whole. In that whole, as in a machine or as in any given animal, you may select one part and call it by a particular name; but if you call that part an individual, then you are suffering from a misconception as great as if you had called the wing of a bird, or even a feather on that wing, an individual. . . . And you talk about essences too, poor philosophers! Forget about your essences. Consider the general mass of the universe, or if your imaginations are too limited for that, consider your first origin and your final end. . . . Oh, Archytas! You who measured the globe, what are you now? A handful of ashes. . . . What is a being? . . . The sum of a certain number of tendencies. . . . Can I be anything other than a tendency? . . . No, I tend always toward my end. . . . And the species? . . . The species, too, are only tendencies toward their own particular and common end. . . . And life? . . . Life is a sequence of actions and reactions. . . . While alive, I act and react as a unified mass . . . when dead, I act and react as separate molecules. . . . Then I do not die? . . . No, I do not die in that sense, that is certain, neither I myself nor anything that is. . . . Birth, life, dissolution—these are but changes of form. . . . And how can one form be better than another? Every form has the happiness and the unhappiness proper to it. From the elephant to the flea, from the flea to the animate and sentient molecule, the origin of everything, there is no point in all nature that does not suffer pain and experience pleasure. . . .

[*D'Alembert goes back to sleep. Bordeu explains to Mlle de Lespinasse how she was formed in the womb.*]

BORDEU: At first, you were nothing at all. You began as an invisible speck, which had been formed from even smaller molecules originally lying scattered through the blood and the lymph of your father or your mother; that speck became a slender thread, then a bundle of threads. Up till that point, not the slightest suggestion of that pleasing shape you have today; your eyes, those lovely eyes of yours, no more resembled eyes than the tip of an anemone root resembles an anemone. Each of the fibers in that bundle of threads was then transformed, by nutrition and its own conformation alone, into organs with particular sense functions—exception being made of those organs in which the fibers of the bundle undergo their metamorphosis and to which they give birth. The bundle is a purely sentient system; if it persisted in that form, it would be susceptible to all those kinds of impression that can be received by pure sentience, such as cold and heat, softness and roughness. These successive impressions—of different kinds, and each varying in intensity within its kind—might perhaps produce memory, self-consciousness, and a very limited power of reasoning. But that pure and simple sentience, that sense of touch, is diversified by the various organs that are produced by each of the fibers; one fiber, by forming an ear, gives rise to a particular sense for apprehending what we call noise, or sound; another fiber forms the palate, thereby producing a second kind of touch, which we call taste; a third, by forming the nose and its lining, produces a third kind of touch, which we call smell; a fourth, by forming an eye, gives rise to a fourth kind of touch, which we call color.

MLLE DE LESPINASSE: But, if I understand you correctly, the people who reject the possibility of a sixth sense or of a genuine hermaphrodite are being very stupid. How can they be certain that nature might not be able to make up a bundle including an additional fiber that would give rise to an organ we've never heard of?

BORDEU: Or a bundle including both the fibers that characterize the two sexes. You are quite right. It's a pleasure to talk to you; you not only grasp the things that are said to you, you also draw conclusions from them that amaze me by their soundness. . . .

MLLE DE LESPINASSE: But to continue. You told me that every fiber in the bundle formed a particular organ. What proof have you that this is so?

BORDEU: Do in your mind what nature sometimes does in reality: deprive the bundle of one of its fibers—of the fiber that is destined to form the eyes, for example. What do you think will happen?

MLLE DE LESPINASSE: That the animal will have no eyes?

BORDEU: Or only one—in the middle of its forehead.

MLLE DE LESPINASSE: Then it would be a Cyclops.

BORDEU: Exactly—a Cyclops.

MLLE DE LESPINASSE: Then the Cyclops may well not be a fabulous creature at all.

BORDEU: It is so far from being fabulous that I can show you one whenever you please.

MLLE DE LESPINASSE: And does anyone know the cause of this peculiarity?

BORDEU: Yes, the man who dissected the creature and found that it had only one optic nerve. Now do in your mind what nature does sometimes in reality. Remove another fiber from the bundle, the fiber that ought to have formed the nose: the animal will be without a nose. Remove the fiber that ought to have formed the ear: the animal will be without ears—or will have only one; and the anatomist, when he dissects the creature, will find neither olfactory nerves nor auditory nerves—or only one of the latter. Continue removing the threads and the animal will be without head, without feet, without hands; and though it may live only a very short while, still it will have lived.

MLLE DE LESPINASSE: And are there real examples of all this?

BORDEU: Certainly. And that's not all. If you duplicate some of the fibers in the bundle, the animal will have two heads, four eyes, four ears, three testicles, three feet, four arms, six fingers on each hand. Disturb the arrangement of the fibers in the bundle and the organs will also be misplaced: the head will be in the middle of the chest, the lungs will both be on the left, and the heart on the right. Make two fibers adhere together and the organs, too, will be fused; the arms will be growing into the body, the thighs, the legs, and the feet will be joined, and you will end up with every imaginable kind of monster.

MILLE DE LESPINASSE: But it seems to me that a functioning physical structure as complicated as an animal, a structure that starts as a speck, that is produced by a seething fluid, perhaps by two fluids randomly mingled, for one scarcely knows what one is doing on such occasions; an organism that progresses toward its final state of perfection through an infinity of successive stages; an organism whose formation, whether it be regular or irregular, depends on a bundle of tiny, slender, flexible threads, on a sort of skein in which not even the smallest fiber can be snapped, torn, misplaced, or missing without some distressing consequence for the whole, such an organism, I repeat, ought to become tangled up and knotted even more often during the course of its development than the silks on my silk winder.

BORDEU: Yes, and, in fact, the organism does suffer from such defects more than people think. There is not enough dissection done, and ideas on the formation of animals are often very far from the truth.

MLLE DE LESPINASSE: Do we have any observable examples of these deformities caused by malformation in the womb—other than hunchbacks and cripples, that is, whose deformities could possibly be attributed to some inherited weakness.

BORDEU: Oh, yes, innumerable ones. There was a carpenter from Troyes, for instance, who died quite recently in La Charité hospital in Paris, at the age of twenty-five, as a result of an inflammation of the lungs. His name was Jean-Baptiste Macé, and he had all the internal organs of his chest and abdomen in the reverse of the normal positions: his heart on the right, whereas yours is in a corresponding position on the left; his liver on the left; his stomach, spleen, and pancreas in the right hypochondrium; the *vena porta* to the liver also on the left, whereas it is on the right if the liver is in the normal position; the intestines similarly reversed; the kidneys, back to back up against the lumbar vertebrae, were horseshoe shaped. So now let them come and tell us about their final causes!

MLLE DE LESPINASSE: It is very strange.

BORDEU: If Jean-Baptiste Macé was married and had children . . .

MLLE DE LESPINASSE: Yes, Doctor, go on. The children . . .

BORDEU: Will be normal in their conformation. But after a hundred or so years, for these irregularities do make such leaps, one or other of their children's children will eventually revert to the unusual conformation discovered in its great-grandfather.

MLLE DE LESPINASSE: What is the cause of these leaps?

BORDEU: Who knows? It takes two people to make a child, as you know. Perhaps one of the participants supplements the other's deficiency, and then the defective network reappears only when the descendant of the malformed breed becomes dominant again and can therefore impose its own defective pattern on the network of the malformed child. The bundle of fibers constitutes the primal and original difference between all the various species of animals. The variations that occur in the bundle of each species give rise to all the malformed variations within that species. . . .

. . . Disturb the origin of the bundle, the brain, and you change the whole animal. Apparently it exists there in its entirety, sometimes controlling the network of organs, sometimes being controlled by it.

MLLE DE LESPINASSE: So that the animal is either being controlled by an absolute despot or else living in anarchy.

BORDEU: An absolute despot, yes, that's very well put. The origin of the bundle gives the orders, and the rest of the organism obeys. The animal is its own master, *mentis compos.*

MLLE DE LESPINASSE: Or else in a state of anarchy, when all the fibers of the network rise up against their ruler, so that there is no longer any supreme authority.

BORDEU: Beautifully put. In strong fits of passion, in attacks of delirium, or when threatened with great danger, if the master directs all the forces of his subjects to bear on a single point, even the weakest animal may display incredible strength.

MLLE DE LESPINASSE: Then there are the vapors—a kind of anarchy to which we women are particularly prone.

BORDEU: Yes, there you have the very image of a weak administration, in which each member is trying to usurp the authority of the master. I know of only one remedy for such a state, one difficult to apply, but infallible. It is for the origin of the sentient network, that part of the animal that constitutes the self, to be suddenly affected by a very powerful motive for regaining its authority. . . .

. . . There was a woman who fell into the most terrifying hysterical condition as a result of giving birth to a child; this condition took the form of involuntary spells of weeping and laughter, convulsions, choking fits, swellings in her throat, periods of gloomy silence, screams, all the most appalling things you can imagine. Now, this woman was passionately in love, and after her symptoms had continued for several years, believing that her lover was growing weary of her sickness and preparing to break with her, she resolved to be cured or to die in the attempt. A kind of civil war then began to take place inside her, in which sometimes the master had the advantage, and sometimes the subjects. Whenever it chanced that the force exerted by the fibers of the network became exactly equal to the reacting force of their origin, the brain, she fell into a state very like death; she would be carried to her bed and lie there for hours on end, motionless and almost lifeless; at other times, she merely suffered from fits of fatigue, a general feeling of exhaustion that seemed bound to end eventually in her extinction. She continued in this state of inner conflict for six months. The rebellion always began in the fibers; she could sense it beginning. At the first symptom, she would get up, run about, and take all the most violent forms of exercise she could think of: she ran up and down stairs, she sawed wood, she went out and started digging. The organ of her will, the origin of the bundle, stiffened its resistance; she said to herself, Victory or death. After an innumerable succession of victories and defeats, the ruler succeeded in regaining his authority, and the subjects became so submissive that, although the woman afterward went through all sorts of domestic troubles and suffered from a variety of illnesses, she never again experienced the slightest symptom of hysteria. . . .

. . . [One of the conclusions to be drawn from this is that] if the origin of the bundle recalls all the powers of the animal into itself, if the entire system starts to reverse itself, so to speak, as I think happens in the case of a man sunk deep in thought or a mystic who sees the heavens opening to his gaze or a savage singing while surrounded by flames or someone in a state of ecstasy or in the case of any form of voluntary or involuntary alienation from reality . . .

MLLE DE LESPINASSE: Well?

BORDEU: Well, then the animal ceases to be sentient, its existence shrinks to a single point. I have not seen the priest of Calamus who was able, according to St. Augustine, to alienate himself from reality to the point of not feeling burning coals; I have not seen those savages who, when bound and tortured, smile at their enemies, jeer at them, and suggest additional torments even more exquisite than those already being inflicted on them; I have not seen those gladiators who never forgot in the arena, even as they lay dying, the grace they had learned in the gymnasium; but I believe in all these things, because I have seen, seen with my own eyes, an effort of the will quite as extraordinary as any of the ones I have mentioned.

MLLE DE LESPINASSE: Oh, do tell me about it, Doctor. I'm just like a child—I love amazing stories. And when they do honor to the human race, I rarely try to question their truth.

BORDEU: In Langres, a small town in Champagne, there used to be a good *curé,* named either Le Moni or de Moni, who was deeply convinced of and imbued with the truth of his religion. He had an attack of the stone, and it became necessary to operate. The day was fixed; the surgeon, his assistants, and myself went to the *curé*'s house. He welcomed us in with every appearance of serenity, undressed, and laid himself down. He would not allow himself to be strapped down. "Just put me in the right position," he said. When this had been done, he asked for the large crucifix at the foot of his bed; when it was brought to him, he clasped it in his arms and pressed his lips against it. The operation was performed; he remained absolutely motionless, wept not a single tear, uttered not a single sigh, and the stone was removed without his even being aware of it. . . .

[*Bordeu then goes on to explain the coordinating function of the brain.*]

MLLE DE LESPINASSE: What is memory, then?

BORDEU: A property inherent in the center, the specific form of sentience peculiar to the origin of the bundle, just as sight is the specific form of sentience proper to the eye. And it is no more surprising that the eye does not possess memory than that the ear is unable to see.

MLLE DE LESPINASSE: But, Doctor, you are evading my questions rather than answering them.

BORDEU: I am evading nothing; I am telling you what I know, and if the structure of the bundle's origin were as familiar to me as that of its dependent fibers, if I had been able to study it with equal facility, then I should know a great deal more. However, though I may be weak on specific phenomena, I make up for it with my triumphs in the field of general phenomena.

MLLE DE LESPINASSE: What general phenomena do you mean?

BORDEU: Reason, judgment, imagination, madness, idiocy, cruelty, instinct.

MLLE DE LESPINASSE: I see what you mean. All those qualities are only consequences of the inherent or acquired relation between the origin of the bundle and its dependent branches.

BORDEU: Precisely. If the origin, or trunk, is too vigorous in relation to the branches, then we get poets, artists, imaginative people, cowardly people, mystics, or madmen. If it is too weak, then we get brutes and wild beasts. If the entire system is slack, soft, lacking in energy, then we get imbeciles. If, on the other hand, it is energetic, in harmony with itself, well governed, then we get able thinkers, philosophers, and sages.

MLLE DE LESPINASSE: And according to which branch of the network is dominant, so we get different instincts predominating in different animals and particular talents in different men:

the dog has a keen sense of smell, the fish a keen sense of hearing, the eagle keen eyes; d'Alembert is a geometrician, Vaucanson an engineer, Grétry a composer, Voltaire a poet. And these different results are caused by one particular fiber in the bundle being stronger in these individuals than any of their other fibers and also than the corresponding fiber in other beings of their own kind.

BORDEU: And those talents are also preserved by the tyranny of habit: an old man will not cease to feel love for women, and Voltaire is still writing tragedies.

(*Here the doctor fell into silent meditation, and Mlle de Lespinasse said to him*)

MLLE DE LESPINASSE: Doctor, you're dreaming.

BORDEU: True.

MLLE DE LESPINASSE: What are you dreaming about?

BORDEU: Voltaire.

MLLE DE LESPINASSE: And?

BORDEU: I was wondering to myself how great men are made.

MLLE DE LESPINASSE: And how are they made?

BORDEU: How? Sensibility. . . .

MLLE DE LESPINASSE: Yes? Sensibility?

BORDEU: Which is to say, an extreme mobility of certain fibers of the network is the predominant characteristic of mediocre minds.

MLLE DE LESPINASSE: Oh, Doctor! What blasphemy!

BORDEU: I thought you'd say that. But what is a man who has great sensibility? A creature entirely at the mercy of his diaphragm. It requires only an affecting phrase to strike his ear, an unusual phenomenon to strike his eye, and suddenly he is filled with a great inner tumult; there is an excitation of all the fibers in the bundle, he begins to shudder, he is gripped by a sacred horror, he weeps, he chokes himself with his own sighs, he becomes unable to speak, and the origin of the bundle becomes completely confused; the man is deprived of all mental calm, all reason, all judgment, all capacity for making distinctions, all self-control.

MLLE DE LESPINASSE: A good description of me.

BORDEU: The great man, if he has been unfortunate enough to

have been endowed with such a disposition by nature, will strive ceaselessly to weaken it, to overcome it, to make himself master of all his emotions, and to preserve the origin of the bundle's position as absolute master. Then he will be able to retain possession of himself amid even the greatest dangers; his judgments will be cold, but always sane. Nothing that might serve to further his ends, to accomplish his goal, will escape him; it will be difficult to surprise him; by the time he is forty-five, he will be a great king, a great minister, a great politician, a great artist, above all a great actor, a great philosopher, a great poet, a great musician, a great doctor; he will be in complete control of himself and of everything around him. He will have no fear of death, that fear which, as the Stoic so sublimely said, is a handle that the strong man seizes in order to lead the weak man where he will; he will have snapped off that handle from himself, and by so doing he will have freed himself from all the tyrannies of this world. Men of sensibility and madmen are on the stage; he is in the audience; it is he who is the wise man.

MLLE DE LESPINASSE: Then may God preserve me from the company of such a wise man!

BORDEU: It is for want of striving to emulate him that you will always be subject alternately to violent pains and pleasures, that you will spend your life laughing and crying, and that you will never be anything but a child.

MLLE DE LESPINASSE: Then that is my choice.

BORDEU: And do you hope to be the happier for it?

MLLE DE LESPINASSE: I have no idea.

BORDEU: Mademoiselle, this quality of sensibility, so highly prized, so unproductive of greatness, can scarcely ever be exercized strongly without pain or weakly without tedium; one is either yawning or drunk with it. You give yourself up unreservedly to the delicious sensations produced by a delightful piece of music, you allow yourself to be carried away by the charm of some pathetic scene: your diaphragm contracts, the pleasure passes, and you are left with nothing but a choking feeling that lasts all the rest of the evening.

MLLE DE LESPINASSE: But what if those are the only conditions on which I can enjoy the sublime music or the touching scene?

BORDEU: But that isn't so. I too can experience pleasure, I too can admire; yet I never suffer pain, except from colic. My pleasure is pure; and as a consequence, my criticisms are more severe, my praise more considered and more welcome. Can there be such a thing as a bad tragedy for souls as easily moved as yours? How many times when reading a play have you not blushed for the ecstasy you experienced while watching it performed—and vice versa?

MLLE DE LESPINASSE: Yes, that has happened, I admit.

BORDEU: So that it is the place not of the sentimental person, like you, but of the calm, cold one, like myself, to say: That is true, that is good, that is beautiful. . . . So we must strengthen the origin of our network as much as we can; that's the most important thing in life. It's a matter of life and death, you know.

MLLE DE LESPINASSE: Of life and death! Can it be as serious as all that, Doctor?

BORDEU: Certainly. There is no one who has not at some time felt sick of life. A single incident may serve to make this feeling an unconscious and habitual one; and then in spite of distractions and varied amusements, of one's friends' advice, of one's own efforts, the fibers stubbornly continue their fatal assaults upon their origin; the unfortunate victim struggles in vain; the whole spectacle of the universe grows dark to him; he walks always with a retinue of melancholy thoughts that never leave him and ends by delivering himself from his own existence.

MLLE DE LESPINASSE: Doctor, you're frightening me. . . .

[*The doctor and Mlle de Lespinasse then go on to discuss sleep and dreams with D'Alembert, who is now awake.*]

D'ALEMBERT: . . . What are the will and the liberty of a dreaming man?

BORDEU: What are they? Exactly what they are in a man who is awake: the most recent impulse of desire or aversion, the most recent result of all that he has been from birth to that precise moment. And I defy even the subtlest mind to perceive the slightest difference between them.

D'ALEMBERT: Do you think that's true?

BORDEU: And you are the one who asks me that! You have spent two-thirds of your life immersed in profound speculations, in a waking dream, acting quite involuntarily, yes, involuntarily, far more involuntarily than in your dream. In your dream you were in control, you were giving orders, you were being obeyed; you were displeased or satisfied, you found yourself being contradicted, you encountered obstacles, you became annoyed, you loved, you hated, you cast blame, you expressed approval, you denied things, you wept, you came, you went. But on days when you have been absorbed in meditation, scarcely were your eyes open in the morning than you were once more in the grip of the idea that had been occupying you the day before; you got dressed, you sat down at your table, you pondered, you drew figures, you made calculations, you ate your dinner, you went back to your problems, sometimes you left the table in order to verify them; you spoke to others, gave orders to your servant, ate supper, went to bed, fell asleep, and all that without having performed a single voluntary action. You existed only as a single point; you were acting, but you were not exercising your will. Can the will be exercised of itself? Will is always brought into action by some interior or exterior motive, by some present impression or some memory from the past, by some passion or intention projected into the future. After which, I have nothing to say about liberty except this: that our most recent action is always the necessary effect of a single cause—ourself; a very complex cause, but a single one.

MLLE DE LESPINASSE: And does that mean the action is inevitable?

BORDEU: Without a doubt. Try to imagine any other action resulting from that cause, assuming that the being performing the action is the same.

MLLE DE LESPINASSE: He's right. Since it is I who act in that particular way, then anyone who could act in a different way would no longer be me. And to say that at the moment when I am saying or doing something, I could be saying or doing another is to say that I am both myself and someone else as well. But, Doctor, what about vice and virtue? "Virtue," a word so sacred in every language, an idea so revered by every nation.

BORDEU: We must replace it with that of doing good, and its opposite with that of doing harm. We are born fortunate or unfortunate; we are carried along, without our being aware of it, in the general torrent that leads one man to glory and another to disgrace.

MLLE DE LESPINASSE: And self-respect and shame and remorse?

BORDEU: They are puerile emotions with no foundation but the ignorance and vanity of a being who attributes to himself the merit or the blame for an inevitable instant in time.

MLLE DE LESPINASSE: And rewards and punishments?

BORDEU: They are means of correcting those beings we refer to as wicked, though they are still capable of alteration, and of encouraging those that we call good.

MLLE DE LESPINASSE: But isn't such a doctrine dangerous?

BORDEU: Is it true or is it false?

MLLE DE LESPINASSE: I think it's true.

BORDEU: Then you are saying that you think there are advantages in falsehood and disadvantages in truth.

MLLE DE LESPINASSE: Yes, I do think that.

BORDEU: And so do I; but the advantages of falsehood are only transitory, whereas those of truth are eternal; the unfortunate consequences of truth, when there are any, soon pass, whereas those produced by a lie last as long as the lie itself. Consider the effects of falsehood on a man's mind and on his conduct. In his mind, either the falsehood becomes mixed up, higgledy-piggledy, with the truth—which makes him incapable of logical thought—or else it is completely and logically linked up with further falsehood—which makes him logically consistent but in error. And what sort of conduct can you expect from a man who is either incapable of logical thought or else logically committed to error?

MLLE DE LESPINASSE: The latter defect, though less contemptible, is possibly more to be feared than the former.

D'ALEMBERT: Very good; now everything has been reduced to questions of sentience, memory, and organic movements—

which suits me well enough. But what about imagination? What about abstract ideas?

BORDEU: Imagination . . .

MLLE DE LESPINASSE: One moment, Doctor. Let us recapitulate. As I see it, according to your principles and by means of purely mechanical processes, I could reduce the greatest genius on earth to an unorganized mass of flesh that would be left with nothing but the capacity for moment-by-moment sentience, and then I could bring this same unorganized mass back from the most complete state of mindlessness imaginable to the condition of a genius once more. One of these processes would consist in amputating the primal skein of a certain number of its threads and of completely mixing up the rest, and the reverse process would consist in returning the threads I had removed to their place in the skein and then leaving the whole to develop happily on its own. Example: I remove Newton's two auditory fibers and he cannot perceive sounds, his olfactory fibers and he cannot perceive smell, his optic fibers and he cannot perceive colors, the fibers that form his palate and he cannot perceive tastes; I remove or tangle up the remaining fibers and farewell to the structure of the brain, memory, judgment, desires, aversions, passions, will, self-consciousness. What remains is an amorphous mass that has nothing left but life and sentience.

BORDEU: Two almost identical qualities: life pertains to the mass as a whole, sentience to each individual particle.

MLLE DE LESPINASSE: I return to the mass; I restore its olfactory fibers and it can smell, its auditory fibers and it can hear, its optic fibers and it can see, its palate fibers and it can taste. Then by untangling the rest of the skein, I allow the other threads to develop; memory, the power of comparison, judgment, reason, desires, aversions, passions, natural aptitudes, talent all return, and there is my man of genius once more, all without the intervention of any heterogeneous and unintelligible agent.

BORDEU: Excellent—always hang on to that; the rest is meaningless twaddle. . . . But what about imagination? What about abstract ideas? Imagination is the recollection of forms and colors. Seeing a view or an object inevitably tunes up the strings of the sensing instrument in some way or another. Later, it can be tuned up to that same pitch again, either by itself or by some external cause. It will then vibrate within or reverberate externally; that is, either it will rehearse the impressions it has received silently and internally or it will expel them as a series of sounds agreed upon by convention.

D'ALEMBERT: But the account that it gives may exaggerate, omit certain circumstances and add others, distort the original fact or embellish it, and the sensitive instruments nearby will receive impressions that are indeed those of the instrument that is sounding but that may not exactly correspond to the original event.

BORDEU: True—the account is historical or poetic.

D'ALEMBERT: But why does this element of poetry or of falsehood find its way into the account?

BORDEU: Because ideas always awaken other ideas, and they awaken one another in this way because they have always been connected. Since you took the liberty of comparing an animal to a harpsichord, you will have no objection, I hope, if I compare the poet's account of his experience to a song.

D'ALEMBERT: No, that's fair enough.

BORDEU: Any song is based on a scale. That scale has intervals; each note in the scale has its harmonics, and those harmonics have theirs. These phenomena enable the melody to be modulated, to be embellished and varied by being heard in another key. The original fact is thus a given theme that every composer feels in his own way. . . .

D'ALEMBERT: And abstract ideas?

BORDEU: There are no such things; there are only habitual omissions, ellipses that make propositions more generally applicable and language swifter and easier to use. The abstract sciences sprang originally from the conventional signs used for speech. A quality common to a number of actions gave rise to the words "vice" and "virtue"; a quality common to a number of objects gave rise to the words "ugliness" and "beauty." We began by saying one man, one horse, two animals; then we learned to say one, two, three, and the whole science of numbers was born. We cannot conceive ideas corresponding to abstract words. It was observed that all bodies have three dimensions: length, breadth, and depth; each of these dimensions was then studied, and from that arose all the mathematical sciences. All abstractions are nothing but signs that correspond to no idea. All abstract sciences are nothing but the study of relations between signs. The idea has been excluded by cutting the sign off from the physical object it represented, and it is only by attaching the sign once more to that physical object that the science can become a science of ideas again. This explains the need, so frequently encountered in conversation and in books, to explain things by means of examples. When, after a long explanation conducted solely by means of signs, you ask for an example, all you are asking of the person speaking is that he now give body, shape, reality, to what he has said—to attach an idea to the series of sounds he has been uttering by linking them up with sensations you have experienced. . . .

Conclusion of the Conversation

The speakers are: Mlle de Lespinasse and Dr. Bordeu.

At two o'clock that afternoon, the doctor returned. D'Alembert was dining out, and the doctor found himself alone with Mlle de Lespinasse. Dinner was served. They talked of more or less inconsequential matters until dessert; but when the servants had withdrawn, Mlle de Lespinasse said to the doctor: Come, now, Doctor, drink a glass of this Malaga, and then you must answer me a question. It has gone through my head a hundred times, but I wouldn't dare to ask anyone about it but you.

BORDEU: Your Malaga is excellent. . . . Now, what is this question?

MLLE DE LESPINASSE: What do you think of interbreeding between species?

BORDEU: And a very good question, too, I may say. Men have always attributed a great deal of importance to the act of generation, and I think they are right to do so; but I'm dissatisfied with both their civil and their religious laws on this matter.

MLLE DE LESPINASSE: And what is your criticism of them?

BORDEU: That they have been made without equity, without purpose, and without any regard to things as they are or to the public good.

MLLE DE LESPINASSE: Try to explain.

BORDEU: That's my intention. . . . But wait . . . *(He looks at his watch.)* I've still got a good hour to give you; if I go quickly, that should be enough. We are alone, you're not a prudish old maid, so you won't go and imagine that I am intending any lack of the respect that is your due; and whatever your opinion of my ideas, I hope for my part that you won't draw any derogatory conclusions from them as to the morality of my own behavior.

MLLE DE LESPINASSE: Of course not, though that's a very disturbing beginning.

BORDEU: Shall we change the subject, then?

MLLE DE LESPINASSE: No, no! Don't let that stop you. One of your friends, who was trying to think of suitable husbands for my two sisters and myself, decided that the youngest ought to be married to a sylph, the eldest to a tall angel of the Annunciation, and I myself to a disciple of Diogenes: he knew us all very well. But all the same, Doctor, a veil, just the slightest veil.

BORDEU: That goes without saying, as far as the subject and my profession will allow.

MLLE DE LESPINASSE: You mustn't let it bother you. . . . But here is your coffee. . . . Take your coffee.

BORDEU *(having drunk his coffee)*: Your question can be considered from a physical, from a moral, or from a poetic point of view.

MLLE DE LESPINASSE: Poetic!

BORDEU: Certainly. The art of creating beings that do not yet exist in the image of those that do—that is true poetry. So much so that I hope you will allow me to quote Horace this time instead of Hippocrates. That poet, or maker, says somewhere, "*Omne tulit punctum qui miscuit utile dulci*": "The supreme merit lies in having mingled the pleasant with the useful." Perfection consists in reconciling these qualities. The pleasant and useful action ought to occupy first place in our aesthetic hierarchy; nor can we deny second place to the simply useful; the third will therefore be the right of the purely pleasant; and the action that produces neither pleasure nor profit, we must relegate to the lowest rank of all.

MLLE DE LESPINASSE: So far I am able to agree with your opinions without blushing. But where is this leading us?

BORDEU: You shall see. Can you tell me, mademoiselle, what profit or pleasure is to be gained, either by the individual involved or by society, from the practice of chastity or strict continence?

MLLE DE LESPINASSE: Good heavens! None.

BORDEU: In that case, despite the magnificent eulogies lavished upon them by religious enthusiasts and the support accorded to them by our civil laws, we shall strike them off our list of virtues, and we shall agree that there is nothing so puerile, so ridiculous, so absurd, so harmful, so contemptible, and nothing in the world worse, with the exception of positive evil, than these two rare qualities.

MLLE DE LESPINASSE: Yes, I can subscribe to that.

BORDEU: Take care. I warn you that you'll want to withdraw in a moment.

MLLE DE LESPINASSE: We never withdraw.

BORDEU: And what about solitary actions?

MLLE DE LESPINASSE: Well, what about them?

BORDEU: Well, since they do at least bring pleasure to the individual, then either our principle is false or . . .

MLLE DE LESPINASSE: What, Doctor! . . .

BORDEU: Yes, mademoiselle, yes, and for the very good reason that although they are just as neutral as chastity and continence, they are also less sterile. It is a need; and even if one were not pressed into it by the need, it is still a pleasant experience. I want people to be healthy, I absolutely insist on that, do you understand? I am opposed to excess of all kinds; but in a society such as ours, there are a hundred and one reasonable considerations, such as lack of means, the dread of a burning repentance for men and of dishonor for women, not to mention the fatal consequences of strict continence combined with a passionate temperament, especially in the young, that reduce a wretched creature who is dying of vapors and boredom or a poor devil who doesn't know where to turn to relieving themselves after the manner of the Cynic. Cato, seeing a young man hesitating on the threshold of a courtesan, said to him, "Courage, my son . . ." But if he were to find the same young man today *in flagrante delicto,* alone, would he not rather say, "Yes, that is better than corrupting another man's wife or endangering your own honor and health"? What! Because circumstances deprive me of the greatest happiness it is possible to imagine—that of mingling my senses with those of a partner chosen by my heart, my ecstasy with her ecstasy, my soul with her soul, and reproducing myself in her and with her—because I cannot set the sacred stamp of utility upon my action, must I forbid myself that delightful and necessary moment? One is bled to relieve an excess of blood. Of what importance is the nature of the superabundant humor, or its color, or the means employed to rid oneself of it? It is quite as superfluous in either form of indisposition. And if it were pumped back out of the vessel where it is stored, redistributed through the whole organism, then disposed of by some longer, more painful, and more dangerous means, would it be any the less wasted, for all that? Nature does not permit waste. And where can the guilt be in my aiding her when she summons me to her assistance by such unequivocal signs? We should never provoke her, but it is permissible to lend her a hand when the occasion requires it. To refuse her request, to remain idle when she calls, seems to me mere foolishness and a wasted opportunity for pleasure. Live an austere life, people will say to me, make sure you tire yourself out. What do they mean? Why, that I should deprive myself of one pleasure and put myself to a great deal of discomfort in order to avoid another. A brilliant idea! . . .

[*Doctor Bordeu then goes on to hint that there are other sexual practices also that he considers preferable to whoring and the ill effects of chastity.*]

MLLE DE LESPINASSE (*covering her eyes*): Doctor, I can see which way your thoughts are tending, and I wager . . .

BORDEU: But I shan't accept the wager: you would win. Yes, mademoiselle, that is my opinion.

MLLE DE LESPINASSE: What! Whether one keeps within the boundaries of one's own species or whether one crosses them?

BORDEU: It is true.

MLLE DE LESPINASSE: You are monstrous!

BORDEU: Not I but, rather, nature or society. Listen, mademoiselle, I refuse to let myself be imposed on by words, and I can express what I believe all the more freely because I have a clear conscience and because the purity of my own way of life is such as to protect me from all suspicion. I shall therefore put to you the following question. Given two actions, both productive of sensual enjoyment, both of which can bring only pleasure without profit, but of which one gives pleasure only to the one performing it, while in the other the pleasure is shared with a fellow being, whether male or female, since the sex or even the use of sex is irrelevant to the question, in favor of which of those two actions will common sense decide?

MLLE DE LESPINASSE: Such problems are too high-flown for me.

BORDEU: Ah, I see! After having been a man for five minutes, now you're retreating again behind your mobcap and your petticoats. You've decided it's time to turn back into a woman again! Very well, so be it! Then I must treat you as one. . . . No sooner said than done. . . . We don't hear much talk about Mme du Barry these days. . . . You see, everything works out in the end. Everyone thought the whole court was going to be turned topsy-turvy, but the master behaved like a sensible man. *Omne tulit punctum;* he has kept the woman who gave him pleasure . . . and the minister who was useful to him as well. . . . But you're not listening to me. . . . What is making you so preoccupied?

MLLE DE LESPINASSE: Those unions of yours that seem to me so wholly against nature.

BORDEU: Nothing that exists can be either against nature or outside nature, not even voluntary continence and chastity, which would be the chief crimes against nature if it were possible to sin against nature and the chief crimes against the social laws of any country where men's actions were weighed on any other scales than those of religious bigotry and prejudice.

MLLE DE LESPINASSE: I'm going back over your beastly syllogisms, and I don't see any way out—one must either reject everything or accept everything. . . . I think, Doctor, that the most decorous and the quickest way out of my dilemma is for us to jump over this nasty, muddy patch and get back to my first question. What do you think of interbreeding between species?

BORDEU: There's no need to jump. We were there already. It is the physical or the moral aspect of the problem you want to know about?

MLLE DE LESPINASSE: The physical, the physical.

BORDEU: So much the better. The moral aspect comes first, but you're still deciding that. So we shall . . .

MLLE DE LESPINASSE: Agreed. . . . But . . . I'm sure it's a necessary preliminary, but I would be grateful . . . if you could separate the cause from the effect. Then we can leave the beastly cause out of it.

BORDEU: You're asking me to begin with the end; since that's what you want, however, I shall tell you that, thanks to our timidity, our aversions, our laws, and our tendency to think we know everything already, very few experiments have been made in this field. Consequently, we do not know in which cases copulation would be entirely unfruitful, in which cases the useful and the pleasurable would be combined, what kinds of new species we could expect from varied and continued experiments, whether Fauns are real or fabulous, whether it would be possible to combine hybrid breeds in a multitude of various ways, and whether those hybrids that we already know of are really sterile. But one startling fact that a great number of learned people will swear to you is true, and that is in fact false, is that they have seen an infamous rabbit in the archduke's poultry yard performing the duties of a cock for twenty infamous hens, all of which were accepting his advances; they may also say that they were shown chickens covered in fur that were the products of this bestiality. Believe me when I tell you that they have been made fools of.

MLLE DE LESPINASSE: But what do you mean by varied and continued experiments?

BORDEU: I mean that developments in nature are always gradual, that the mutual assimilation of two species must be prepared beforehand, and that in order to achieve success in such experiments, we should have to start a long way back and try first of all to make the two species more like each other by giving them a similar diet.

MLLE DE LESPINASSE: It will be difficult to make men graze.

BORDEU: But not to persuade them to drink a great deal of goat's milk. And there will be no difficulty in making goats eat bread. I have selected the goat for reasons peculiarly my own.

MLLE DE LESPINASSE: Oh? What reasons?

BORDEU: You are very bold! Well, the reasons are . . . that from such a combination, we should be able to produce a breed of vigorous, intelligent, indefatigable, and swift-footed creatures that we could then train to be excellent servants.

MLLE DE LESPINASSE: Oh, yes, that's excellent, Doctor! I fancy I can already see five or six great, insolent footgoats behind all our duchesses' carriages. It's a sight to gladden the heart!

BORDEU: And consequently we should no longer degrade our fellow men by forcing them to fulfill functions unworthy of both themselves and us.

MLLE DE LESPINASSE: Still better.

BORDEU: And should no longer reduce men in our colonies to the status of mere beasts of burden.

MLLE DE LESPINASSE: Quickly, quickly, Doctor, you must get to work right away and make all these footgoats for us.

BORDEU: And you have no scruples about allowing it to be done?

MLLE DE LESPINASSE: Oh, stop, one has just come to me: your footgoats would all be appallingly lascivious.

BORDEU: I certainly can't guarantee that they would be particularly moral.

MLLE DE LESPINASSE: There will be an end of all safety for honest women; they will breed unceasingly—in the end, we shall either have to slaughter them or submit to them. I don't want them any more, I don't want them any more. You can relax.

BORDEU (*preparing to leave*): And what about the problem of whether or not to baptize them?

MLLE DE LESPINASSE: It would cause a wonderful to-do in the Sorbonne.

BORDEU: When you were in the Jardin du Roi, did you ever see that orangutan there in the glass cage? The one that looks for all the world like St. John the Baptist preaching in the wilderness?

MLLE DE LESPINASSE: Yes, I've seen him.

BORDEU: The Cardinal de Polignac said to it one day, "Speak and I shall baptize thee!"

MLLE DE LESPINASSE: Good-bye, then, Doctor. Don't stay away for centuries on end the way you usually do, and try to remember sometimes that I love you to distraction. If people only knew all the horrors you've been telling me!

BORDEU: I'm quite sure that you, at least, won't tell them.

MLLE DE LESPINASSE: Don't be too sure. I listen only for the pleasure of repeating what I've heard. But just one more word, and then I'll never mention the subject again.

BORDEU: What is it?

MLLE DE LESPINASSE: Those abominable tastes, what is the cause of them?

BORDEU: Generally speaking, they are caused by an organic weakness in the young and by mental corruption in the old. But there can be more specific causes: in Athens, the attraction of beauty; in Rome, the scarcity of women; in Paris, a fear of the pox. Good-bye, good-bye.

Supplement to Bougainville's *Voyage*, or Dialogue Between A and B

[1772]

A persistent current of primitivism runs throughout the eighteenth century, nourished by the streams of travelers' tales. It was put to various uses, often leading to an anarchistic utopianism that was set in opposition to civilized cultures, which were portrayed as artificial and morally degenerate. But primitivism was itself subject to the disillusioning corrosion of reality; its geographical realm kept receding, until it reached at last the isolated islands of Oceania. Louis-Antoine de Bougainville's account of his voyage around the world was published in 1771. Diderot was inspired by it but took liberties with the facts, in his Supplement, *changing them to suit his own theses. The three focuses of his polemic are civilization and colonialism, religion, and sexual restraints; the dialogue culminates in a brief general discussion of morals and culture. It must be added that the work is in good measure paradoxical and speculative. Diderot defended civilization more often than he attacked it. It is true that he criticized sexual restraints rather more often than he defended them, but, then again, he never reached a clear understanding of the role of sex in the total affective economy of the self. Similarly, his comments on morality, law, and culture are superficial and inconsistent, and the dialogue closes on a note of general retreat. The* Supplement *is one of the most piquant of Diderot's dialogues but philosophically is one of the weakest. Diderot composed it in 1772; it was published in 1796. (Sec. A-T, Vol. 2.)*

Supplement to Bougainville's Voyage, *or Dialogue Between A and B*

Judgment on Bougainville's *Voyage:*

A: And what is his opinion of the primitive races?

B: It appears that the cruel character sometimes observed in them is the result of their having constantly to defend themselves against wild beasts. Wherever there is nothing to disturb their rest and security, they are innocent and gentle. All wars are caused by a common claim to the same property. When two civilized men living at opposite ends of a field both lay claim to that field, then it becomes a subject of dispute between them.

A: And the tiger has a common claim with the savage to the possession of the primeval forest: that is the first of all claims and the oldest cause of war. . . . Did you see the Tahitian that Bougainville took on board and brought back to this country?

B: Yes, I saw him; his name was Aotourou. He took the first land he saw to be the explorers' home country, either because they had deceived him about the length of the voyage or else because the apparently short distance from the seashore where he lived to the point at which the sky seemed to meet the horizon had naturally misled him as to the true extent of the earth. The communal enjoyment of women was a custom so firmly established in his mind that he hurled himself upon the first European woman he encountered and prepared in all seriousness to pay her his best Tahitian respects. He found life among us very tedious. Since the Tahitian alphabet has no b, c, d, f, g, q, x, y, or z, our own language presented too many strange articulations and new sounds for his inflexible speech organs to master, and he never learned to speak it. Nor did he ever cease to yearn for his own country, and I am not surprised. Bougainville's voyage is the only one that has ever made me feel the slightest attraction for any country other than my own. Until I read his book, I always thought there could never be any other place as good as home, and I assumed this to be true for every other inhabitant of the earth: a natural effect of the attraction exerted by our native soil, an attraction derived from the commodities that it yields for our enjoyment and which we cannot feel the same certainty of finding elsewhere.

A: What! Don't you think the Parisian is quite convinced that the Roman Campagna produces exactly the same kind of grain as the fields of La Beauce?

B: Good heavens, no! And after providing for his expenses and ensuring his safe-conduct, Bougainville sent Aotourou back home.

A: Oh, Aotourou! How glad you will be to see your father, your mother, your brothers, your sisters, and your fellow Tahitians again! I wonder what he will tell them about us?

B: Very little. And even that they won't believe.

A: Why very little?

B: Because he understood very little while he was here and because he won't find any terms in his own language to correspond to the little he did understand.

A: And why won't they believe him?

B: Because having compared our customs with their own, they will prefer to consider Aotourou a liar than to believe we could be so mad.

A: Really?

B: I'm certain of it: the life of the savage is so simple, and our social machinery is so complicated! The Tahitian is still at a primitive stage in the development of the world, whereas the European is part of its old age. The gulf between us is even greater than that between a newborn infant and a senile old man. The savage either understands nothing of our customs or else sees them as fetters tricked out in a hundred different disguises, fetters which can only excite indignation and contempt in a being for whom there exists no deeper feeling than his love of freedom.

A: Are you beginning to subscribe to this Tahitian myth?

B: It's no myth, and you would have no doubts about Bougainville's veracity if you were acquainted with the supplement to his *Voyage*.

A: Where can one find this supplement?

B: Over there, on that table.

A: Will you allow me to borrow it?

B: No, but we can run through it together if you'd like.

A: Indeed I would. . . .

B: Here you are, then, let's start here. The preamble is of no importance; let's go straight to the farewell speech one of the Tahitian chiefs made to the explorers. It will give you some idea of this people's eloquence.

A: How could Bougainville understand this farewell if it was spoken in a language he didn't know?

B: You'll see later on.

The Old Man's Farewell

It is an old man speaking, the father of a numerous family. When the Europeans first arrived, he looked upon them with nothing but disdain, showing neither astonishment nor fear nor curiosity. When they approached him, he turned his back on them and retired into his hut. His silence and his air of anxiety revealed what he was thinking only too clearly: he was lamenting inwardly at the eclipse now threatening to obscure his country's days of glory. When Bougainville left the island, as the other natives ran down in a crowd onto the shore, clinging to the explorer's garments, clasping his companions in their arms, and weeping, this old man advanced among them with a great air of sternness and said, "Weep, wretched people of Tahiti, weep! But let it be for the coming and not for the going of these wicked and ambitious men. One day you will know them better. One day they will come back, that piece of wood you see hanging from that man's belt in one hand and the steel hanging by that man's side in the other, preparing to enslave you, massacre you, or subject you to all their own extravagances and vices. The day will come when you will be their slaves, as corrupted, as base, and as wretched as they themselves. But I have one consolation: I am now nearing the end of my time on earth; I shall not live to see the calamity I am warning you of. Oh, people of Tahiti! Oh, my friends! There is a way for you to escape this tragic future, yet I would rather die than counsel you to take it. Let them depart, and let them live."

Then, turning to Bougainville, he added, "And you, chief of

these brigands who obey you, remove your vessel quickly from our shores. We are innocent, and we are happy; you can only destroy that happiness. We follow the pure instincts of nature, and you have tried to erase its impress from our souls. Here, everything belongs to everyone, and you have preached to us this distinction you make between *yours* and *mine*. Our daughters and our wives are common to us all. You shared that privilege with us, and you have inflamed them with passions they did not know before. They turned into madwomen in your arms, and you turned into wild beasts. They have begun to hate one another. You have butchered one another for their favors, and they have come back to us stained with your blood. We were free, and now you have planted in our earth your claim to be our future masters. You are neither a God nor a devil. Who are you, then, that you should make other men your slaves? Orou! You understand the language of these men; tell all those gathered here, as you told me, what they have written on that sheet of metal: 'This land is ours.' Yours! Why? Because you have set your feet upon it? If a Tahitian were to land someday on your shores and if he were to carve on one of your rocks or on the bark of one of your trees: 'This land belongs to the people of Tahiti,' what would you think then? You are the stronger! Yes, but what difference does that make? When one of us took away one of those despicable trinkets with which your ship is filled, you made an outcry and you exacted vengeance. Yet at that very moment, in the depths of your hearts, you were planning to steal a whole country! You are not a slave, you would rather die than be so—yet you wish to enslave us. Do you think a Tahitian cannot defend his liberty, and die for it, as well as you? You are trying to capture him as though he were a wild animal, and he is your brother. You are both children of nature. What rights have you over him that he does not have over you? You came here. Did we attack you? Did we plunder your ship? Did we capture you and expose you to the arrows of our enemies? Did we make you work with our animals in the fields? No, we respected our own image in you. Leave us to our ways; they are wiser and more honest than yours; we do not wish to barter what you call our ignorance for your useless knowledge. Everything necessary and good for us we already possess. Do we deserve contempt because we have never discovered how to create superfluous desires in ourselves? When we are hungry, we have food to eat. When we are cold, we have clothes with which to cover ourselves. You have been into our huts. What do they lack, in your opinion? You may pursue your hunt for what you call the amenities of life as far as you wish, but permit men of good sense to stop when a continuation of their laborious efforts would bring them nothing but imaginary benefits. If you were to influence us into exceeding the narrow limits of our needs, when would our toil ever cease? When would we find time for pleasure? We have reduced our daily and annual labors to the smallest possible amounts, because nothing is better in our eyes than repose. Go back to your own country; torment and agitate yourselves there as much as you please, but leave us in peace; stop disturbing our minds with your unreal needs and your imaginary virtues. Look at these men; see how straight they stand, how healthy and strong they are. Look at these women; see how straight they stand, how healthy and fresh and beautiful they are. Take this bow of mine; call two or three or four of your companions to help you, then try to draw it. I can draw it unaided. I plow the land, I climb the mountains, I cut my way through the forest, I can run a league across the plain in less than an hour. Your youngest companions have difficulty keeping up with me, yet I am more than ninety years old. Woe to this island! Woe to all the Tahitians now alive, and woe to all those as yet unborn, from the moment that you visited these shores! We knew only one disease, that to which all men, all animals, all plants have been condemned: old age. But you have brought us another; you have infected our blood. Perhaps we shall be forced to massacre our daughters, our wives, our children with our own hands: all those men who have lain with your women, all those women who have lain with your men. Our fields will be soaked with the impure blood that has passed from your veins into ours or our children will be condemned to nourish and perpetuate the sickness that you gave to their fathers and their mothers and then to transmit it in their turn, forever, to their descendants. Wretched man! You must henceforward bear the guilt either of the ravages that your tainted caresses are destined to make among this people or of the murders we shall commit to halt the poison's progress. You talk of crimes! Can you conceive of any crime greater than your own? What is the punishment in your country for one who kills his neighbor? Death by the sword. What is the punishment in your country for the coward who poisons another? Death by fire. Compare your own offense with this second crime and tell us, poisoner of nations, what terrible punishment you deserve. But a short while ago, the young Tahitian maiden yielded herself in ecstasy to the embraces of the Tahitian youth; she waited impatiently for her womanhood to ripen, so that her mother could lift her veil, according to the custom, and bare her breast. She was proud when she stirred up the desires and excited the amorous glances of strangers, of her relatives, of her brother. Without fear and without shame, in the presence of all, surrounded by a circle of innocent Tahitians, to the sound of flutes, between two dances, she accepted the caresses of the man her young heart and the secret voice of her senses had chosen. The idea of crime and the danger of disease were first brought to us by you. The delights we shared with one another, once so sweet, are now attended with fear and remorse. That man in black, the one standing by your side and listening to me now, has talked with our young men. He has said things to our young women. I do not know what those things are, but our young men hesitate now, our young women blush. You may plunge into the dark forest if you wish, accompanied by the perverted companion of your desires, but allow the good and simple Tahitians to reproduce themselves without shame, under the wide sky, and by the light of day. . . .

". . . You have walked as it pleased you on our island, you and your companions; you have been respected; you have enjoyed all that we had; no gate has ever been shut to you, nothing was ever refused; we invited you into our homes, you sat down, and all the abundance of our country was spread before you. When you desired young women, all those not prevented by their youth from showing their faces and their breasts were presented to you naked by their mothers; you became the possessor of a tender victim to the duties of hospitality; the ground was strewn with flowers for you and the one you had chosen; the musicians tuned their instruments for you; nothing disturbed the sweetness or hindered the freedom of your caresses or hers. Your hosts chanted the hymn we have for these occasions, exhorting you to be a man and our daughter to be a woman, a yielding companion and a giver of pleasures. They danced around your flowery bed. And it was at the moment that you left that woman's arms, after experiencing the sweetest of all ecstasies upon her breast, that you slew her brother, her friend, perhaps her father. You did worse still. Look there; turn your eyes upon that enclosure bristling with spears. Look well upon those arms that have never threatened any but our enemies: you see them turned now upon our children. Those are the unhappy partners of your pleasures: look well upon their misery, upon their fathers' grief, upon their mothers' despair. In that place they are condemned to perish, either by our hands or from the diseases that you have given them.

"Now go, unless your cruel eyes take pleasure in the spectacle of death. Now depart, go, and may the guilty seas, which spared you on your voyage hither, now expiate that crime and avenge us of our wrongs by swallowing you up before you can return! And you, people of Tahiti, go back into your huts, go, all of you! And may these unworthy strangers, as they leave, hear nothing but the roaring sea, see nothing but the foaming fury of the waves as they whiten a deserted shore!"

He had scarcely finished speaking before the crowd of islanders had all vanished. A vast silence reigned through all the island, and there was nothing to be heard but the whistle of the keening wind and the muffled noise of the waves breaking along the whole length of the coast. It was as though the air and the sea had heard the old man's words and were preparing to obey him. . . .

The Discussion Between the Chaplain and Orou

B: When the Tahitians first divided Bougainville's crew up among their homes, it was decided that the chaplain should become the guest of Orou. The chaplain and the Tahitian were both about the same age, thirty-five or thirty-six. Orou at that time had only his wife and three daughters, named Asto,

Palli, and Thia. They undressed the chaplain, washed his face, hands, and feet, and served him a wholesome and frugal meal. When he was about to go to bed, Orou, who had withdrawn from the room with the rest of his family, reappeared with his wife and three daughters, all of whom were naked. Presenting them to the chaplain, he said, "You have eaten, you are young, you are healthy; if you sleep alone, you will sleep badly; a man needs a companion beside him at night. Here is my wife, and here are my daughters; choose whichever of them suits you best. But if you wish to oblige me, you will give your preference to my youngest daughter, for she has had no children as yet."

The mother then added, "Alas! But I have no reason to reproach her for it. Poor Thia, it isn't her fault."

The chaplain replied that his religion, his calling, morality, and decency all prevented him from accepting this offer.

Orou then replied, "I don't know what this thing you call religion is, but I can only think ill of it, since it prevents you from enjoying an innocent pleasure—and one to which nature, the sovereign mistress of all things, invites us all—from giving existence to one of your own kind, from rendering a service that a mother, a father, and all their children have asked of you, from repaying a host who has made you as welcome as he was able, and from enriching a nation you are visiting by providing it with an extra citizen. I don't know what this thing is that you refer to as your calling, but your first duty is to be a man and to show gratitude. I do not ask you to take the ways of Orou and his people back to your own country; but Orou, your host and your friend, begs you to accept the ways of Tahiti while you are here. Whether the ways of Tahiti are better or worse than the ways of your country is an easy question to decide. Has the land where you were born more people on it than it can feed? In that case, your ways are neither worse nor better than ours. Could it feed more people than it does? Then our ways are better than yours. As to the decency that you say prevents you, that I understand; I admit that I was wrong, and I ask your pardon. I am not asking you to injure your health; if you are tired, then you must rest. But I hope that you will not continue to make us unhappy. Look at the sorrow you have spread on all these faces: they are afraid that you may have observed blemishes in them and that these are the cause of your disdain. But even if that were so, surely the pleasure of making my daughter honored among her companions and her sisters and that of doing a good deed are still sufficient reasons for you to accept. Be generous!"

CHAPLAIN: It's not that. They are all equally beautiful. But my religion! My calling!

OROU: They are mine, and I am offering them to you. They are their own, and they too give themselves to you. Whatever the purity of conscience that is prescribed you by the thing *religion* and the thing *calling*, you may accept them without scruple. I am in no way abusing my authority; rest assured that I know and respect the rights of individuals.

At this point, the truthful chaplain admits that Providence had never exposed him to such urgent temptation. He was young; he was in an agony of torment and agitation; he averted his eyes from the lovely suppliants, then gazed at them again; he raised his eyes and his hands to heaven. Thia, the youngest, threw her arms around his knees and said, "Stranger, do not make my father unhappy, do not make my mother unhappy, do not make me unhappy! Make me honored in my home and among all my kinsfolk; raise me to the same rank as my sisters, who mock me now. Asto, the eldest, already has three children; Palli, the second, has two; and Thia has none at all! Stranger, honest stranger, do not reject me! Make me a mother; give me a child that I may one day lead by the hand, here in Tahiti, by my side; that will be seen in nine months' time sucking at my breast; of which I can be proud; who will be a part of my dowry when I go from my father's hut into another's. Perhaps I shall be more fortunate with you than with our young Tahitians. If you grant me this favor, I shall never forget you; I shall bless you all my life; I shall write your name on my arm and on the arm of your son; we shall never cease to speak it with joy; and when you leave these shores, my good wishes will accompany you across the seas until you arrive in your own land once more."

The ingenuous chaplain says that she clasped his hands in hers; that she gazed into his eyes with such moving, such expressive looks; that she wept; that her father, her mother, and her sisters withdrew; that he was left alone with her; and that, still saying "my religion, my calling," he found himself next morning lying there beside the young girl as she overwhelmed him with kisses and invited her father, her mother, and her sisters, when they approached the bed after sunrise, to join their expressions of gratitude to hers.

Asto and Palli, after withdrawing for a while, returned bearing food, drinks, and fruits. They kissed their sister and expressed wishes for her happiness.

After they had all broken fast together, Orou stayed with the chaplain in the hut; and when they were alone, he said, "I see that you have made my daughter happy, and I thank you. But could you tell me now what exactly you mean by this word 'religion,' which you have uttered so many times and with such pain in your voice?"

The chaplain, after musing for a moment, answered, "Who made your hut and the things with which it is furnished?"

OROU: I did.

CHAPLAIN: Well, we believe that this world and everything in it was also made by someone.

OROU: So he must have feet and hands and a head?

CHAPLAIN: No.

OROU: Where does he live?

CHAPLAIN: Everywhere.

OROU: Here as well?

CHAPLAIN: Here as well.

OROU: We've never seen him.

CHAPLAIN: No one ever sees him.

OROU: He must be an indifferent sort of father, then! And he must be very old, because he must be at least as old as all the things he made.

CHAPLAIN: He doesn't grow old. He spoke to our ancestors and gave them laws. He told them how he wished them to honor him. He ordered them to do certain things because they are good and forbade them to do others because they are bad.

OROU: I understand. And one of the things he forbade because they were bad was to lie with a woman or a girl? But if so, why did he make two sexes?

CHAPLAIN: So that they may be joined. But only on certain strict conditions and only when certain preliminary ceremonies have been performed, after which a man then belongs to a woman, and only to her, and a woman belongs to a man, and only to him.

OROU: For as long as they live?

CHAPLAIN: For as long as they live.

OROU: So that if a woman should happen to lie with someone other than her husband, or a husband with a woman other than his wife . . . But, of course, that never happens. Since he is always there and such things displease him, he can stop people from doing them.

CHAPLAIN: No, he lets them do it, and then they are sinning against the law of God—that is the name we give to the workman who made the world—and against the law of their country. They are committing a crime.

OROU: I should be grieved if I were to offend you with my words; but if you were to permit it, I should tell you my opinion of all this.

CHAPLAIN: Speak.

OROU: I find these singular precepts contrary to nature, against all reason, and certain not only to breed crimes but also to be a constant cause of anger to the old workman who made everything without a head, without hands, and without tools, who is everywhere and is never seen anywhere, who is here now and will be still tomorrow without being a day older, who gives orders and is not obeyed, who has the power to stop people disobeying him and yet doesn't stop them. They are contrary to nature, these precepts, because they presuppose that a sentient, thinking, free being can be the property of another being of the same kind. On what could such a right of possession be founded? Don't you see that in your country you have confused things that have no sentience, thought, desire, or will, things that one can pick up, put down, keep, or exchange without them suffering or complaining, with things that cannot be exchanged, that cannot be acquired, that possess freedom, will, and desires, that can give themselves or refuse to give themselves as they will, either for a moment or for always, that can complain, that suffer, and that cannot become articles of commerce without their particular nature being ignored and without violence being done to nature as a whole? They are also contrary to the general law of beings. Can you, in fact, think of anything more senseless than a precept that proscribes the perpetual change that is within us, that orders us to show a constancy not in our nature, and that violates the natures and the liberties of both male and female by chaining them to each other for their whole lives? Can you think of anything more senseless than a fidelity that limits the most capricious of all our pleasures to a single object, than a vow of immutability taken by two beings made of flesh in the sight of a sky that does not remain the same for a single instant, beneath caverns constantly threatening collapse, at the foot of a rock that is slowly turning to powder, beneath a tree that is shedding its bark, on a stone that is rocking in its bed? Believe me, you have made the condition of man worse than that of the animals. I don't know what your great workman is like exactly, but I am heartily glad he never spoke to our fathers, and I hope he will never speak to our children; for he might chance to tell them the same foolish things, and they might be foolish enough to believe them. Yesterday, at supper, you talked about people you call "magistrates" and "priests," who have the authority to regulate your conduct. But, tell me, have they authority over good and evil also? Can they make what is unjust become just and what is just become unjust? Have they the power to make good result from evil actions and evil from innocent or useful actions? You cannot think so, for if such were the case, then there would be no true or false, no good or evil, and no beautiful and ugly—or, at any rate, only insofar as your great workman, your magistrates, and your priests decreed such things to exist, in which case you could be obliged to change your ideas and your conduct from one moment to the next. One day someone would come and tell you, on behalf of one of your three masters, "Kill," and you would be obliged by your conscience to kill; another day, "Steal," and you would be forced to steal; or, "Do not eat of this fruit," and you would not dare to eat it; "I forbid you this plant or this animal," and you would refrain from touching them. There is no sort of goodness that could not be forbidden you, no sort of evil that might not be required of you. And what a plight you would be reduced to if your three masters, unable to agree among themselves, took it into their heads to allow you, enjoin you, and forbid you the same thing all at the same time—as I suspect must happen quite often! In that case, in order to please the priest, you will be forced to set yourself at odds with the magistrate; in order to satisfy the magistrate, you will be forced to arouse the anger of the great workman; and in order to accommodate the great workman, you will be forced to fly in the face of nature. And do you know what will happen then? You will come to despise all three of them, and you will then be neither a man nor a good citizen nor a true believer; you will be nothing; you will be frowned upon by all three forms of authority, at odds with yourself, evildoing, tormented by your own heart, persecuted by your illogical masters, and as wretched as I beheld you yesterday evening, when I presented my daughters to you and you cried, "But my religion! And my calling!" Would you like to know what is good and what is evil, in all times and in all places? Then hold fast always to the nature of things and of actions, to your relations with your fellow man, to the influence your conduct has upon your own private good and upon the general good. You are a raving madman if you believe that there is anything in the whole universe, whether in the sky above or the earth below, that can either add anything to or subtract anything from the laws of nature. The eternal will of nature is that the good should be preferred to the bad, and the general good to the private good. You may decree the contrary, but you will not be obeyed. You will merely breed crime and misery from fear, from punishment, and from guilt; you will deprave your people's consciences, you will corrupt their minds, for they will no longer know what they should do and what they should not do. Uneasy when in a state of innocence, at peace only in crime, they will have lost all sight of their guiding star and strayed from their true path. Answer me honestly. In spite of these express orders given by your three lawgivers, does no young man in your country ever lie with a young woman without their consent?

CHAPLAIN: I should be lying if I made such as assertion.

OROU: And the woman who has sworn to belong to no one but her husband, does she never give herself to another?

CHAPLAIN: Nothing is more common.

OROU: Your lawgivers either punish these crimes or do not. If they do punish them, then they are savage beasts fighting against nature; if they do not punish them, then they are fools who have exposed their authority to contempt by instituting futile prohibitions.

CHAPLAIN: Those culprits that escape the severity of the law are punished by general reprobation.

OROU: Which is to say that justice is administered by the entire nation's lack of common sense and that you have substituted the folly of public opinion for laws.

CHAPLAIN: A girl who has lost her honor can never find a husband.

OROU: Lost her honor! Why?

CHAPLAIN: An unfaithful wife is more or less despised.

OROU: Despised! Why?

CHAPLAIN: The young man is called a cowardly seducer.

OROU: A coward! A seducer! But why?

CHAPLAIN: The lives of the father, the mother, and the child are laid waste. The unfaithful husband is a libertine. The betrayed husband shares his wife's shame.

OROU: What a monstrous tissue of extravagance is this you have laid before my eyes! Yet, even so, you have not told me everything. For as soon as a people allows itself to dispense at its own pleasure with the ideas of justice and propriety, to add arbitrary characteristics to things or to take away those they essentially have, to attribute or to deny the terms "good" or "evil" to their actions according to no principle but their own caprice, then they begin to reproach one another, accuse one another, suspect one another, tyrannize over one another; they become envious, jealous, and deceitful; they deceive one another, bring sorrow on one another, and conceal what is in their hearts; they spy, quarrel, cheat, and lie; daughters deceive their parents, husbands their wives, wives their husbands. I have no doubt, too, that young women will smother their children, that suspicious fathers will despise and neglect theirs, that mothers will abandon them and leave them to the mercy of fate. Crime and debauchery will appear in every kind of shape. I know all this as well as if I had lived among you. It is so because it could not be otherwise; and the society that your chief praises to you as a well-ordered state can be nothing but a garbage heap of hypocrites secretly trampling your laws underfoot, or of unfortunates who are themselves the instrument of their own sufferings simply because they submit to them, or of imbeciles in whom prejudice has entirely stifled the voice of nature, or of abnormal creatures in whom nature does not clamor for her rights. . . .

OROU: What a moment of joy it is for a young woman and her parents when it becomes evident that she is pregnant! She leaps to her feet, she runs to them, she throws her arms about their necks; and it is with transports of mutual joy that she tells them and they learn of this event. "Oh, Mother, Father, kiss me! I'm with child!" "Are you sure?" "Oh absolutely sure!" "And who is the father?" "I made it with so and so. . . ."

CHAPLAIN: How is she able to tell who the father is?

OROU: Why should she not be able to? The duration of our love affairs is governed by the same principle as that of our marriages: both must last at least from one moon to the next.

CHAPLAIN: And is this rule scrupulously observed?

OROU: You may judge of that yourself. First of all, the interval between two moons is not a long one; but, also, when two men both have a well-founded claim to being the father of a child, then the child no longer belongs to its mother.

CHAPLAIN: To whom, in that case, does it belong?

OROU: To that claimant to whom it pleases the mother to give it; that is her sole privilege in the matter. And since a child is in itself a source of benefit and riches, you can understand that loose-living women occur only rarely among us and that the young men avoid them.

CHAPLAIN: You do have loose-living women among you, then? That comforts me a great deal.

OROU: We even have more than just one kind. But you are making me digress from my subject. When one of our daughters is pregnant, if the father of the child is a good-looking, well-made, courageous, intelligent, and hardworking young man, the hope that the child will inherit its father's good qualities renews the expressions of joy. The only shame our sons and daughters have to fear is that of a bad choice. You can easily conceive what value we attach to health, beauty, strength, industry, and courage; and you can imagine how, without our interference, the prerogatives of blood are bound to be perpetuated among us. You who have visited so many different countries, tell me whether you have ever beheld in any of them as many fine-looking men or as many beautiful women as you see in Tahiti! Look at me. What do you think of me? Well, there are ten thousand men here who are taller and as strong, but there is not one more brave than I; that is why many mothers urge their daughters to lie with me.

CHAPLAIN: But of all these children that you are able to beget outside your own hut, how many come to you?

OROU: One-fourth, male or female. Among us, there has been established a circulation of men, women, and children—of people of every age and profession, that is to say—based upon a wholly different concept of value from that implied in your own circulation of commodities, for commodities are only what people produce.

CHAPLAIN: I can understand that. But what are these black veils that I see some of your people wearing sometimes?

OROU: They are the mark of sterility, whether caused by a defect at birth or by advancing age. Any woman who takes off that veil and consorts with men is considered loose, and any man who lifts that veil and consorts with the sterile woman is also considered loose.

CHAPLAIN: And the gray veils?

OROU: They are the sign of woman's periodic indisposition. The woman who removes that veil and consorts with men is considered loose, and the man who lifts it and consorts with the indisposed woman is also considered loose.

CHAPLAIN: Do you have punishments for this loose behavior?

OROU: None, except the blame.

CHAPLAIN: May a father lie with his daughter, a mother with

her son, a brother with his sister, or a husband with the wife of another?

OROU: Why not?

CHAPLAIN: Well, we'll say nothing about the fornication, but adultery, incest!

OROU: What do these words of yours mean—"fornication," "adultery," "incest"?

CHAPLAIN: Crimes, monstrous crimes, for any one of which people are burned to death in my country.

OROU: Whether you burn people in your country or whether you don't is of no great importance to me. But you will not condemn the ways of Europe because they are not those of Tahiti, nor, consequently, those of Tahiti because they are not the same as those of Europe. We must have a more reliable criterion of judgment than that, so what shall it be? Do you know of any other besides that of the general good and private advantage? Now, tell me what there is in this crime you call "incest" that is contrary to either of these two goals we have set for our actions. You are in error, my friend, if you think that once a law has been promulgated, a shameful word invented, or a punishment decreed that all has been said. Answer me, now, what do you mean by "incest"?

CHAPLAIN: I mean . . . committing incest. . . .

OROU: Committing incest? . . . Tell me, is it a long time since your great workman without a head, without hands, and without tools made the world?

CHAPLAIN: No.

OROU: Did he make all the human race at the same time?

CHAPLAIN: No, he created only one man and one woman.

OROU: Did they have children?

CHAPLAIN: Certainly.

OROU: Suppose that these first two parents had produced only girl children and that their mother had died first—or that they had produced only boys and that the woman lost her husband.

CHAPLAIN: You put me in a difficult position; but whatever you say, incest is a monstrous crime. Let us discuss something else.

OROU: Easily said, but I am not going to speak until you have explained what this monstrous crime of "incest" is.

CHAPLAIN: Very well, then! I grant that incest perhaps does no harm to nature, but isn't it enough that it is a threat to the political constitution? How could the leader be secure or the state tranquil if a whole nation composed of several million men were split into fifty family groups, each centered around one father?

OROU: At the very worst, it would mean that instead of one large society, there would be fifty small ones, a great deal more happiness, and one less crime.

CHAPLAIN: And yet I don't believe that a son often lies with his mother, even here.

OROU: No, not unless he has a great deal of respect for her and a feeling of tenderness sufficient to outweigh the disparity in age and make him prefer a woman of forty to a girl of nineteen.

CHAPLAIN: And intercourse between fathers and daughters?

OROU: Scarcely more frequent, unless the daughter is ugly and little sought after. If her father loves her, then he makes it his task to see that she acquires her dowry of children. . . .

CHAPLAIN: Apparently, then, jealousy is very little known among you. But conjugal affection and paternal love, those two feelings that we consider so powerful and sweet, even if they are not completely unknown here, they must at least be very weak.

OROU: We have replaced them with another, one that is altogether more universal, more powerful, and more lasting: interest. Now, be honest with me; leave aside all that self-righteous prattle about virtue that is continually on your companions' lips and completely absent from their hearts. Tell me if, in any country whatsoever, there is a father who, supposing he were not held back by shame, would not rather lose his child, or a father who would not rather lose his wife, than his wealth and his comfort for the rest of his life. You may rest assured that wherever men's concern for the preservation of their fellows is sufficiently bound up with their beds, their health, their peace of mind, their huts, their fruits, and their fields, they will do everything within their power to help them. It is here in Tahiti that tears moisten the pillow of a sick child; it is here that mothers are well tended when they are sick; it is here that we prize a fertile woman, a daughter ripe for marriage, or an adolescent boy; it is here that we take over their upbringing—because here their preservation always means an increase in our fortunes, and their loss a diminution in our wealth.

CHAPLAIN: I am very much afraid that this savage is right. The wretched peasant in our country will kill his own wife with work to save his horse and let his child perish for want of attention while he calls in the doctor to look at his ox. . . .

The good chaplain then tells us that he spent the remainder of the day walking about the island and visiting the huts; that in the evening, after supper, the father and mother having begged him to lie with the second of their daughters, Palli was presented to him in the same state of undress as Thia, whereupon he was obliged to exclaim several times during the night, "My religion! My calling!"; that during the third night, he was agitated by similar fits of remorse with Astro, the eldest; and that he granted the fourth, as a matter of politeness, to his host's wife.

Continuation of the Dialogue

A: I have a high regard for that polite chaplain.

B: And I have even more for the ways of Tahiti and Orou's powers of discourse.

A: Though he does seem to have been influenced by European models. . . .

A: Then what do you mean by morality?

B: I mean a general obedience to good or bad laws and a form of conduct determined by those laws. If the laws are good, then morals are good; if the laws are bad, then morals are bad; if the laws, whether good or bad, are not observed at all —the worst condition of all for any society—then there is no morality at all. Now how can you expect laws to be observed when they contradict one another? Look back over the history of all ages and nations, ancient as well as modern, and you will find that men have always been subject to three separate bodies of law—the laws of nature, civil law, and the laws of religion—and constantly placed in the unavoidable position of having to infringe at least one of these codes at any given time, since they have never been in agreement. And the result of this is that there has never existed in any country, as Orou guessed of ours, anyone who was truly a man, truly a good citizen, or truly religious.

A: From which you will doubtless conclude that by basing morality on the eternal relations that exist between men, the laws of religion may become superfluous and the civil law ought to be no more than a formulation of the laws of nature.

B: Yes, and the penalty of doing otherwise is to breed wicked people rather than to produce good ones.

A: Or, if it be judged necessary to keep all three codes, that the last two should be no more than strict copies of the laws of nature, which we all carry engraved in our hearts and which will always be the strongest.

B: That is not quite true. We are born with no more in common with other human beings than a similarity of structure, the same needs, an attraction toward the same pleasure, and a common aversion for the same kinds of pain; these are the things that make man what he is, and they alone can form the proper basis for a morality suited to his needs.

A: It won't be easy to formulate such a morality though.

B: On the contrary, it is so easy that I am inclined to believe Tahitian people—which is to say, the most backward people in the world and the one that has adhered most closely in every point to the laws of nature—nearer to possessing a truly good code of law than any civilized people.

A: Because it is easier for them to shake off some of their excessively primitive ways than for us to retrace our steps and reform our abuses.

B: Especially those connected with the relations between men and women.

A: That may be so. But let us begin at the beginning. Let us put the question to nature quite openly and see what answers she provides on this point.

B: Yes, I agree to that.

A: Does marriage exist in nature?

B: If you mean by marriage the preference that one female accords to one particular male over all others or the preference that one male accords to one particular female over all others—that is to say, a mutual preference that results in a more or less lasting union and one that perpetuates the species by the reproduction of individuals—then marriage does exist in nature.

A: I agree with that, for this preference is to be observed in other species as well as our own—as witness the large number of males that we see chasing the same female in our own countryside in spring, only one of which is finally accepted as her mate. But what about courtship?

B: If by courtship you mean the variety of means, whether delicate or violent, that passion inspires, either in the male or in the female, as a method of obtaining this preference, which then leads to the most pleasurable, the most important, and the most universal of enjoyments—then courtship exists in nature.

A: Again, I agree with you. Witness all the various tender attentions paid by males of all species to the female in order to attract her and by the female to the male in order to excite his passion and fix his attention upon her. But what about flirtation?

B: Flirtation is a falsehood that consists in simulating a passion that one does not feel and in promising a preference that one is not in fact going to grant. The male flirt is making sport of the female; the female flirt is making sport of the male: it is a treacherous game that sometimes leads to the most terrible catastrophes, a ridiculous farce in which the deceiver and the deceived are equally punished by losing the most precious moments of their life.

A: Then, according to you, flirtation does not exist in nature?

B: No, I don't say that.

A: And constancy?

B: I cannot express myself better on that subject than by repeating Orou's words to the chaplain: it is a vain delusion entertained by two children who know nothing about themselves and who are blinded by a momentary ecstasy to the mutability of all that is around them.

A: And that rare phenomenon, marital fidelity?

B: In our country it is almost always a form of torture produced by the obstinacy of a respectable man and a respectable woman. In Tahiti it is a fantasy with no real existence.

A: And jealousy?

B: The passion of a starved and miserly creature who is afraid of going without; in man, an unjust attitude created by our false moral standards and by extending our property rights to apply to a sentient, thinking, conscious, free being.

A: Then, according to you, jealousy does not exist in nature?

B: No, I don't say that. Everything that exists, vices as well as virtues, exists in nature.

A: A jealous man is a gloomy man.

B: Like the tyrant: because he is aware of the defect in him.

A: And modesty?

B: Really! You are forcing me into a course of lectures on the "Ethical Principles of Lovemaking." A man does not wish to be either disturbed or distracted during his pleasures. Further, the pleasures of love are followed by a period of weakness that would leave him at the mercy of his enemies. Exception made of this fact, there is nothing natural in modesty at all; all the rest is social convention. The chaplain has remarked, in a third fragment that I omitted to read to you, that the Tahitian does not blush for the involuntary movements excited in him by the proximity of his wife, even when he is surrounded by his daughters. The daughters may sometimes be moved by this sight but are never embarrassed. As soon as woman became a property of man and as soon as another man's secret enjoyment of another man's woman came to be regarded as a theft, then the terms "modesty," "reserve," and "propriety" came into being, accompanied by a whole retinue of imaginary virtues and vices. In short, there was an attempt to create a barrier between the two sexes that would prevent them from tempting each other to violate the laws that had been imposed on them. Though, in the event, these barriers often produced the contrary effect, by heating people's imaginations and exciting their desires. When I see trees planted around our palaces or the bodices that both conceal and display the bosoms of our women, I seem to detect a secret wish to escape deep into the forest, a call to return to the primal liberty of our ancestral dwelling place. The Tahitian would say to us: Why are you hiding yourselves? What are you ashamed of? Are you doing wrong when you yield to the noblest urge of nature? Man, show yourself openly if you are attractive. Woman, if this man pleases you, then welcome his advances with the same honesty.

A: There's no need to get worked up. Though we may begin like civilized men, it is rarely that we don't conclude matters much like the Tahitians.

B: Yes, but a man of genius can waste half his lifetime on these preliminaries that convention demands of us.

A: True, But what does it matter—if that pernicious impulse in men's minds, against which you were inveighing a moment ago, is commensurably impeded by them? One of our present-day philosophers, when asked why it was always men who paid court to women and never women who paid court to men, replied that it was natural for the request to be made to the one who was always in a position to give.

B: That explanation has always struck me as more ingenious than sound. Nature, though you may call her immodest for it, impels both sexes toward each other indiscriminately. And in a wretched and completely primitive state of nature, which possibly exists nowhere but in our minds . . .

A: Not even in Tahiti?

B: No. . . . the gap separating a man from a woman would be crossed by whichever was the more amorously inclined of the two. If one or other of them hesitates or runs away or gives pursuit or avoids the other or attacks the other or defends herself from the other, then that is merely because passion, more abrupt in its onset in the one than in the other, is not producing its effects in them both with equal force at the same time. The consequence being that sensual enjoyment has already risen, been consummated, and died in the one, while it is still scarcely beginning to develop in the other, so that they are both left unsatisfied. That is a realistic picture of what would happen between two young, free, and perfectly innocent people. But when a woman has learned, either through experience or education, what more or less painful consequences can ensue from a moment of pleasure, then she trembles at the approach of a man. The man's heart does not tremble: his senses issue the orders, and he obeys them. The woman's senses make it clear to her what they want, but she is afraid to listen to them. It is the man's task to make her forget her fears, to intoxicate her, and to seduce her. The man preserves all his natural urge toward the woman, whereas the woman's natural urge toward the man is, as a geometrician would say, directly proportional to the passion she feels and inversely proportional to the extent of her fears. But these ratios are complicated by a multiplicity of different elements in our social customs—elements that almost all conspire to increase the timidity of the one sex and the length of time spent by the other sex in pursuit of the first. The result is a sort of tactical problem in which the resources of the defense and the means at the disposal of the attackers have remained constantly abreast of one another. We have sanctioned the woman's resistance, and we have placed a stigma upon violence on the part of the man. Such violence, though it would constitute no more than a trifling wrong in Tahiti, has become a crime in our cities.

A: But how is it that an act so sacred in its aims, an act to which nature incites us by the most powerful of attractions, an act that is a source of the greatest, the sweetest, the most innocent of pleasures, has become the most fruitful source of the ills and depravations that beset us?

B: Orou explained that ten times over to the chaplain. Listen again to what he said, and try to remember it. The result you mention may be attributed to the following causes:

To the tyranny of man, who converted the physical possession of women into a law of property.

To our morality and customs, which overloaded the union of husband and wife with an excess of conditions.

To the civil laws, which subjected the marriage union to endless formalities.

To the nature of our society, in which the disparities of wealth and rank have given rise to the notions of privilege, propriety, and impropriety.

To a strange contradiction, common to all existing societies, by which the birth of a child, though regarded as an increase in the wealth of the nation as a whole, often proves nothing but an added source of poverty to the individual family.

To the political views of sovereigns, who consider everything only in relation to their own interest and security.

To the religious institutions that have applied the terms "virtue" and "vice" to actions that are not susceptible of moral qualifications at all.

How far we are from both nature and happiness! Yet the rule of nature cannot be overthrown: no matter what means we use in our attempts to thwart it, it must always prevail. You may write as much as you like on tables of bronze that—to borrow the expression of the wise Marcus Aurelius—the pleasurable friction of the two membranes is a crime; the heart of man will merely be torn between the threat of your inscription and the violence of its own desires. The rebellious heart will never cease its claims, and a hundred times in the course of all our lives, your terrible tables will fade before our mortal eyes. You may carve it in marble: Thou shalt not eat of the eagle and the ossifrage and the ospray; thou shalt have carnal knowledge of no woman save only thy wife; thou shalt not take thy sister in marriage—but you must not forget also to increase the severity of the punishments in proportion to the outlandishness of your prohibitions. And yet, no matter how cruel and savage you make them, you will never be able to kill my natural impulses.

A: How brief a nation's list of laws would be if those laws were all drawn up in strict accordance with the dictates of nature! And how many vices and errors would man be spared!

B: Shall I give you a brief historical account of almost all our misfortunes? It is as follows. There was once a natural man, then an artificial man was created inside him. Whereupon a great war broke out inside that man, a struggle that is destined to continue as long as he lives. Sometimes the natural man proves the stronger; at others, he is beaten to the ground by the moral and artificial man. But in both cases the miserable monster is plagued, racked, tortured, and stretched on the wheel—ceaselessly groaning, ceaselessly wretched, whether he is being transported and made drunk by some false and frenzied striving for glory or whether he is being battered and crushed by some equally imaginary feeling of shame. Yet there are extreme circumstances that can still force man back to his original simplicity.

A: Poverty and sickness, those two great exorcists.

B: Yes, you have hit my meaning. For what, in fact, becomes of our conventional virtues in such circumstances? A man in the grip of poverty is entirely without scruples, and a sick woman completely devoid of modesty.

A: Yes, I have had occasion to observe it.

B: But another phenomenon that will likewise not have escaped you is that the moral and artificial man subsequently reappears, gaining ground step by step as the sickness gives way, first to convalescence, then to full recovery. The moment the sickness finally disappears is also the exact moment at which the civil war inside the man is renewed, the immediate result almost always being a setback for the invader.

A: That is true. I have myself experienced how during a period of convalescence the natural man seems to display a vigor against which the artificial and moral man is almost powerless. But, now, tell me in a word: is it better to civilize man or to leave him to his instincts?

B: You want an absolutely clear-cut answer?

A: Of course.

B: If you want to gain a tyrannical power over him, then civilize him; poison him as far as you are able with a morality that is contrary to nature; fetter him in every way you can think of; impede his every movement with a thousand obstacles; saddle him with terrifying phantoms; make sure that the civil war inside him never ceases and that the natural man lies perpetually chained beneath the heel of the moral man. But if you want him to be happy and free, then leave him to his own devices (for there will be quite enough unforeseen events to lead him toward either enlightenment or depravity), and never allow yourself to forget that it is for their own sakes and not for yours that all those wise lawgivers have forced you into your present unnatural and rigid molds. And as evidence of this, I need only produce all our political, civil, and religious institutions. Examine them thoroughly, and either I am very much mistaken or you will find that mankind has been forced to bow, century after century, beneath a yoke that a mere handful of scoundrels has conspired, in every age, to impose upon it. Beware of the man who wants to set things in order. Setting things in order always involves acquiring mastery over others—by tying them hand and foot. . . .

B: We must speak out against senseless laws until they are reformed; and in the meantime, we must abide by them. Anyone who breaks a bad law on no other grounds than his private authority thereby authorizes everyone else to break the good ones. Life is always less difficult for a madman living among madmen than for a wise man all on his own. We must tell ourselves—and shout it to the world—that shame, punishment, and dishonor have been made the consequences of actions that are innocent in themselves. But we should not commit those actions, for there are no greater evils than shame, punishment, and dishonor. Let us follow the good chaplain's example: let us be monks in France and savages in Tahiti.

A: Put on the costume of the country we go to visit, but always pack a suit of clothes to return home in.

B: And, above all, be scrupulously honest and open with those frail creatures who cannot make us happy without sacrificing the most precious advantages of our society. And now what's become of that thick fog?

A: It has cleared.

B: So that we shall have a choice between staying in after dinner or going out?

A: I think that will depend rather more on the ladies' feelings in the matter than on ours.

B: Ah, those women again! You can't walk a step without running into them at the first corner.

A: Perhaps we should read them the conversation between Orou and the chaplain?

B: What do you think they would say about it?

A: I have no idea.

B: And what would they think of it?

A: Perhaps the opposite of what they would say.

Conversation with a Christian Lady

[1774]

The Entretien avec la Maréchale de —— *was written by Diderot during his second stay in Holland, in September, 1774, after his return from Russia, and was included two years later in the secret* Correspondance littéraire. *Unlike most of Diderot's philosophical writings, it was published during his lifetime, in 1777, in a collection attributed to "Thomas Crudeli."*

This dialogue is light, gay, and Gallic, though it deals with serious subjects. We may perhaps take it as a model of the brilliant conversation in the polished salons of the eighteenth century, when ladies who had charm, wit, and intelligence delighted in fencing with serious writers who, in their turn, were graceful, gay, and unpedantic. Reading a dialogue such as this, one can understand why the somber, awkward Jean-Jacques Rousseau was ill at ease in this society.

The Entretien *actually adds nothing new to Diderot's philosophic views. It does admit us to his intellectual personality. We see him as a materialist and an atheist, but neither a dogmatist nor a fanatic, and as a man who loved to play with ideas. (See A-T, Vol. 2.)*

Conversation with a Christian Lady

HAVING some business or other with the Maréchal de ——, I called at his town house one morning. He was out, but I went in to pay my respects to Mme La Maréchale. She is a charming woman, not only beautiful but as pious as an angel; her sweetness of character is apparent in her every feature, while the gentle quality of her voice and the simplicity of her speech are in complete accord with her physiognomy. She was at her toilette. A chair was brought for me; I sat down, and we talked together. After I had made several remarks that both edified and surprised her (for she was of the opinion that any man who denies the Holy Trinity can be nothing but a thoroughgoing scoundrel, fit only for the gallows), she asked me:

LA MARÉCHALE: Are you not Monsieur Crudeli?

CRUDELI: Yes, madame.

L.M.: Then you're the man who doesn't believe in anything.

CRUDELI: In person, madame.

L.M.: Yet your moral principles are the same as those of a believer?

CRUDELI: Why should they not be—as long as the believer is an honest man?

L.M.: And do you act upon those principles?

CRUDELI: To the best of my ability.

L.M.: What? You don't steal? You don't kill people? You don't rob them?

CRUDELI: Very rarely.

L.M.: Then what do you gain by not being a believer?

CRUDELI: Nothing at all, madame. Is one a believer from motives of profit?

L.M.: I cannot say, but certainly a concern for our personal interests does no harm to our affairs, either in this world or the next. Though it reflects little credit upon poor humanity, and I am sorry for that. But tell me, do you really not steal?

CRUDELI: No, upon my honor.

L.M.: Then if you neither steal nor murder, you must admit that you are inconsistent.

CRUDELI: Why do you say that?

L.M.: It seems to me that if I had nothing to hope for or fear in the next world, there are a great many little indulgences of which I should certainly not deprive myself in this one. I confess that I expect God to pay me a high rate of interest on all the virtue I am banking with Him.

CRUDELI: Is that how you imagine it?

L.M.: There's nothing imaginary about it; it's a fact.

CRUDELI: And may one ask you what these little indulgences are that you would permit yourself if you were an unbeliever?

L.M.: Without wishing to offend—no. I keep such things strictly for the ear of my confessor.

CRUDELI: I invest my virtue without any guarantee of returns.

L.M.: A sure way to end up a beggar.

CRUDELI: Would you prefer me to be a usurer?

L.M.: Certainly. One can play the usurer with God as much as one likes—there is no danger of ruining Him. Oh, I know perfectly well that such a proceeding is slightly unscrupulous, but does it matter? Since the whole point is to get into heaven, by hook or by crook, we must make everything work on our behalf and neglect no opportunity for profit. Alas, no matter how vast the amount we invest, it is still as nothing to the return we expect! But you, you expect no return, you say?

CRUDELI: None.

L.M.: That is very sad. But you must admit that in that case, you are either very wicked or very foolish!

CRUDELI: To be honest with you, madame, I cannot say.

L.M.: But what motive can an unbeliever possibly have for being good, supposing he isn't mad? I should very much like to know.

CRUDELI: Then I will tell you.

L.M.: That is extremely kind of you.

CRUDELI: Don't you think it possible that we might be so fortunate as to be born into this world with a natural desire to do good?

L.M.: Yes, I think that possible.

CRUDELI: And that we might receive an excellent education calculated to strengthen this natural inclination toward the good?

L.M.: Certainly.

CRUDELI: And that later in life, experience might convince us that, all things considered, we are more likely to achieve happiness in this world by being honest than by being rogues?

L.M.: Of course. But how is it possible to be virtuous if one has bad principles? They ought to reinforce one's passions and make temptation irresistible.

CRUDELI: One is simply inconsistent. And is there anything commoner in this world than inconsistency?

L.M.: Alas, no, unfortunately! One may be a believer and yet behave constantly as though one weren't.

CRUDELI: And one may also be an unbeliever and behave all the time as though one were.

L.M.: That's as may be. But what harm would there be in having one more reason for doing good—religion—and one less reason for doing evil—unbelief?

CRUDELI: None at all, if religion were a motive for doing good and unbelief a motive for doing evil.

L.M.: Can there be any doubt about that? Is it not the very essence of religion to thwart our horrid, corrupted nature, and the essence of unbelief to abandon it to its own evil ways, by freeing it from all fear?

CRUDELI: That question, madame, will plunge us into a very long discussion.

L.M.: What does that matter? The Maréchal will not be back for some while, and it is certainly better that we should spend our time in rational discussion than in speaking ill of our neighbors.

CRUDELI: I shall be forced to go rather a long way back.

L.M.: Oh, you may go as far back as you like, provided I understand you.

CRUDELI: If you did not understand me, it would certainly be my fault.

L.M.: You are very kind. But you must know that my reading has always been confined to my missal and that my experience of life has been limited entirely to practicing the teachings of the Gospels and producing children.

CRUDELI: Two duties of which you have acquitted yourself admirably.

L.M.: As far as the children are concerned, yes. As you saw, I had six around me when you came in, and if you had come a few days later, you might well have found me with another in my arms. But begin.

CRUDELI: Madame, is there any kind of good in this world that is entirely free from drawbacks?

L.M.: No, none.

CRUDELI: Or any evil that does not do some good?

L.M.: No, none.

CRUDELI: What, then, do you mean by good and evil?

L.M.: Evil must be that which brings more drawbacks than advantages, and good, on the other hand, must be that which brings more advantages than drawbacks.

CRUDELI: I hope, madame, that you will be good enough to bear this definition you have given of good and evil in mind.

L.M.: Yes, I will bear it in mind. But do you call that a definition?

CRUDELI: Yes.

L.M.: It was philosophy, then?

CRUDELI: Excellent philosophy.

L.M.: I never thought to see the day when I became a philosopher!

CRUDELI: So, then, you are convinced that religion has more advantages than drawbacks. And that is why you call it good. Is that so?

L.M.: Yes.

CRUDELI: And I, for my part, do not doubt that your steward robs you rather less on Good Friday than on Easter Monday or that religion does from time to time prevent a number of little evils and produce a number of little benefits.

L.M.: They mount up too—little by little.

CRUDELI: But do you believe that such miserable little advantages as these can ever prove sufficient compensation for the terrible ravages that it has caused in past ages and that it will continue to cause in the future? Remember the violence of the antipathies that it has created, and is still perpetuating, between nations. There is not a Musselman alive who would not imagine that he was performing an action pleasing to God and his Holy Prophet by exterminating every Christian on earth, while the Christians are scarcely more tolerant on their side. Remember that it has created, and is still perpetuating, violent dissensions within nations of a kind that are rarely resolved without bloodshed. Our own history presents us with only too many recent and frightful examples of this kind. Remember that it has created, and is still perpetuating, the strongest and most ineradicable feuds between members of the same society and even between members of the same family. Christ said he had come to separate husband from wife, mother from children, brother from sister, friend from friend—and his prophecy has been only too faithfully accomplished.

L.M.: Those are the abuses; they are not the thing itself.

CRUDELI: It is the thing itself if the abuses are inseparable from it.

L.M.: And how can you prove to me that the abuses of religion are inseparable from religion itself?

CRUDELI: Very easily. Tell me, if a man who hated mankind had made the unhappiness of the whole human race his life's goal, could he have invented anything more likely to accomplish this end than an incomprehensible being about whom men could never agree and to whom they would attach more importance even than to their own lives? Further, is it possible to conceive of a divinity not endowed with the profoundest incomprehensibility and the utmost importance?

L.M.: No.

CRUDELI: Then draw your own conclusion.

L.M.: I conclude that it is an idea that probably makes sense to madmen.

CRUDELI: But you should then add that madmen always have been and always will be in the majority, that the most dangerous madmen are those created by religion, and that people whose aim is to disrupt society always know how to make good use of them on occasion.

L.M.: But there must be something to frighten men away from the bad actions that escape the rigor of the law. And if you destroy religion, what will you put in its place?

CRUDELI: Even if I had nothing to put in its place, there would at least be one terrible prejudice less in the world, without counting the fact that there has never been any age in which religious opinions have provided the foundation for any nation's moral practices. The gods worshiped by the early Greeks and the early Romans, the most moral folk who ever lived, were nothing but a set of low-living libertines: a Jupiter who deserved to be burned alive, a Venus who should have been locked up, and a Mercury fit only for penal servitude.

L.M.: And do you think that it makes no difference whether we are Christians or pagans, that we would be no worse if we were pagans, and that the fact that we are Christians has made us no better?

CRUDELI: Yes, I am convinced of it, with the one exception that if we were pagans, we should be rather merrier.

L.M.: That can't be true.

CRUDELI: But, madame, are there any Christians, in fact? I have never seen any.

L.M.: You say that to me? To me?

CRUDELI: No, madame, I was not saying it to you. I was addressing myself to a lady of my acquaintance, one who is good and pious, just as you are, and who believed herself to be a Christian as sincerely as it is possible to do, just as you do.

L.M.: And you made her see that she was wrong?

CRUDELI: In a trice.

L.M.: How did you set about it?

CRUDELI: I opened her copy of the New Testament, which she must have read a great deal, for it was very worn, and then, reading out the Sermon on the Mount to her, I stopped after each article and asked her, "Do you do that? And that? And that as well?" I went further. But first I must tell you that she is a very beautiful woman and that although she is very good and very religious, she is not unaware of her beauty. She has a very white skin, and although she herself does not attach any great value to this ephemeral advantage, still she is not displeased when it excites praise. Her throat and bosom are as perfect as it is possible for such things to be, and although she is in fact a modest woman, she is not averse to their perfections being observed.

L.M.: I see nothing wrong—provided only she and her husband are aware of these things.

CRUDELI: I believe that her husband has a nearer acquaintance with them than anyone else, but for a woman who prides herself on the strictness of her religious principles, that is not enough. I said to her, "Is it not written in the Scriptures that he who has coveted his neighbor's wife has committed adultery in his heart?"

L.M.: And she answered yes?

CRUDELI: I said to her, "And adultery committed in the heart damns a man as surely as adultery committed in more favorable conditions, does it not?"

L.M.: And she answered yes?

CRUDELI: I said to her, "And if the man is damned for the adultery he has committed in his heart, what will be the fate of the woman who incites all those who come near her to commit that crime?" This last question embarrassed her somewhat.

L.M.: I understand: she was not in the habit of concealing that throat and bosom—which are as perfect as it is possible for such things to be—as completely as she might.

CRUDELI: I'm afraid that's true. She replied that it was a matter of social custom, as though there were nothing more customary than to call oneself a Christian and not to be one; that it would be wrong to dress ridiculously, as though there were some comparison possible between being scoffed at momentarily and damning her own and those poor men's souls to hell for all eternity; that she left it to her dressmaker to decide what she wore, as though keeping one's dressmaker were more important than keeping one's religion; that her husband liked to see her like that, as though any husband would be mad enough to require of his wife that she forget all duty and decorum and as though a true Christian wife ought to push obedience to the absurd demands of a husband so far as to sacrifice her obedience to the will of God and flout all the threats of her Redeemer!

L.M.: I knew all those childish excuses already. I might even have answered you exactly as your beautiful neighbor did—but it would have been dishonesty on both our parts. Tell me, what decision did she make after you had remonstrated with her?

CRUDELI: The day after our conversation—it was a holy day—I met my pious and beautiful neighbor as I was going up to my lodging and she was coming down on her way out to mass.

L.M.: Dressed as usual?

CRUDELI: Dressed as usual. I smiled at her, she smiled at me, and we passed by each other without exchanging a word. And she was a good woman, madame! A Christian woman! A deeply religious woman! After this example and a hundred others of the same kind, what real influence can I grant religion to possess on our behavior? Hardly any—and so much the better.

L.M.: So much the better? You cannot mean it.

CRUDELI: But I do. What if twenty thousand of the people now living in Paris suddenly took it into their heads to behave exactly as they are told to in the Sermon on the Mount? . . .

L.M.: Well, we should see a great deal less of several beautiful bosoms I can think of.

CRUDELI: And there would be so many madmen that the Lieutenant of Police wouldn't know what to do with them—there wouldn't be room in the madhouses for even half of them. There are always two kinds of morality present in inspired writings: one universal, common to all nations and all religions, which we abide by more or less; and another specifically suited to a particular nation or religion, which we believe in, which is preached in the church or the temple, which is advocated in the home, and which has no influence whatsoever upon our conduct.

L.M.: And what is at the root of this strange inconsistency?

CRUDELI: The impossibility of subjecting a whole people to a way of life that is suitable only for a few melancholy men and that has been patterned by those men on their own characters. It is the same with religions as with the laws of monasteries: both relax with the passage of time. They are follies that cannot hold out against the constant assaults made on them by nature as she urges us to return to her laws. But once see to it that the good of individuals is so closely bound up with the public good that no citizen can harm society without harming himself; once make sure that virtue is rewarded as inevitably as wickedness is punished; once make it customary for merit, without any distinctions of sect or social position, to assume the highest places in the state, and you may count on evil dying out in any society, with the exception of a small number of men who will always be led into vice by a natural perversity of character that nothing can root out. Temptation is too close to us, madame, and hell too far away. There is no use in expecting anything worth the attention of wise legislators from a body of beliefs that is too outlandish even to take in a child, that encourages crime by the ease with which it grants absolutions, that sends a man who has committed injuries against mankind to ask forgiveness of God, and that debases all our natural and moral duties by subordinating them to a series of chimeras we refer to as our "higher" duties.

L.M.: I don't understand you.

CRUDELI: I will explain. . . . But I think I can hear M. le Maréchal's carriage. He has arrived just in time to prevent me from saying something I might regret.

L.M.: But say it, say this thing you might regret. I won't hear it —I have learned how to hear only what I wish to hear.

CRUDELI: (Here, I went close to her and whispered in her ear.) Madame, ask your parish priest which is the more appalling crime of the two—pissing in a holy vessel or blackening the name of an honest woman. He will shudder with horror at the idea of the first and cry out that it is sacrilege. And the civil code, which scarcely pays any attention to calumny, whereas it punishes people who commit sacrilege by burning them at the stake, will complete this confusion of our ideas and this corruption in our minds.

L.M.: I know of more than one woman who would think it a sin to eat meat on Friday, and yet . . . But, there, I too was about to say something I should regret. Go on.

CRUDELI: But, madame, I really must go and speak to M. le Maréchal.

L.M.: Just a moment more, then we shall go in and see him together. I can think of no arguments to use against you, and yet you don't seem to be trying very hard to make me think as you do.

CRUDELI: It was never my intention to make you think as I do. Religion is much like marriage in this respect. Though it makes most people unhappy, marriage has brought you and M. le Maréchal great happiness, so that you were both of you right to marry. And religion, which has made, which is making, and which will make so many people wicked, has in fact increased your goodness, so that you are right to keep it. It is a sweet consolation for you to imagine beside you or above your head a great and powerful being who is watching you as you journey through your life, and this idea strengthens your steps. So continue, madame, to enjoy the presence of this venerable keeper of your thoughts, of this spectator, of this sublime model for all your actions.

L.M.: You obviously don't have a passion for making converts.

CRUDELI: Not in the slightest.

L.M.: I think the more of you for that.

CRUDELI: Everyone may think as they like, as far as I am concerned, provided they allow me to think as I like. And, besides, the people who are destined to free themselves from these prejudices have no need of indoctrination anyway.

L.M.: Do you think mankind can manage without superstition?

CRUDELI: No—not as long as it remains ignorant and fearful.

L.M.: Well, then! Superstition for superstition, I think ours is as good as any other.

CRUDELI: I'm afraid I don't.

L.M.: Tell me truly, aren't you repelled by the idea of not existing after you're dead?

CRUDELI: I should prefer to go on to another existence, even though I can see no reason why a being who has already shown himself capable of making me unhappy without reason once should not amuse himself at my expense a second time.

L.M.: But if, despite that disadvantage, the hope of a life to come seems to you a consoling and pleasant prospect, why try to deprive us of it?

CRUDELI: Since my desire for a life after death is unable to conceal from me the futility of hoping for it, I myself do not entertain such a hope. But I do not wish to deny it to others. If people can believe that they will see when they no longer have eyes, hear when they no longer have ears, think when they no longer have brains, love when they no longer have hearts, feel when they no longer have senses, or exist as objects when they have no extension and occupy no space, then they are quite free to do so, as far as I am concerned.

L.M.: But this world of ours! Who made it?

CRUDELI: I cannot say. Can you?

L.M.: God made it.

CRUDELI: And what is God?

L.M.: A spirit.

CRUDELI: If a spirit can make matter, why should matter not be able to make a spirit?

L.M.: But why should we think it can?

CRUDELI: Because I see it do so every day. Do you believe that animals have souls?

L.M.: Certainly I do.

CRUDELI: Then can you tell me, to take one example, what becomes of the soul of the Peruvian snake when it is hung up in a fireplace to dry and left there in the smoke for years on end?

L.M.: What becomes of it? Why, let it become what it will. What's that to me?

CRUDELI: Ah, then perhaps you are not aware, madame, that this same snake, after it has been smoked and dried, comes back to life and is born again.

L.M.: I don't believe a word of it.

CRUDELI: Yet we are assured that such is the case. And by Bouguer, a very able man.

L.M.: Then your able man was lying.

CRUDELI: But what if he was speaking the truth?

L.M.: Then I should be forced to believe that animals are machines.

CRUDELI: And man? Who is, after all, only an animal a little more perfect than the rest . . . But M. le Maréchal is . . .

L.M.: One more question—the last. Are you quite untroubled by your unbelief?

CRUDELI: No one could be more so.

L.M.: But—what if you were wrong, after all?

CRUDELI: Well?

L.M.: Everything you believe to be false would be true, and then you would be damned. Monsieur Crudeli, it is a terrible thing to be damned. To burn for all eternity; that's a very long time.

CRUDELI: La Fontaine believed that we should take to the flames like a fish to water.

L.M.: Yes, yes, I know, but La Fontaine became very serious at the very end. That's when I'd like to know what you'd say.

CRUDELI: If my brain is addled first, then I won't answer for what I say; but if I am carried off by any of the diseases that leave a man all his capacity for reason right to the end, then I shall be no more disturbed at that last moment you seem to set such store by than you see me now.

L.M.: Your boldness takes my breath away.

CRUDELI: To me, there is far more boldness in the dying man who believes in a strict judge, a judge that weighs even our most secret thoughts, a judge in whose scales even the most upright man can lose his soul through vanity, yet still does not tremble at the thought of proving too light. If that man, on the point of death, were given the choice between annihilation and being tried by that judge, then I should think him bold beyond everything if he so much as hesitated before taking the former course, unless he were even more out of his senses than St. Bruno's companion or even more intoxicated with his own merit than Bohola.

L.M.: I have read the story of St. Bruno's companion, but I've never heard of Bohola.

CRUDELI: He was a Jesuit at the college of Pinsk, in Lithuania. When he died, he left a coffer full of money and a note, written and signed by himself.

L.M.: What sort of note?

CRUDELI: It read more or less as follows: "I request the dear colleague to whom I have entrusted this coffer that he will open it when I have performed a sufficient number of miracles. The money it contains is to be used to cover the cost of my beatification. I have also added several authentic documents, written by myself, attesting to my virtues. These will be of considerable use to those who undertake accounts of my life."

L.M.: What a hysterically funny story!

CRUDELI: For me, madame, yes. But I don't think your God likes that sort of joke.

L.M.: Yes, you're quite right.

CRUDELI: It is only too easy to sin gravely against your code, is it not, madame?

L.M.: I must admit it is.

CRUDELI: And the justice that will decide your fate is exceedingly rigorous.

L.M.: True.

CRUDELI: And if you are to believe what the oracles of your religion say about the number of the elect, they are very few.

L.M.: Oh, I'm not a Jansenist, you know! I look only at the consoling side of it all. The blood of Jesus Christ can cover a multitude of sins, it seems to me. And since the Devil didn't give up his only son to death, I should think it very odd if he were still to end up with the larger share of souls.

CRUDELI: And what about Socrates, Phocion, Aristides, Cato, Trajan, and Marcus Aurelius? Have you consigned them all to hell?

L.M.: Certainly not. No one but a wild beast could even think of such a thing. St. Paul says that every man shall be judged by the law that he has known. And St. Paul is quite right.

CRUDELI: And by what law is the unbeliever to be judged?

L.M.: Your case is a little different. You are one of those accursed inhabitants of Chorazin and Bethsaida who closed their eyes to the light that shone upon them and stopped their ears that they might not hear the voice of truth as it spoke to them.

CRUDELI: Madame, if those people of Chorazin and Bethsaida were so completely masters of themselves that they could believe or not believe at will, then no others like them have ever existed anywhere in the world.

L.M.: But they were shown miracles that would have sent the prices of sackloth and ashes sky-high if they'd been done in Tyre and Sidon.

CRUDELI: Yes, but, then, the people of Tyre and Sidon were very clever, whereas the people of Chorazin and Bethsaida were fools. Do you think, though, that whoever created them as fools is going to punish them for being so? I told you an anecdote a moment ago; now I should like to tell you a little story. There was once a young Mexican. . . . But M. le Maréchal.

L.M.: I shall send in to see if he's at liberty. Now! Your young Mexican?

CRUDELI: Tired after his day's work, he was walking one day

along the seashore, when he saw a plank lying on the beach, one end in the water and the other resting on the shore. He stopped to rest for a while on this plank, and as he gazed out across the vast and watery expanse before him, he said to himself, "It is quite certain that my grandmother's brains have become addled in her old age. The stories she tells about those people, whoever they are, who came here, whenever it was, from some country or other that's supposed to be across the sea—well, they're all nonsense. It would be against common sense: anyone can see that the sea and the sky meet out there. So how, against the evidence of my senses, can I be expected to believe an old wives' tale that everyone tells differently, that no one knows the date of, and that is nothing but a tissue of absurd impossibilities over which they all eat out their own hearts and scratch out one another's eyes?" As he lay there pondering these things, the movement of the waves continued to rock the plank on which he was resting, and he fell asleep. While he was asleep, the wind rose, the tide caught up the plank on which he was lying, and in no time at all our young philosopher was drifting out to sea.

L.M.: Alas, yes! What a true picture that is of us: we are all of us floating on our own little plank—the wind blows and the tide takes us out to sea.

CRUDELI: He was already a long way from land when he woke up. And surprised though he was to find himself in mid-ocean, he was even more surprised when he saw that the sea and the sky, now that the shore on which he had been walking only a moment ago had disappeared, came together all the way around him. Perceiving this, he began to suspect that he might have been mistaken and that if the wind went on blowing him in the same direction, he might possibly be carried finally to the coast belonging to those people his grandmother had so often told him about.

L.M.: But you're leaving out all his fear and anxiety.

CRUDELI: He had none. He said to himself, "What does it matter, as long as I reach land? I have reasoned stupidly, it's true, but I was honest with myself, and no one can ask any more of me than that. If being clever isn't a virtue, then not being clever can't be a crime." Meanwhile the wind continued to blow, the young man and the plank drifted on, and the unknown shore began to rise above the horizon. He reached it, and he stepped ashore.

L.M.: We shall meet on that shore one day, Monsieur Crudeli.

CRUDELI: I hope we shall, madame. And in whatever place that shore may chance to be, I shall always be delighted at any opportunity of paying you my respects. . . . Scarcely had he left his plank and set foot upon the beach than he perceived a venerable old man standing beside him. He asked where he was and to whom he now had the honor of speaking. "I am the ruler of this country," the old man replied. At this, the young Mexican bowed to the ground. "Stand up," the old man said. "Now, you denied my existence, I believe?" "Yes, I did." "And that of my empire?" "Yes, that too." "I pardon you, because I am he who sees into the bottom of all men's hearts and because I have looked into yours and seen that you acted in good faith. However, all your thoughts and deeds have not been equally innocent." Whereupon, taking him by one ear, the old man reminded him of all the errors he had committed in his life, and as each one was named, the young Mexican bowed down, beat his breast, and asked forgiveness. . . . Now, madame, put yourself for a moment in the old man's place and tell me what you would have done. Would you have seized that foolish young man by the hair and spent all eternity delightedly hauling him around the beach?

L.M.: No, to be frank, I wouldn't.

CRUDELI: If one of these six pretty children of yours ran away from the house, did a lot of stupid things, then came back repentant, what would you do?

L.M.: Oh, I should rush out to meet him and hug him and cry all over him with thankfulness, but the Maréchal, his father, is made of much sterner stuff than I.

CRUDELI: But the Maréchal isn't exactly a tiger.

L.M.: Oh, far from it.

CRUDELI: You would have to pester him for a while, but he would give his forgiveness in the end.

L.M.: Without a doubt.

CRUDELI: Especially if he were to consider that he knew the child's whole life before it was created and that punishing it would bring no advantage to himself or to the culprit or to the culprit's brothers.

L.M.: But the Maréchal and the old man are not the same, you know.

CRUDELI: Do you mean that the Maréchal is better than the old man?

L.M.: God forbid! I mean that, just as my justice is not the same as the Maréchal's, so the Maréchal's may not be the same as the old man's.

CRUDELI: Ah, madame! You do not see the consequences of that reply. Either the general definition of justice applies equally to you, to the Maréchal, to myself, to the young Mexican, and to the old man or else I no longer know what justice is and I am entirely ignorant of what things will please the old man and what things will displease him.

At this point, we were advised that the Maréchal was ready to receive us. As I offered my arm to Mme la Maréchale, she said, "It's enough to make one's head spin, isn't it?"

CRUDELI: Not if the contents are sound, I think.

L.M.: When all is said and done, I think the easiest way out is to behave as though the old man does exist.

CRUDELI: Even if one doesn't believe it.

L.M.: And even when one does believe it, not to count on his being kind.

CRUDELI: It may not be the politest way, but I agree that it's the safest.

L.M.: By the way, if you were summoned to give an account of your principles before the magistrates, would you tell them the truth?

CRUDELI: I should do my best to spare those magistrates the responsibility of an appalling crime.

L.M.: Oh, you coward! And if you were at the point of death, would you submit to receiving the last rites of the church?

CRUDELI: Most conscientiously.

L.M.: Oh, for shame! You wicked hypocrite!

Elements of Physiology

[1774–1780]

The Elements of Physiology *is a series of notes jotted down by Diderot during his reading of the Swiss physiologist Albrecht von Haller, probably between 1774 and 1780. A large variety of topics is covered. Some of Diderot's speculations, reflecting the state of knowledge of his time, are absurdly quaint. At other moments, he reaches deep into biological and psychological problems, and his intuitions are occasionally startling by their modernity. This work was not published until 1875. (See A-T, Vol. 9.)*

Elements of Physiology

Contradictory Beings

These are the beings whose structure does not fit in with the rest of the universe. Blind nature, which creates them, also exterminates them; she permits only those to subsist that are able to reach a tolerable state of coexistence with that universal order of hers so much lauded by all her eulogists.

Animal and Plant

What is an animal, a plant? A coordination of infinitely active molecules, a chain of small, living forces that everything is conspiring to disrupt.

Is it surprising, then, that these beings last so short a while?

Vegetable Matter

Heat and fermentation can cause vegetable matter enclosed in a vessel to become animal.

It also becomes animal in me; and once animalized in me, it becomes reanimalized in the vessel.

The only difference is in forms.

The tiny worms generated in flour paste are viviparous.

Animals

We must not believe that they have always been or will always remain as we see them now.

Their present appearance is the effect of an infinite lapse of time; their forms appear to remain always the same to us, but it is no more than an appearance.

. . . Why should the long list of animals we see today not all be different developments stemming from a single animal?

Do Animals Have Morality?

Behavior of birds during incubation period difficult to explain mechanically.

Animal Functions

Tell me how a young swallow builds its first nest and I will explain all the actions appropriate to man before he acquires experience, belonging to man as an animal.

One observation we ought not to neglect is that during the nine months a mother carries her child within her, there are tendencies, tastes, and organic aptitudes passing from the woman into the fetus whose force it is impossible for us to estimate with any accuracy.

Two absurd suppositions are commonly made on this subject. They are then used to deduce insoluble difficulties.

One of these suppositions is that there exists on the surface of this earth a being, an animal, that has been since the beginning of time exactly what it is now.

Animal and Machine

The peasant who sees a watch moving and then, because he is unable to understand the mechanism, assumes that the hands are being controlled by a spirit is neither more nor less foolish than our spiritualists.

Sentience

Take away sentience and you are left with nothing but the inert molecule. . . .

Someday it will be proved that sentience, sensitivity to touch, is present in every part of nature. We already know of phenomena that point in this direction. This once proved, matter in general will be seen to possess five or six essential properties: active or inactive energy, length, breadth, depth, impenetrability, and sentience.

I should have added attraction to this list if it were not perhaps a consequence of motion or energy.

Irritability

This form of energy, irritability, is different from all other known kinds of energy: it is life—sentience.

Man

A rather able man began his book with these words: "Man, like all animals, is composed of two distinct substances: the soul and the body. If there is anyone who denies this proposition, it is not for him that I am writing."

I almost closed the book. Ridiculous man! If once I were to accept those two distinct substances of yours, there would be nothing more you could tell me. For you certainly don't know what the thing you call soul is, still less how the two substances are united, and no better what reciprocal action they would have upon each other.

On the Perfectibility of Man

Man's perfectibility springs from the fact that all his senses are so weak that none of them can ever predominate over the organ of his reason.

If he had the nose of a dog, he would always be smelling; the eye of an eagle, he would never stop looking; the ear of a mole, he would be a creature who listens.

On Abstract Man and Real Man

Two philosophers arguing without understanding each other. About man's free will, for example.

One says: Man is free; I feel it. The other says: Man is not free; I feel it.

The first is talking about abstract man, man not moved by any motive, man as he exists only in sleep or in the mind of our first philosopher.

The other is talking about real man—man acting, occupied, reacting to stimuli. . . .

Let us suppose this real man to be a geometrician. He wakes up; as soon as his eyes begin to open, he starts thinking again about the problem he embarked upon the day before. He finds his dressing gown and gets dressed without knowing what he is doing. He sits down at his worktable; he picks up his ruler and compass; he draws lines; he writes down equations, combines figures, calculates—all without knowing what he is doing. His clock chimes; he looks to see what time it is; he hurriedly writes several letters that must be sent by that day's mail. His letters written, he dresses, goes out, and starts to walk to the Rue Royale, where he is to dine. The street is strewn with stones; he picks his way among them; he suddenly halts his steps. He remembers that his letters are still lying on his worktable, open, without seals on, not dispatched. He goes back home; he lights his candle, seals his letters, and takes them himself to the post office. From the post office, he continues on to the Rue Royale and goes into the house where he was intending to dine. There, he finds himself in the company of several philosophers, his friends. They are talking about free will, and he maintains vociferously that man is free. I let him talk; but as night falls, I draw him into a corner and ask him to give me an account of his actions that day. He can tell me nothing, absolutely nothing, about what he has been doing, and I can see that, far from being free, he has been purely and simply a passive mechanism acted upon by the various motives that have set him in motion, that he has not produced even one single purposeful act of his own will. He has thought, he has felt, but he has acted no more freely than an inanimate body, than a wooden automaton made to execute all the same movements as he himself.

Life and Death

As long as the vital principle is not destroyed, even the extremest cold cannot freeze the fluids of an animal exposed to it or sensibly diminish its body heat. This last assertion is false. Effects of the cold in Russia.

Without life, nothing can be explained, nothing. Or without sentience. Or without living and sensitive nerves.

Without life, no distinction between the living man and his corpse.

Death

The infant runs toward it with its eyes closed, the adult is stationary, the old man approaches it with his back turned. The child can perceive no end to its own duration; the man pretends not to believe that he will die; the old man lulls his fears, even as he trembles, with a hope that springs afresh each day. It is tactless and cruel to talk about death in the presence of an old man. Old age is honored but not loved. Even if we were to gain no more by an old man's death than a cessation of the tedious attentions we are forced to pay him, we should soon be consoled for it; even not being secretly glad of it is a great deal. I myself was a good sixty-six years old before I faced up to these truths.

Organs Compared to Animals

Every organ may be considered as a separate animal. What damages and irritates one may cause another pleasure. . . .

From molecule to man, there is a chain of beings ascending from a state of living stupor to the highest form of intelligence.

. . . Man, a grouping of various animals all retaining their own functions.

Every organ or animal has its own character first of all, then its influence on the others. . . .

How do organs acquire habits? This is perhaps the only point where they are forced to cooperate and work as a society. Each one sacrifices a part of its well-being to the well-being of another. . . .

An organ in pain will quiver involuntarily. This action belongs to that organ alone and proves it to be an animal distinct from the rest.

Our virtues and vices are closely related to our organs.

The blind man who cannot see the outward aspect of a man in pain, the deaf man who cannot hear his cries, the man whose nerves are rigid and calloused and whose sensations are consequently dulled, the man who lacks imagination and cannot recall the sensations aroused by past events—none of these can be expected to possess great compassion or a particularly refined awareness of goodness and beauty or any passionate love for truth.

It is true that a natural defect in one organ may sometimes be compensated for by a more intensive use of another. Though a blind man is deprived of all sensations produced by visual forms, and therefore of all the emotions aroused by such sensations, nevertheless he is much more sensitive to cries: the sound of the voice is to him what facial expression is to those who can see.

I once knew a young blind girl who could receive sensations and ideas through her ears that are entirely strange to us; she distinguished between *blond* voices and *brunet* voices. . . .

Every organ has its particular kind of pleasure and pain, its individual construction, type of flesh, function, accidental or hereditary diseases, aversions, appetites, remedies, sensations, will, movements, food, stimuli, appropriate treatment, birth, and development.

On the Structure Peculiar to Each Species

Structure determines functions and needs. But needs sometimes reverse this process: their influence is sometimes sufficient to create new organs and always sufficient to modify existing ones.

Three small children: very large penises, together with an abundance of sperm; minds entirely preoccupied with coitus; dull-witted, sad, and wild, but excessively salacious.

Will, Freedom

The will is no less mechanical in operation than the understanding. There is no such thing as an act of will without a cause.

It has been said that nature makes no leaps.

The animal, man, everything in nature, is subject to this universal law.

It is said that desire is a product of the will, but the converse is in fact true: will is a product of desire. Desire is the offspring of structure. Happiness and unhappiness are the offspring of comfort and discomfort. We direct our wills toward happiness.

There is only one passion, the passion for happiness. It is given different names according to the objects it fixes upon; it becomes vice or virtue according to its violence, the means it employs, and the effects it creates.

Correspondence of Ideas with the Motion of Organs

Fury inflames the eyes, clenches the fists and teeth, and pulls apart the eyelids.

Pride raises the head; gravity strengthens it.

These physical effects of emotion may be observed in both man and animals. They are the whole basis of study for all those concerned with the imitation of nature.

Every passion has an action proper to it. This action is expressed in bodily movements.

There are organic sympathies between the different parts of the body.

Speech or cries arise from the linking of emotions and organs. Whether it is a Chinese child or a European child that experiences a sharp pain in its intestines, the instrument, the string, the harpist are all the same, so why should the sound or cry be any different? Exclamations are the same in all languages.

Therefore, any given sound is necessarily linked with one particular sensation.

It is to this correspondence that we must look for an explanation of the tender eyes of a passionate lover, of erection, perhaps of the increased strength observable in moments of passion, terror, fever, etc.

Why have recourse to a little harpist (the soul) that is unintelligible, isn't atomic, lacks organs, occupies no space, is essentially different in substance from the instrument, has no senses, and yet plucks the strings?

Good music is very close to primitive language.

Sleep

The dreams of young girls still in a state of innocence come to the brain from the very extremities of the fibers, bringing with them dark desires, vague sensations of unease, and a melancholy of which they cannot tell the cause. They do not know what they want, because they lack experience. They take this state for one of inspiration, for a desire to shut themselves away, to be alone, to go into a convent.

Dreams go either up or down; they either rise through the fibers to the brain or descend from the brain into the fibers. If the organ designed for the venereal act becomes agitated, then the image of a woman will be excited in the brain; if the image is first excited in the brain, then the organ of enjoyment will be agitated as a result.

Memory

I am inclined to believe that everything we have ever seen, known, perceived, heard, even all the trees on a long forest ride—what do I mean, all the trees?—even the arrangement of their branches, the shapes of their leaves, the variety of their colors, all the different greens and light effects—even the appearance of the grains of sand on a seashore, even the uneven surface of the waves, whether they were ruffled by a gentle breeze or lashed into a foaming tumult by a gale, even the multitude of human voices, of animal cries and inanimate noises, even the melodies and harmonies of all the tunes, of all the pieces of music, of all the concerts we have ever heard—all of it still exists inside us without our realizing it.

Even now, awake as I am, I can see all the forests of Westphalia, of Prussia, of Saxony and Poland.

In dreams, I see them in color—as brilliant as though they were in a Vernet painting.

I have been taken back in sleep to concerts that were repeated all over again exactly as I first heard them. . . .

A workman whose habit it was to spend his leisure hours at the theater fell victim to an acute attack of fever caused by the juice of a poisonous plant that had been carelessly administered to him. Whereupon the man started to recite whole scenes from plays of which he had not the slightest recollection when in good health. Worse still, this attack left him with an unfortunate inclination to write verse. He doesn't know the first thing about the verse he spouted in his fever, yet he is mad to write verses of his own.

The Power of Memory over Reason

The sound of a voice, the presence of an object, the sight of a certain place—and there before me is an object—what do I mean, an object?—there before me is a whole period of my life brought back from the past. And there I am, plunged into pleasure, into regrets, or into grief.

This power is exerted over us either in moments when we have become entirely unaware of self or when our minds are wandering.

It seems to me that the organ of memory is always passive: it can recall nothing of itself; it needs a cause to call it into play. . . .

Without memory, the sentient being would be aroused from

sleep by every sensation and then fall asleep again as soon as the sensation had passed; it would hardly have time to be aware of its own existence. It would experience nothing but a momentary feeling of surprise at each sensation; it would emerge from nothingness, then slip back into it again.

Will

Pain, pleasure, sensitivity, emotions, comfort, discomfort, needs, appetites, internal and external sensations, habits, imagination, instinct, the individual actions of each organ—these are what control the machine. And they control it independently of the will.

What is will, in fact, if we take away all these causes? Nothing. *Will* is merely a word: examine it closely and you will find nothing but impulse, awareness, and acquiescence; involuntary impulse, awareness or aseity, acquiescence or felt attraction.

To think. Voluntary action, involuntary action. The one we call voluntary is in fact no more so than the other; its cause is merely one stage further removed, for we cannot will anything of ourselves: will is always the effect of a cause that sets it in motion and determines its effect.

Freedom

If free will exists, then it does so only in the ignorant. Only when we have a choice between two actions and no motive for giving the preference to either can we do what we will to do. . . .

Self-interest is produced and determined in each organ by its position, its structure, and its functions; so it is an animal subject to comfort and discomfort, the first of which it seeks to attain, the second of which it attempts to avoid.

Soul

Marat[1] doesn't know what he is talking about when he discusses the action of the soul on the body. If he had thought

[1] Jean-Paul Marat, the revolutionary demagogue, was a doctor and had written a mechanistic work entitled *De l'homme* (*On Man*), 1773.

about it more carefully, he would have seen that the action of the soul on the body is merely the action of one part of the body on another. . . .

The animal is a whole, a unity, and it is perhaps this unity—with the help of memory—that constitutes the soul, the self, and consciousness.

There is nothing free in intellectual operations, nor in sensation, nor in the perception, visual or otherwise, of relations between sensations, nor in reflection or meditation or any degree of attention paid to such relations, nor in the act of judging or in acquiescing with what seems true.

Uterus

The uterus is not essential to the life of a woman; the Ancients used to remove it by surgery in certain diseases without fatal results. . . .

No menstruation when there is no milk. The milk passes from the uterus to the breasts and from the breasts to the uterus. . . .

According to this doctor [Soranus], a certain and infallible sign that a woman is bearing a male child is that the pulse in her right arm will be faster and stronger than that in her left. And, conversely, if the left pulse has these characteristics, then she is bearing a girl.

Generation

The first elements of man are to be found in that very place where he is born. They wait there for the male seminal fluid, without which they cannot develop.

Sperm

Similar organisms to be found in all body fluids, even in the lubricants produced by the natural parts—even in capons. . . .

The sperm flows back into the blood and spreads throughout the body. It can be detected by the sense of smell.

Children resemble the father more than the mother.

Disease and defects passed on from father to son.

Worms, the dominating principle in the animal kingdom. . . .

Excess of spermatic fluid produces cancer and tuberculosis. The remedy is simple. . . .

There are animalcules in the semen, and in that secretion only. But decay will engender them in all parts of the animal.

Semen

Nature lays down the use to which it shall be put, wisdom regulates it, continence retains it, vice makes it into a poison, religion blesses it, debauchery is prodigal of it.

It is a fluid that is produced in the brain, then flows down through the great sympathetic nerve. This fluid contains a tiny brain, the seed or nucleus from which the fetus is born. . . .

The woman is actually impregnated by a vapor; that appears to be proved.

Preexisting Germs

. . . A man is made just as an eye is made. What is there in common between a particle taken from the bark of a willow tree and the willow tree? Nothing. Yet that particle produces a willow tree.

How? By an inherent tendency that cannot, given nutrient matter, produce any other effect.

Monsters

Why should man, why should all animals not be simply more enduring kinds of monsters?

The monster, or abnormal being, is born and dies. Nature exterminates the individual in less than a hundred years. Why should nature not also exterminate the species in a longer period of time?

The whole universe sometimes seems to me no more than a conglomeration of monstrous beings.

What is a monster? A being whose duration is incompatible with the present order of things.

But the universal order is constantly changing. How can the duration of any species remain unchanged amid such constant change? Only the molecule remains eternal and unalterable.

The defects and virtues of the preceding order have led to the order we now see, and this order's defects and virtues will lead to the order that succeeds it, without it being possible for us to say whether the process as a whole is for the better or for the worse. Improvement and deterioration are terms that have no relevance except when comparing two individuals of a species or two different species.

There are as many kinds of monsters as there are organs and functions in man. . . .

If a man had two heads, one might be a Catholic and the other an unbeliever. He would be solicited at every moment by two contradictory sets of desires: one might want to go to Mass, the other to take a walk; one might conceive a passion for a certain woman, the other a loathing for her—unless perhaps, with time, they managed to establish such a conformity between them that they could act as though they had only one head.

Diseases

Gaiety—a quality of ordinary men. Genius always presupposes some disorder in the machine.

Conclusion

The world is the house of the strong. I shall not know until the end what I have lost or won in this place, in this vast gambling den where I have spent more than sixty years, dicebox in hand, shaking the dice.

Felices quibus, ante annos, secura malorum
Atque ignara sui, perludum elabitur aetas.[2]

[2] "Fortunate ones, whose life slips away prematurely,
Careless of evils and, in its play, unaware of its own passing!"

What do I perceive? Forms. And what else? Forms. I know nothing of things. We walk among shadows. And we are shadows too, both to ourselves and to others. . . .

There is only one virtue: justice; only one duty: to achieve happiness; only one corollary: not to expect too much of life and not to fear death.

Refutation of the Work of Helvétius Entitled *On Man*

[1773–1776]

By 1758, Diderot had already felt uneasy about Helvétius' notorious work On the Mind (De l'Esprit). *Helvétius' posthumous treatise* On Man *(1772) was even more naïvely simplistic and rigorously systematic in its reduction of all human action and thought to physical sensation and in its moral-political conclusions. Diderot had never been a pure sensationist. Closer to the "man-machine" school, he had always placed greater weight on structure—that is, on the active contribution of each individual to his own experience. In this work, moreover, he rebels against some of the extreme conclusions of eighteenth-century materialism, even though he had sometimes speculated in those very directions. The humanist that Diderot essentially was refused to imprison the human self within the bounds of any mechanical system. For him, the human element is truly unique in nature and quite inexplicable by a total reduction to laws which may explain lower forms of life. The human is an emergence into a new realm of moral experience and value. Diderot, though sometimes he wrote as a nihilist, did not compromise on this, his deepest article of faith.*

The Refutation, *written and revised between 1773 and 1776, was first published in 1875. (See A-T, Vol. 2.)*

Refutation of the Work of Helvétius Entitled On Man

To feel is to judge.[1]

THIS assertion, as it is phrased, does not seem strictly true to me. A stupid man feels but does not necessarily judge. A being totally deprived of memory feels, but it does not judge: judgment presupposes the comparison of two ideas. The difficulty consists in knowing how this comparison is performed, since it presupposes the simultaneous presence of two ideas in the mind. Helvétius would have removed a terrible stumbling block if he had given a clear explanation of how we entertain two ideas simultaneously or how, if we do not entertain them simultaneously, we can nevertheless still compare them.

Perhaps I was in an ill humor when I read this sixth chapter, but here are my remarks on it—good or bad, I shall set them down just as they came to me at the time. From all the author's metaphysics, there emerges the fact that judgment, or the comparison of objects with each other, presupposes some motive for comparing them. Helvétius then concludes that this motive arises necessarily from the desire for happiness, which, in its turn, arises from physical sensitivity. This conclusion is very farfetched; it is more applicable to animals in general than to man. To leap suddenly from physical sensitivity, *i.e.*, the fact that I am not a plant, a stone, or a metal, to the desire for happiness, from the desire for happiness to self-interest, from self-interest to attention, from attention to the comparison of ideas—these are generalities I cannot accept. I am a man, and I must have causes particular to man. The author also adds that by climbing two rungs higher or descending one rung lower, he could go on from physical sensitivity to structure, from structure to existence and could then say, "I exist, and I exist in this form; I feel, I judge; I try to be happy because I feel; my self-interest leads me to compare my ideas because I have a will toward

[1] The italicized passages heading each entry are from Helvétius and are the points against which, in each instance, Diderot proceeds to conduct his polemic.

happiness." But what possible utility can I derive from a string of consequences that is equally applicable to a dog, a weasel, an oyster, or a dromedary? . . .

Descartes said, "I think, therefore I am."

Helvétius wants us to say, "I feel, therefore I wish to feel pleasantly."

I prefer Hobbes. He claims that if we wish to draw any meaningful conclusion, we must say, "I feel, I think, I judge, therefore a portion of matter organized as I am can feel, think, and judge." . . .

If he had started with the single phenomenon of physical sensitivity, accepting it as either a universal property of all matter or a result of structure, and clearly deduced from it all the operations of the understanding, then he would have done something new, difficult, and extremely fine.

But I shall hold in even greater esteem the man who, by means of experiments or observation, either provides us with rigorous proof that sentience is as essential to matter as impenetrability or demonstrates it irrefutably to be an effect of structure.

I urge all physicists and all chemists to attempt the discovery of what living, sentient, animal substance is.

In the development of the egg and in some other operations of nature, I can clearly see matter that is apparently inert, although possessing structure, passing from this inanimate state to a state of sentience and life as a result of purely physical agents, but the necessary link in this transition escapes me.

Our notions of matter, structure, motion, heat, flesh, sentience, and life must still be very far from complete.

We must all agree on this: the organization or coordination of inert parts most certainly does not produce sentience. Secondly, the presence of universal sentience in all molecules of matter is only a supposition, and a supposition of which the whole strength is derived from the difficulties from which it extricates us; and in good philosophy, that is not enough. But now let us go back to our author.

Is it really true that physical pleasure and pain, which are possibly the only principles of action in animals, are also the only principles of action in men?

It is certainly necessary to possess a structure like ours and to feel in order to act. But it seems to me that those are merely the essential and primal conditions, the data *sine qua non*, and that the immediate and most direct motives of our aversions and desires are something else.

Without alkali and sand, there can be no glass, but are those elements the *cause* of transparency?

Without uncultivated land and without a pair of arms, we cannot clear new land, but are those the *motives* of the farmer when he clears a stretch of forest?

To take conditions for causes is to lay oneself open to childish paralogisms and meaningless conclusions.

If I were to say: One must be in order to feel; one must feel in order to be an animal or a man; one must be an animal or a man in order to be miserly, ambitious, and jealous; therefore jealousy, ambition, and avarice have as their primary causes structure, sentience, and existence—well, would you be able to refrain from laughing at me? And why not? Because I would be confusing the conditions for all animal actions in general with the motives for the actions of one individual taken from one particular species of animal called man.

Admittedly I do everything I do in order to feel pleasure or in order to avoid pain, but has the word "feel" only one connotation?

Is there only physical pleasure in possessing a beautiful woman? Is there only physical pain in losing her, either to death or to another?

Is the distinction between the physical and the moral not as solid as that between the merely feeling animal and the thinking animal?

Is it not true that what appertains to the feeling being and what appertains to the thinking being are sometimes united and at other times separated in almost all the actions that make for happiness or unhappiness in our lives, a happiness and an unhappiness that both presuppose physical sensation as a prerequisite condition—which is to say, quite simply, that it is necessary to be something more than a cabbage?

Thus we see how important it was not to make *feeling* and *judging* two perfectly identical operations.

> *Pleasure and pain are, and always will be, the sole causes of men's actions.*

I agree. And this work contains a multitude of other maxims and observations of which I should say likewise, "I agree"—but I should then add, "though I deny the conclusion you have drawn. You admit only corporal pleasures and pains, whereas I have experienced other kinds. And you attribute the causation of these latter to physical sensitivity, whereas I claim that physical sensitivity is only an ultimate, essential, but primitive condition of such pleasures and pains. 'I contradict you, therefore I exist.' Very well. But 'I contradict you because I exist' is no more tenable a proposition than 'I need a pistol to blow a man's brains out, therefore I am blowing a man's brains out because I have a pistol.' "

> *There are learned men, it is said, who condemn themselves to lives spent in isolation, withdrawn from society. Now, how can we convince ourselves that the passion these men have for their work is based on the love of physical pleasures, especially on a desire for women? How are we to reconcile these irreconcilables?*

The fact is that they cannot be reconciled. The objection you have made to yourself is insoluble. And yet you answer it. But do you answer it well? Ah, that is another matter. What a waste of a good mind![2]

Why not dispense with all those subtleties, which no good mind could ever accept from itself, and believe that when Leibniz shut himself away at the age of twenty and spent thirty years in his dressing gown, buried in the deeps of geometry or lost in the dark regions of metaphysics, he was no more thinking of obtaining an appointment or of lying with a woman or of filling an old chest with gold than he would have been if faced with imminent death. He was a thinking machine, just as the stocking loom is a weaving machine. He was a being who enjoyed thinking. He was a sage or a madman, whichever you

[2] Helvétius answers the problem by saying that the state of desire is a state of pleasure, as with misers.

wish, who attributed an infinite value to the praise of his fellow men and who loved the sound of applause as much as any miser ever loved the ring of gold coin. . . .

"Since he is happy," you say, "he likes women."

I don't know whether that's true or not.

"Since he likes women, he is using the only means at his disposal to obtain their favors."

If that is true, then go into his room, present him with all the most beautiful women you can find, and let him enjoy them—on condition that he renounces any further attempt to solve his problem. He will not accept.

"He is ambitious for high position."

Offer him the post of Prime Minister if he will throw his *Treatise on Preestablished Harmony* onto the fire. He will certainly not do so. . . .

The fact is that there is a principle our author has not grasped: that man's reason is an instrument corresponding to animal instinct and covering the same wide range, that mankind includes within itself analogues of all the various kinds of animals, and that it is no more possible to take a man out of his own particular subdivision than it is to take an animal out of its species—not, at least, without denaturing them both and without putting oneself to a great deal of trouble simply in order to make them into two stupid beasts. I grant that man combines ideas, just as a fish swims and a bird flies; but each man is impelled by his particular structure, character, temperament, and natural aptitude to combine such and such ideas rather than such and such other ones. Chance and, to an even greater extent, the pressures of life dispose of us according to their caprice. Who knows this better than I? It is the reason why, for almost thirty consecutive years, against my personal taste, I worked constantly on the *Encyclopedia* and wrote only two plays. It is the reason why talents are misplaced, why every calling in our society is filled with unhappy men performing their tasks in a mediocre fashion, why the man who might have been a great artist ends up merely a poor scholar or an indifferent jurist. And that is the true story behind our lives, not all these sophistical suppositions, in which I can see much wisdom but not an atom of truth, charming details accompanied by absurd conclusions, and everywhere the portrait of the author presented to us as a portrait of man.

For what do we learn from all these assertions Helvétius has made? That he was born with a great deal of sensuality and that, in his wanderings through society, he has run up against a great many lackeys and swindlers.

And from all that I have just said, what conclusion should we draw? That men do not seek glory, wealth, and honors merely as coin with which to pay for sensual pleasures. . . .

Avarice is the vice of the old, and there are children who are miserly. I have seen two brothers, both young children, one of whom always gave everything away, while the other always hoarded everything, and yet they were both exposed daily, without the slightest effect, to constant reprimands from their parents telling each to do the opposite. The elder has remained a spendthrift to this day, and the younger a miser.

Prince Galitzin[3] has two children, a good, sweet, simple little boy and a cunning, clever little girl who is always intent on getting her own way—and always by devious means. Their mother is very unhappy about this. Up till now, she has tried every possible means she can think of to make her little daughter more straightforward in her habits, but without success. What has caused this difference between these two children, both of whom are about four years old and both of whom have been brought up and cared for by their parents in exactly the same way? Whether Mimi mends her ways or whether she doesn't, Dimitri, her brother, will never have the talent for coping with court intrigues that she will. A teacher's lessons can never equal those we receive from nature.

And what have you to say about all those philosophers, our friends and contemporaries, who have so nobly taken priests and even kings to task? They cannot use their names; their aim cannot be either fame, self-interest, or sensual gratification, for where is the woman they wish to lie with, the appointment their ambition has singled out for them, or the flood of wealth that is to inundate their lives? We both of us know men of this kind

[3] Prince Dimitri Galitzin, Russian ambassador to France and close friend of Diderot.

who, though already enjoying all these advantages, disdain them because such things cannot bring them happiness and who, moreover, could be deprived of them by the slightest indiscretion on the part of their friends or the least suspicion in the minds of the civil authorities. How can you reduce this generous enthusiasm that is exposing them to the loss of their personal liberty, of their fortunes, of even their honor and their lives—how, without the most pitiable abuse of words, can you in the final analysis reduce all this to mere sensual pleasures? They are outraged by our prejudices, they groan at the errors with which we make our lives into a hell; from the midst of the darkness where we are all milling blindly, scourging one another on, their voices can be heard calling us to a better fate: that is how they satisfy their impulse to reflect and meditate, that is how they yield to their natural inclinations, which have been reinforced by education, and to the goodness ever present in their hearts—hearts weary of being merely spectators of the ills to which the wretched human race has been so cruelly and for so long subjected without protest. They will avenge mankind; yes, they will avenge it; that is what they say to themselves. And what the final goal of their intention is, I do not know, unless it be this dangerous honor itself.

I know what you will say, "They flatter themselves that their names will someday come to be known and that their memory will be eternally honored among men." I agree. But what does such heroic vanity have in common with physical sensitivity or with the sort of abject reward that you would reduce it to?

"They are gratified in advance by hearing the sweet strains of future voices raised in concert to celebrate their glory, and their hearts leap with joy at the sound."

"And so?"

"Does that leaping in their hearts not presuppose physical sensitivity?"

"Yes, since it presupposes a heart that can leap. But does a condition without which something is impossible also constitute its motive? Again and again, always the same sophistry. . . ."

> *What is the mind in itself? An aptitude for seeing the resemblances and differences, the congruities and incongruities existing among various objects.*

—Is this aptitude natural or acquired?

—It is natural.

—Is it the same in everyone?

—In all men with normal structures.

—And what is its primary cause?

—Physical sensitivity.

—And sensitivity?

—Is like aptitude, whose effects vary only as a result of upbringing, chance, and self-interest.

—And structure, provided that it is not abnormal and deformed, has nothing to do with it?

—Nothing.

—What difference, according to you, is there between a man and a beast?

—Structure.

—So that if you lengthen the ears of a Sorbonne theologian, if you cover him with hair and line his nose cavities with an extensive pituitary membrane, instead of smelling out heretics, he will run after hares and he will be a dog.

—A dog!

—Yes, a dog. And if you shorten a dog's nose . . .

—I know what you're going to say: he will most certainly turn out to be a Sorbonne theologian, a creature that ignores partridges and hares but runs baying after heretics.

—Are all dogs equally good hunters?

—Certainly not.

—What! There are some that neither the trainer's instructions nor punishment nor chance will ever make into good hunters?

—Beyond a doubt.

—And you still don't see the inconsistencies in your reasoning?

—What inconsistencies?

—The inconsistency of attributing the difference between man and beast, the two extremes of the animal chain, to structure, of using the same cause to explain the difference between one dog and another, and then rejecting it when you have to explain the varying degrees of intelligence, sagacity, and cleverness between one man and another.

—Oh, man, man . . .

—Well? Go on, what about man?

—The difference between the senses of one individual and those of another are of no importance.

—Very well. But when it is a question of estimating the aptitude of two different men for the same thing, is there nothing else to consider except their feet and hands, their noses, their eyes, their ears, and their sense of touch?

—What else would you have us consider, since those are the only organs we possess that are capable of sensation?

—But does the sensation the eye receives stop in the eye? Is it the eye that affirms or denies? Does the sensation received by the ear stop in the ear? Is it the ear that confirms or denies? Would an imaginary man who consisted of nothing but a living eye or a living ear be able to judge, think, reason like a whole man? . . . You have neglected to examine an organ [the brain] without which the varying degrees of perfection in the other organs mean nothing, the organ that gives rise to all the astonishing differences men display in the sphere of intellectual operations. . . .

And do not think that I am joking; without a common judge to which all sensations may be referred, without an organ capable of storing the memories of everything that happens to us, the sensitive and living instruments provided for receiving various kinds of sensation would perhaps possess a moment-by-moment awareness of their existences, but there would certainly be no consciousness of the animal or man as a whole. . . .

. . . But apart from the physical sensitivity common to all parts of the animal, there also exists a different and extremely powerful kind of sensitivity, one common to all animals and appertaining to one specific organ—though whether this second sort of sensitivity is in fact identical in origin with the first, being merely infinitely more intense in this organ than elsewhere, or whether it is a special kind of sensitivity, I shall not attempt to decide—I mean the sensitivity present in the diaphragm, that thin, extremely tough membrane we find dividing the internal cavity of the torso into two sections. It is this organ that is the seat of all our pains and pleasures; its vibrations or contractions vary in strength from one being to another; it is the action of this organ that characterizes cowardice or bravery. . . . The head makes wise men, the diaphragm compassionate and moral men. . . .

Since you attribute so much power to the impulse that drives one sex toward the other, you must recognize that the vigorous but insensitive man will be impelled by his passion toward a woman only in the way that a bull is impelled toward a cow; he is the wild beast we read of in Lucretius, its flanks transfixed with a mortal arrow, yet still charging upon the hunter and covering him with blood. Such a man will scarcely be given to madrigals and elegies; his intention is simply to gratify his desires; he cares little about moving or pleasing others. There is a burning, abundant, and acrid fluid irritating his organs of pleasure; such a man does not sigh, he roars. He does not direct tender and languishing looks at the object of his passion from between tear-stained eyelids: his eyes flash fire, and his gaze devours her. Like the stag in autumn, he lowers his horns and drives the timid doe before him. In the dark corner of the forest to which he has directed her steps, he expends all his energy on his own satisfaction, without a thought for that of the being he has forced to submit to him. And then, once satisfied, he abandons her and goes his way. Try to make a delicate and tender poet out of that animal if you can. . . .

We are all born with good minds!

But what is a good mind? It is one that denies those things that ought to be denied and affirms those things that ought to be affirmed. Do we really all bring this precious gift into the world with us when we are born? And even if nature did give it to us, would it be in our power to conserve it?

However much I should like to share the opinion of Helvétius in this matter, I cannot. Why not? Why do I persist in my conviction that one of this writer's greatest inconsistencies lies in his attributing the difference between man and beasts to the difference in their structures and then excluding that same cause when it comes to explaining the difference between one man and another? Why does it seem to him to be proven that every man is equally fitted for everything and that his dull-witted janitor has as much intelligence as he himself, potentially at least, when such an assertion seems to me the most palpable of absurdities? Why are all his subtlety, his eloquence, and his arguments insufficient to make me agree with him that all our likes and dislikes may be reduced in the last analysis to a desire for or a fear of sensory and physical pain or pleasure?

Any man possessing a normal structure is capable of everything.

. . . Here, I must make the following comment: though I have met with problems that seemed at first glance to be rather complicated, yet turned out to be quite simple when I looked into them, there have also been others, apparently quite simple at first glance, that I was subsequently forced to recognize as being beyond my powers. For example, I am convinced that even in a society as badly ordered as ours, one in which vice when it succeeds is often acclaimed and virtue when it fails almost always mocked, I am convinced, I say, that when all is said and done, the best way of achieving happiness is to be virtuous. To my way of thinking, the most important and interesting work yet to be written is one dealing thoroughly with this subject; it is the achievement I would recall with greatest satisfaction in my last moments. It is a subject I have considered a hundred times, and with all the intellectual concentration of which I am capable. I was in possession, I believe, of all the necessary data. And yet, though I hesitate to admit it, I have never dared to take up my pen and write even so much as the first line of it. I said to myself, "If I do not emerge victorious from this attempt, then I shall have made myself an advocate of wickedness; I shall have betrayed the cause of virtue; I shall have encouraged man to be vicious. No, I am not equal to this sublime task; even if I were to devote my whole life to it, it would be in vain."

Would you like a simpler problem? Here it is: Should the philosopher, if summoned before a court of law, confess his true opinions at the peril of his life?

Was Socrates right or wrong to stay in prison? . . . And think how many other subjects there are that have more to do with character than with logic! Will you dare to cast blame upon the sincere and courageous man who prefers to die rather than to retract and, by that retraction, to sully his own reputation and that of his fellow believers? If such a role is noble and beautiful in a tragedy or any other work of art, why should it be senseless or ridiculous in reality?

What is the best form of government for a great empire? And what reliable precautions could we devise that would effectively limit its sovereign power?

Is there any case at all in which it is permissible for a subject to raise his hand against his king? And if perchance such a case does exist, what is it? In what circumstances may a private individual consider himself to be the interpreter of the wills of all other individuals? . . .

Is the savage state preferable to the civilized state?

None of these are problems for children. Do you really believe that all men are endowed by nature with the capacity to resolve them? Without foolish modesty, I beg you to except me. They are questions that would have taxed even Montesquieu's powers to the full and taken up most of his life. . . .

General Refutations

Helvétius says: Climate has no influence whatever on men's minds. *Substitute:* Its influence is usually exaggerated.

Helvétius says: Legislation and government alone can make a people either stupid or enlightened. *Substitute:* This is true of the mass of people; but even under the reign of the caliphs, there were great doctors and a poet like Saadi. . . .

Helvétius says: Love makes even the weakest animal bold. *Substitute:* Yes, the weakest animal—but man, delicate and tender man, will stammer, tremble, become embarrassed, lose control of his speech and actions. . . .

Helvétius says: Innumerable experiments have proved that men everywhere are essentially the same. *Substitute:* If he means one society of free and civilized men is much like another society of free and civilized men, then that is more or less true. If he means that man is everywhere a man as opposed to being a horse, then that is a platitude. If he means that in any society, one man is essentially the equal of another, then that is a mistake. Since the definition of a man is not the same as the definition of an intelligent man and since every definition contains two ideas, one of which is the neighboring class and the other the essential and specific difference from it, intelligent man not only must be essentially different from man but also must be as essentially different as man is from an animal.

A good or bad nervous structure constitutes a difference between men for which nothing perhaps can compensate. Anatomists, doctors, and physiologists will prove this to you by citing an infinite number of different phenomena. Open their books and you will see that this prime motor, whatever it is, of all our intellectual operations suffers in an almost supernatural way from the slightest change that occurs in the rest of the machine; you will see, for example, how even a slight attack of fever can either clear a man's head or make him dull-witted. Have you never had a headache? And you don't even mention the insane, yet insanity is a phenomenon that would have led you, if you had considered it aright, to conclusions quite different from the ones you have drawn. The inmates of our asylums have an ability to see, hear, smell, taste, and touch things no less keen than your own as you sit at home in your study, but they reason quite differently. Why did you not ask yourself the reason for this? It is a question that would have added more than one essential chapter to your book. It might even have led you to the true origin of the differences between minds and led you to search for the ways, if they exist, of repairing the flaw in a vital organ, in that feeling, thinking, judging, dulled, darkened, and shattered mirror to whose decisions all our sensations are submitted. Do you experience no difficulty in convincing yourself that in a machine such as man, in which everything is so closely linked, in which all the organs are constantly acting and reacting upon one another, one of its parts, whether solid or fluid, can be defective without any adverse effect upon the others? Do you find it so very simple to persuade yourself that the nature of the body's secretions, of the blood, of the lymph, or the capacity of the various blood vessels ramifying through the whole body, or the system of glands and nerves, the *dura mater*, the *pia mater*,[4] the condition of the intestines, the heart, the lungs, the diaphragm, the kidneys, the bladder, the reproductive organs can vary with-

[4] Membranes of the brain.

out affecting the brain and the cerebellum? Can you really make yourself believe such a thing, even though the twitching of one nerve fiber is enough to produce the most appalling muscular spasms; even though a decrease or increase in the rate of the blood flow can produce lethargy or delirium; even though the unconsidered loss of a few drops of semen is enough to slow down or increase bodily activity; even though the cessation or blockage of one secretion can cause sustained discomfort; even though the removal or crushing of two glands that are apparently unrelated to the intellectual functions can produce or preserve a certain timbre of voice, dissipate energy and courage, and almost metamorphose one sex into the other? If you can convince yourself of such a thing, then you cannot concur in the opinion that there is scarcely any man born who does not come into the world without some of these structural defects or that, in any case, it does not take long for time, diet, exercise, pain, and pleasure to produce them in us. And you will therefore persist in the opinion that either the head is not affected by them or the effects they do have will be without influence on our powers of combining ideas or on our capacity for concentration, reasoning, and judgment. Consider, then, how far you are from providing a solution to the problem you set yourself. . . .

> *There is no better form of government, said the King of Prussia in a speech made to the Academy of Berlin, than the arbitrary rule of a just, humane, and virtuous prince.*

And it is you, Helvétius, who quote this tyrant's maxim with approbation! The arbitrary rule of a just and enlightened prince is always bad. His virtues are the most dangerous and the surest form of seduction: they lull a people imperceptibly into the habit of loving, respecting, and serving his successor, whoever that successor may be, no matter how wicked or stupid. Such a prince deprives his people of the right to deliberate, to will or not to will, even to oppose his will when he orders what is good. For such a right of opposition, senseless though it is, is also sacred; without it, subjects resemble nothing but a herd of cattle whose protests are ignored on the pretext that they are being led to fat pastures. By governing according to his own pleasure, the tyrant is committing the greatest of crimes. For what is it that characterizes the despot? Is it goodness or wickedness? By no means; those two notions do not even enter into the definition. It is the extent of the authority he arrogates to himself and the use to which he puts it. One of the greatest misfortunes that could befall a nation would be two or three successive periods of rule by a just, gentle, enlightened, but arbitrary power: the people would be led by their happiness into complete forgetfulness of their privileges, into the most perfect slavery. I do not know whether there has ever been a tyrant who, together with his children, thought to put this formidable political strategy into practice, but I have no doubt at all that it would have been successful. Woe to those subjects in whom all sensitivity to their own freedom has been destroyed, even by the most apparently praiseworthy means. For such an appearance only makes those means the more fatal for the future. That is how a people is lulled into a sleep that may be sweet but also like death, a sleep during which patriotic feelings flicker out and citizens become strangers to the government of their own State. If the English had been ruled by three Elizabeths in succession, they would now be the basest slaves in all Europe.

Observations on the Drawing Up of Laws

[1774]

This work belongs to a group of papers composed by Diderot for his benefactress Catherine the Great during or after his stay at her court. It is one of a number of writings in which we can see how far he has turned away from the weak and abstract generalities of his political articles in the Encyclopedia. *In the intervening years, he had developed a greater sense of political realities, a belief in representative political processes, and a strong awareness of the need to limit the sovereign power in order to protect the inalienable rights and freedoms of individuals. Composed in 1774, the* Observations *was first published in 1921, by Paul Ledieu. (Not in A-T.)*

Observations on the Instructions of the Empress of Russia to the Deputies for the Drawing Up of Laws

THERE is no true sovereign but the nation; there can be no true legislator but the people. It is only rarely that a people will submit itself sincerely to laws imposed on it; but it will respect, obey, and defend as its own work laws that it has created itself. . . . Laws are useless if there is a single member of society who may infringe them with impunity. . . .

The first line of a well-conceived code of law ought to bind the sovereign. It should begin thus: "We the people and we the Sovereign of this people conjointly swear to uphold these laws, by which we are both to be judged; and if it should happen that we the Sovereign change or break these laws, thus becoming the enemy of our people, it is just that our people should become our enemy also, that it should be freed from its oath of fidelity, that it should prosecute us, depose us, and even condemn us to death should the case require it. Such is the first law of our code: woe to the Sovereign that treats the law with contempt, and woe to the people that suffers the law to be treated with contempt."

One question that merits discussion is whether political institutions ought to be placed under the sanction of religion. I am averse to allowing a share in acts of sovereignty to men who preach the existence of a being superior to the sovereign and who have the power to put into the mouth of that being whatever pleases them. I am equally averse to making what is a matter for reason into a matter for fanaticism, to making what is a matter of rational conviction into a matter of faith, and to giving weight and consideration to those who speak in the name of the Almighty. Religion is a buttress that never fails to bring the whole house down in ruin.

The distance between altar and throne can never be too great. Experience in all places and all ages has proved the danger of proximity between the altar and the throne.

. . . There is no place in the world where it has proved possible to reduce priests to the status of citizens pure and simple without the use of violence. . . . They have everywhere claimed the right to a special jurisdiction. . . . A wise and enlightened policy would prescribe very strictly what they are permitted to say [to the people], and any transgression of those limits would be punished by severe penalties. For disturbances in society are never more fearful than when those who are stirring up the trouble can use the pretext of religion to mask their true designs.

Because they intercede for them with God, who alone has the power to exact vengeance for the oppression of kings, subject peoples, if too much oppressed, grow accustomed to regarding priests as their protectors. . . .

The priest, whose philosophic system is a tissue of absurdities, secretly tends to maintain ignorance; reason is the enemy of faith, and faith is the foundation of the priest's position, his fortune, and his prestige. . . .

What man with a little common sense, after a single impartial glance at all the religions to be found on this earth, will not recognize them as a tissue of fanciful falsehoods, as a system in which the ranks have been ordered thus: God, the priesthood, royalty, the people. . . .

Woe to that people among whom the education of the crown prince is entrusted to a priest. He will bring him up to the glory of God—in other words, to the glory of himself. What are the two main principles that he will inculcate in his charge? Abnegation of his reason, or total submission to religion, and intolerance, or his own independence of all kind of authority except that of God. Everything he tells him in a hundred devious ways can be reduced to the following: "You are nothing in the sight of God; you are absolute master of your people"—but he excepts himself.

The philosopher speaks very ill of the priest; the priest speaks very ill of the philosopher. But the philosopher has never killed any priests, whereas the priest has killed a great many philosophers. Nor has the philosopher ever killed any kings, whereas the priest has killed a great many. . . .

Morals are in all countries the result of legislation and government; they are not African or Asian or European: they are good or bad. . . . Whatever Peter the Great brought to Russia, if it was good in Europe, then it was good everywhere. . . .

One thing that would seem to me to be very wise would be to start by moving the capital [of Russia] to the center of the country: the heart is badly placed at the tip of a finger. Once the capital is at the center, highways, communication routes with the whole empire will come into being. . . .

It is clear that in a well-ordered society, the wicked person cannot do harm to society without also harming himself.

The wicked man knows this. But he knows even better that he

can gain more by being wicked than he will lose as a member of the society he is harming. . . .

Here, however, we encounter a difficulty. Natural laws are eternal and universal. Positive laws are merely corollaries of natural laws. Therefore positive laws are also eternal and universal. And yet it is also certain that such and such a positive law may be good and useful in one set of circumstances and bad and harmful in another; it is certain that there is no code of laws that does not have to be revised with the progress of time. Perhaps this difficulty is not insoluble, but it remains to be solved. . . .

It is against this master [the ruler], potentially the most dangerous evildoer of all, that the laws ought principally to be directed. Other evildoers may disturb the social order; he alone has the power to overthrow it. . . .

Three excellent and successive despots would accustom a nation to blind obedience. Under such a rule, the people would forget their inalienable rights; they would be lulled into apathy and a fatal sense of security; they would no longer feel the continual sense of alarm that is the necessary guardian of their liberty. . . .

In any country whatsoever, the sovereign authority must therefore always be limited, and the limits imposed must be lasting ones. The difficult problem that faces us is not, therefore, how to give a people laws or even how to give it good ones; it is how to protect those laws from any attempt at infringement that might be made upon them by the ruler. . . .

Since it is the law of nature that there should be twenty madmen for each wise man, a good government will be one under which the liberty of individuals is as great as possible and the liberty of the sovereign as restricted as possible. . . .

. . . It seems to me that the source of all political and civil power can only be the consent of the nation, a consent expressed either by the nation itself in assembly or by its deputies. . . .

If the depository [of the legislative power] is subordinated to and dependent upon the supreme power, then all legislation is useless. . . .

. . . Nevertheless, one should enlighten and instruct [the people], though without expecting too much from this means.

The rights of the intermediary powers between sovereign and people ought to be fixed, and fixed in such a way that they cannot be revoked either by the legislator himself or by his successors: if the intermediary powers are dependent upon the supreme power, then they are nothing. A free people differs from a nation of slaves only by the inalienability of certain privileges that belong to man as man, to each class of citizens as a branch of the social order, and to each citizen as a member of society. . . . For a sovereign to bind himself and also to bind his successor, that is the height of heroism, humanity, and love for his subjects—but it is also one of the most difficult things to achieve by legislation. I know only three or four ways of doing it: public awareness or instruction, brevity of the code and the laws, education, a national oath and periodic assembly of the Estates-General, and, above all, confirmation of rights by the enjoyment of them over a long period of time.

If the right to be a representative can be purchased, then the richest men will always be the representatives. If it cannot be purchased, then the representative himself will be the more easily bought. I am sometimes tempted to believe that there is little to choose between the venality of political office in England and the venality of civil-service appointments in France: they are two necessary evils.

The equality of citizens consists in their all being subjected to the same laws. The sentence should read "*equally subjected.*"[1] This paragraph must necessarily lead to the abolition of all the privileges of the nobility, the clergy, and the magistracy. But I should like to know what precautions will be taken to ensure that citizens who are unequal in power, in influence, in means of all kinds will still be all equal in the courts of law. It should be so, it has always been supposed that it is so, but it never has been so,

[1] A quotation from the *Instructions to the Deputies*, on which Diderot is commenting.

and perhaps it has never been possible for it to be so. It is a goal well worth our consideration.

. . . The general interest of the masses might take the place of the insight of genius if it were allowed freedom of action. . . .

We could console ourselves for all past and present evils if these things were destined to be different in the future, but that is a hope with which it is impossible for us to delude ourselves. Indeed, if we were to ask the philosopher what purpose is served by the advice he stubbornly continues to give to nations and to those that govern them and if he were to give us an honest answer, it would be that he is simply satisfying an invincible inclination to speak the truth, even at the risk of exciting anger and perhaps of being obliged to drink from the same cup as Socrates.

It is for legislation to conform to the spirit of the nation.[2] I believe this to be untrue: it is for legislation to mold the spirit of the nation.

The laws are particular and precise institutions of the legislator. All good laws have already been made by nature; it is the legislator's task to utter them. To sovereigns, I should say, "If you want your laws to be obeyed, let them never contradict nature"; to the priests, I should say, "Let your morality never forbid innocent pleasures." Thunder, threaten us all as much as you like, show us the dungeons yawning and the fires of hell burning beneath our feet—you will never stifle the desire that is in me to be happy. I wish to be happy: that is the first article of a code that takes precedence over all legislation, over any religious system whatever.

I believe that morality is determined by the laws. . . .

Resentment is the sole law of nature, and social law has taken its place. Resentment varies according to the character of the offense and of the injured person; civil law ignores resentment and takes into account nothing but the nature of the offense. Submission to the law has made the forgiving person vindictive and the vindictive person forgiving.

[2] This quotation from the *Instructions* was based on the theory of Montesquieu.

Patriotism is an ephemeral motive that scarcely ever outlasts the particular threat to society that aroused it.

Shame and the fear of disapproval, which act as checks to a small number of decent people, will never be sufficient to form the spirit and morals of a large nation. These means must be replaced by freedom, by security of persons and property, and by happiness. The punishment for a bad action ought not to be legal conviction, yet no bad action ought often to go unpunished —that is to say, it ought to punish itself, which will always happen if any good or ill that befalls society is always indissolubly linked with the good or ill that befalls those who compose it.

There are no constant and universal morals except those founded upon laws.

The decisions of law courts should never be printed: in the long run, they form a counterauthority to the law. Commentators on the Scriptures have committed a thousand heresies; commentators on the laws have buried those laws beneath their glosses. Let there be no other authority or means of defense in courts of law than law itself, reason, and natural justice. Once a sentence has been pronounced or executed, the court's decision must be obliterated: it should be illegal to cite it. If the court was in error, then citing that erroneous judgment is simply asking it to commit the same injustice again. All citing of precedents must be forbidden.

The limits of unhappiness or oppression have been laid down by nature. . . .

Men united to form societies by instinct, just as the weaker sorts of animal gather into herds. There was certainly no kind of covenant actually drawn up in such primitive societies.

Before everything else, a society must be happy. It will be happy if the freedom and property of individuals are secure, if trade is unrestricted, if all classes of citizens are equal before the law, if taxes are levied in proportion to the ability to pay and do not exceed the needs of the State, if virtue and talent are assured of a just reward. . . .

If man was made only to plow and reap, to eat and sell, then it is no great matter. But it seems to me that a being capable of feeling was intended to achieve happiness through all his thoughts. Is there any reason for setting a limit to the mind and senses and for saying to man: You shall think only thus far; you shall feel only thus far? I believe that this kind of philosophy tends to keep man in a state of brutishness and to restrict his pleasures and happiness in a way quite contrary to his nature. Any philosophy that goes against human nature is absurd, as is all legislation that continually forces the citizen to sacrifice his own tastes and happiness to the good of society. I want society to be happy, but I also wish to be happy myself, and there are as many ways of being happy as there are individuals.

All true duties must have our own happiness as their foundation. . . .

All these just and reasonable ideas—that the members of a society were not made by the ruler, but the ruler by the members; that there exist a tacit pact, inalienable rights, freedom, right of ownership—are all quite new in relation to the original formation of society. They are the cry of man oppressed, the product of a long series of evils all brought about by abuses of authority. So that reason was already well advanced when man first asked what a man is, the individual what society is, the subject what a sovereign is. On all these points, enlightenment has been carried in our time to the limits of the possible. What has this enlightenment produced? Nothing. Amid the demands of all civilized peoples, clamoring with the voices of their magistrates and philosophers, despotism is spreading on every side. That moment is still a long way off when we shall read at the head of an edict: "Louis, Frederick, Catherine, by the grace of their subjects," and not "by the grace of God." The first sovereign to introduce that innovation would be certain of immortality.

. . . In any country where talent and virtue produce no advancement, money will be the national god. Its inhabitants will either have to possess money or make others believe that they do. Wealth will be the highest virtue, poverty the greatest vice. Those who have money will display it in every imaginable way. If their ostentation does not exceed their fortune, all will be well.

But if their ostentation does exceed their fortune, they will ruin themselves. In such a country, the greatest fortunes will vanish in the twinkling of an eye. Those who don't have money will ruin themselves with vain efforts to conceal their poverty. That is one kind of affluence: the outward sign of wealth for a small number, the mask of poverty for the majority, and a source of corruption for all.

But let us suppose that a country has an excellent administration, great freedom of trade, a protected agriculture, taxation determined by the true needs of the state and the individual's ability to pay—in short, an opulent and happy nation—that is a second kind of affluence: the sign of wealth and sufficient means in all classes. In such a state, since gold cannot be eaten, it will be used for all kinds of pleasurable purposes: gilt, statues, and even grotesque art. It will produce no crimes, but all those vices that produce happiness in this world and damnation in the next.

The first kind of affluence, on the other hand, combines both vice and crime: the vices of affluence and the crimes of poverty.

It is those not engaged in agriculture yet obliged nevertheless to find a way to live who double and triple the farmer's work. It is therefore the manufacturer who makes agriculture thrive and not agriculture that makes manufacturing thrive. . . .

All I have to say is that a government should never interfere with trade by instituting rules or prohibitions. . . .

It is impossible to provide universal education in a large nation. I know of no people, however numerous, that is unable to provide small schools in which the children of the lower classes may be given bread, lessons in reading, writing, and arithmetic, and also moral and religious instruction. I know of no nation that cannot provide public art schools, colleges with boarders and day students, paying students, and scholarship students.

Do you want a great many students and bad teachers? Then let the State pay the teachers. Do you want fewer pupils and excellent teachers? Then the teachers must be paid by the students.

There is no mention of divorce in Her Imperial Majesty's instructions. Yet I should feel no embarrassment at advocating it myself, whether on the grounds of natural law or on account of the harm that is caused by the indissolubility of the marriage tie. I should require, however, that both partners be left free to remarry, for without that clause a divorce condemns both of them to a life of sexual license. But the children, whom shall we appoint as their guardians? I have no idea. The Moscow orphanages? Why not?

The possibility of divorce renders both marriage partners stricter in their observance of the duties they owe to each other. Divorces help to improve morals and to increase the population. . . .

But is it necessary for the divorce to be asked for by both partners at once? If the answer to this is in the affirmative, then divorce will simply be more infrequent. But the marriage was made by the consent of both partners. . . .

. . . It is not arts and letters that have corrupted men's morals; it is not the sciences that have made them depraved. Study history closely and you will see that, quite to the contrary, the corruption of morals produced by entirely different causes has always preceded and brought in its train a corruption of taste, a degradation of the arts, scorn for the sciences, ignorance, imbecility, and barbarousness—not that barbarousness from which the nation had already once emerged, but a new barbarousness from which it can never again escape.

On Women

[1772]

This essay is of interest not only because of its psychological content and the spirit in which it is written, but also as a sample of Diderot's "creative" literary criticism, or intellectual habit of finding his point of departure in the reading of a book with which he strongly agreed or disagreed. The book in question was Antoine-Léonard Thomas's Essay on the Character, Morals, and Mind of Women in Different Centuries *(1772). Diderot's essay was written in the same year, for Grimm's* Correspondance Littéraire. *(See A-T, Vol. 2.)*

On Women

. . . [WOMAN is] a being extreme both in strength and in weakness, a creature who will faint at the sight of a mouse or a spider and who can sometimes brave the greatest terrors that life has to offer. It is above all when they are gripped by passionate love, by jealousy, by the transports of maternal tenderness, by superstition, or by popular and epidemic emotions that women are most astonishing—as beautiful as Klopstock's seraphim, as terrible as Milton's fallen angels. I have seen love, jealousy, superstition, and rage carried to a point in women that no man ever felt. The contrast between the violence of their impulses and the gentleness of their features renders them hideous; it adds to their disfigurement. The distractions of a busy and contentious life break off our passions. But a woman will brood over hers: they become a fixed point to which her gaze is allowed to remain constantly attached by her idleness or the frivolity of her duties. This point then expands until it has no bounds, and in order to become insane, a woman gripped by passion would need only to attain the complete solitude that she is seeking. Submission to a master she finds distasteful is a torment to her. I have seen a decent woman shudder with horror at the advances of her husband; I have seen her plunge into her bath as though she felt it impossible ever to wash herself clean from the soil of duty. This kind of revulsion is almost unknown to us. Our organ is less fastidious. There are some women who will die without ever having experienced the climax of sensual pleasures. That sensation, which I am inclined to think of as a momentary epilepsy, is rare for them, though it never fails to obey our summons. This sovereign happiness evades them even in the arms of the man they adore, while we can experience it with any obliging woman, no matter how unattractive we may find her. Since they have much less control over their senses than we, the rewards they receive from them are less certain and less prompt. Their expectations are being continually belied. With a physical structure so much the opposite of our own, the cue that sets their sensuality in play is so delicate and its source so far removed that we cannot be surprised at its not reaching fulfillment or becoming lost on the way. If you hear a woman speaking ill of love or a man of letters decrying public acclaim, you may be sure that the one is losing her charms and the other his talent. No man has ever sat, at Delphi, on the sacred tripod: the role of Pythoness could never suit any but a woman. None but a woman's head could be so prevailed upon by ecstasy as to sense in all seriousness the approach of a god, to shake from side to side, to become disheveled, to foam at the mouth, to cry out, "I feel him, I feel him coming, he is here, the god," and to find the right words for such a moment. A hermit whose ideas were as fiery as his expressions once said to the Heresiarchs of his time, "Go and speak to the women; they receive ideas promptly, because they are ignorant; they spread them swiftly, because they are giddy; they remember them for a long time, because they are stubborn."

Impenetrable in their dissimulation, cruel in their vengeance, tenacious in their purposes, unscrupulous as to their methods, animated by profound and hidden hatred for the tyranny of man—it is as though there exists among them an ever-present conspiracy toward domination, a sort of alliance like that subsisting among the priests of every country. They all know its articles without ever having told them to one another. They are naturally curious: they desire knowledge about everything, so that they may then use it or abuse it as they choose. In times of revolution, this curiosity prostitutes them to the party leaders. Anyone who fathoms them is their implacable enemy. If you love them, they will ruin you and they will ruin themselves. If you thwart the ambitions they have set for themselves, then they feel in the bottoms of their hearts what the poet has put in Roxane's mouth:

Malgré tout mon amour, si dans cette journée
Il ne m'attache a lui par un juste hyménée;
S'il ose m'alléguer une odieuse loi;
Quand je fais tout pour lui, s'il ne fait tout pour moi;
Dès le même moment, sans songer si je l'aime,
Sans consulter enfin si je me perds moi-même,
J'abandonne l'ingrat, et le laisse rentrer
Dans l'état malheureux d'où je l'ai su tirer.[1]

Racine, *Bajazet*, I, iii

And they all deserve to hear the words that another poet, albeit a less elegant one, has addressed to one of their number:

C'est ainsi que, toujours en proie à leur délire,
Vos pareilles ont su soutenir leur empire;
Vous n'aimâtes jamais; votre coeur insolent
Tend bien moins à l'amour qu'à subjuguer l'amant.
Qu'on vous fasse régner, tout vous paraîtra juste;

[1] "In spite of all my love, if within this day he does not join me to him by a just marriage; if he dares to offer an odious law as an excuse; if he does not do all for me, when I am doing everything for him; from that very instant, without thinking whether I love him, without even considering whether I am condemning myself, I shall abandon the ungrateful wretch and let him sink back into the wretched state from which I found the means to remove him."

Mais vous mépriseriez l'amant le plus auguste,
S'il ne sacrifiait au pouvoir de vos yeux
Son honneur, son devoir, la justice, et les dieux.[2]

They will feign the ecstasy of passion if their reason for deceiving you is strong enough. But even when they experience it, it is without forgetting themselves. And the moment when they yield themselves utterly may also be the moment when they are wholly oblivious of everything but their schemes. They deceive themselves more than we do about what they like. Pride is more their vice than it is ours. . . .

. . . Woman bears within her an organ capable of the most terrible spasms, one that controls her completely and excites phantoms of every kind in her imagination. In her hysterical frenzy, she can return to the past or leap forward into the future; all times can become the present to her at such moments. And it is from the organ peculiar to her sex that all her extraordinary ideas arise. The woman who is hysterical in her youth becomes devout in her old age; the woman who still has a certain energy when old was doubtless hysterical in her youth. Her head still speaks the language of her senses even when they themselves are mute. No connections are closer than those between ecstasy, visions, prophecy, revelation, exalted poetry, and hysteria. When the Prussian woman Karsch lifts her eyes toward a heaven lit with lightning flashes, she sees God in the clouds; she sees him shaking down thunderbolts from a fold of his black cloak onto the head of the sinner; she sees the head of the sinner. Meanwhile, the recluse in her cell feels herself rising in the air; her soul pours itself out into the bosom of the Divinity; her essence mingles with the divine essence; she swoons, she is dying; her breast heaves rapidly; her companions, who have filed in and gathered around her, cut the laces of the gown that is constricting her. Night comes; she hears the choirs of heaven; her own

[2] "And so it is that, always a prey to its frenzy, your sex has always known how to maintain its sway; you never loved; your proud heart is intent much less on love than on subjugating the lover. Place you upon the throne, and everything will seem just to you; but you would scorn the most august lover if he did not sacrifice his honor, his duty, justice, and the gods themselves to the power of your eyes." (The poet is Crébillon.)

voice mingles with their concerts. Afterward, she descends to earth once more; she speaks of ineffable joys; they listen to her; she herself is convinced; she sways them to her beliefs. A woman in the grip of hysteria experiences an indefinable influence that may be infernal and may be heavenly. Sometimes such women have made me shiver. It was in the fury of the wild beast that is a part of her that I saw it, that I heard it. . . . There was a woman walking through the streets of Alexandria, barefooted, hair falling down her back, a torch in one hand, a pitcher in the other, saying, "I shall burn down heaven with this torch and put out the fires of hell with this water, so that man shall love his God only for His own sake." Such a role is suited only to a woman.

Yet that wild imagination, that spirit apparently so wholly incoercible can be crushed with a single word. A doctor in Bordeaux merely told some women who were suffering from the most terrible hysterics that they were in danger of contracting epilepsy, and they were immediately cured. A doctor shook a piece of red-hot iron in the faces of a group of young epileptic girls, and they were immediately cured. The magistrates of Miletus proclaimed that the first woman to kill herself would be exposed naked in the public square, and the women of Miletus were immediately reconciled to life. Women are subject to contagious ferocity: the example of a single one will sweep a whole multitude of others along with her. Only the first is criminal; the others are merely sick.

Oh, women, what extraordinary children you are! And you, Monsieur Thomas, with a little sensibility, a little feeling for pain, what tender emotions you might not have aroused in us by showing us women subjected, just as we are, to the infirmities of childhood; more confined and neglected in their upbringing; abandoned to the same whims of fate, but with more changeable souls, more delicate organs, and without any of that natural or acquired resolution that prepares us to face them; reduced to silence in adulthood; and suddenly subject to an indisposition that is preparing them to become wives and mothers. Whereupon they become sad, restless, melancholy, in the homes of parents who are alarmed not only for their daughter's health and life, but also for her character—for it is at this critical moment that a girl becomes what she will remain all her life: intelligent or stupid, sad or gay, serious or giddy, good or wicked, her mother's hope either realized or betrayed. For many years after this, each moon will bring back that same indisposition. The moment that is to free her from her parents' despotic rule has arrived; her imagination opens upon a future full of fantasies before her; her heart is bathed by a hidden joy. Be joyful while you can, poor, sad creature: time would progressively have weakened the tyranny that you are leaving; time will make progressively harsher the new tyranny that is about to be imposed on you. A husband is chosen for her. She becomes a mother. The state of pregnancy is difficult for almost all women. They give birth to their children in pain, at the peril of their lives, at the cost of their charms, and often to the detriment of their health. The child's first home and the two reservoirs provided for its nourishment—those organs that characterize the sex—are all three subject to two incurable diseases. There is perhaps no other joy comparable to that of the mother as she first looks upon her first-born child, but she will have paid dearly for that moment. The father unloads the burden of his sons' education upon someone who will perform that office for money; the mother is always left with the onus of bringing up her daughters herself. Age comes on; beauty vanishes; the years of neglect, of ill humor, of boredom are upon her. And having prepared her to become a mother by means of a periodic indisposition, Nature now takes away that power by means of a long and dangerous illness. What is a woman then? Neglected by her husband, abandoned by her children, of no account in society, her last and only recourse is her religion.

In almost all countries, the civil laws have merely served to reinforce nature's original cruelty to women: they have been treated like imbecile children. There is no kind of harassment that a man may not inflict on a woman with impunity in civilized societies. The only reprisal within her power is followed by domestic quarrels and punished by a more or less open scorn, according to whether the country she lives in is more or less moral. Nor is there any kind of harassment that a savage does not inflict on his wife. Woman, unhappy in the city, is even more unhappy still in the depths of the forest. . . .

Women, how I pity you! There is only one possible compensation for your sufferings, and if I had been a legislator, perhaps it would have been accorded you. Freed from all forms of bondage, you would have been sacred in whatever place you appeared.

When we write about women, we should dip our pens in the rainbow and dry what we have written with the dust from butterfly wings; as with the pilgrim's little dog when it shakes its paw, at every quiver of the pen a pearl should fall. But M. Thomas has not let fall a single one. It is not enough to talk about women, M. Thomas, or even to talk well about them: you must also make me see them. Suspend them before my eyes like so many thermometers recording the slightest changes in morality and manners. Set out, with all the rigor and impartiality at your command, the various prerogatives of men and women. But do not forget that, for want of principles and powers of reflection, nothing ever penetrates far enough into a woman's mind to carry true conviction; that the ideas of justice, virtue, vice, goodness, and wickedness all merely float on the surface of their souls; that their self-love and self-interest still retain all the energy they would have had in the state of nature; and that, though they may be more civilized than we are on the outside, they have remained true savages within—all Machiavellians more or less. The symbol for women in general is that of the Apocalypse, on whose brow is written: "MYSTERY." What to us is a wall of bronze is often no more than a spider's web to them.

Many people have questioned whether women make good friends. There are women who are men, and men who are women; and I admit that I shall never take a man-woman as a friend. If we have more reason than women, they have much more instinct than we. The only thing they have ever been taught is how to wear the fig leaf they have inherited from their original ancestress. Everything that is told to them, repeated to them for eighteen or nineteen consecutive years, may be reduced to the following: Now, my girl, take good care of your fig leaf; your fig leaf is in good shape, your fig leaf is in bad shape. Among a people given to gallant manners, there is nothing men and women appreciate the value of less than a declaration of love. They neither of them see it as anything more than the prelude to an exchange of sensual pleasures. Yet what is the meaning of that phrase, so lightly uttered, so frivolously interpreted, "I love you"? Its true meaning is: "If you would only sacrifice your innocence and your morals to my desires, lose your self-respect and the respect bestowed on you by others, walk in society with lowered eyes, at least until you have become sufficiently accustomed to wantonness to acquire the effrontery that accompanies it, give up all idea of a respected position in society, kill your parents with grief, and give me a moment of pleasure, then I should think it vastly obliging of you." Mothers, read these lines to your daughters; they are an explication, a résumé, of all the flattering words that will ever be spoken to them. And you cannot set them on their guard too early in life. So much importance has been attached to such lovemaking that the girl who once takes this step is apparently deprived immediately of every sort of virtue. It is like the hypocritically pious woman and the bad priest, in whom incredulity is almost the seal of depravity. Once they have committed that great crime, nothing else can hold any horror for them.

While we are reading books, they are perusing the great book of life. So that their ignorance makes them quick to recognize the truth when it is shown to them. They have never been forced to submit to any intellectual authority; whereas truth is always encountering a Plato, an Aristotle, an Epicurus, a Zeno on guard at the entrance to our skulls, all armed with pikes and ready to repel it. Women are rarely systematic in their thought, always swayed by what is before them at the moment.

Thomas has no word to say about the advantages a man of letters may obtain from conversing with women, and this proves him to be ungrateful. Women are no more decorous than we at heart, but because convention does not permit them to speak with the same frankness as men, they have devised a delicate bird language for themselves, a mode of speech that permits the expression of anything one has to say with the utmost decency, once one has been taught the secret. Women either remain silent or else, quite often, seem to have an air of not daring to say the very things they are in fact saying. It is easy to see that Jean-Jacques[3] has wasted a great deal of his time at women's feet and that Marmontel[4] has spent a great deal of his very profitably in their arms, whereas one is inclined to suspect that Thomas and d'Alembert have been rather too well behaved in this respect. Women also accustom us to making even the driest and thorniest of subjects clear and entertaining. Since we are always addressing ourselves to them, wanting to make them listen, fearing lest we may be boring or fatiguing them, we gradually acquire a certain facility of expression that passes from our conversation into our style of writing. When they have genius, I believe its imprint is more original in them than it is in us.

[3] Rousseau.

[4] Marmontel (1723–1799), popular novelist and man of letters.

Paradox on Acting

[1773–1778]

Written in 1773 and revised in 1778, this provocative work was first published in 1830. It represents the culmination of a gradual evolution in Diderot's thinking about the role of passion, emotion, and enthusiasm in aesthetic creativity. It has evoked continual discussion and debate, especially among actors and writers interested in the thespian art, but its reach extends to the arts of creation as well as to those of performance. *(See A-T, Vol. 8.)*

Paradox on Acting

FIRST SPEAKER: . . . The natural actor is usually detestable and occasionally excellent. . . . And how could nature form a great actor without the aid of art, since nothing happens on the stage exactly as it does in reality and since dramatic works are all composed according to a fixed system of principles? . . .

. . . If the actor were actually experiencing emotions, do you honestly believe he could play the same role with the same fire and the same success twice in a row? He would be bursting with ardor at the first performance, drained and cold as marble at the third. Whereas the acting of one who is an observant imitator and a thoughtful disciple of nature, the first time he presents himself upon the stage under the name of Augustus, Cinna, Orosmane, Agamemnon, or Mahomet, since he is rigorously copying what he has observed in himself and in others and continually observes our reactions—his acting, I repeat, instead of growing weaker, will be progressively strengthened by the new ideas he will have gathered. He will judge how far to raise or lower his tone and will thus satisfy you the more. If he is himself when he is acting, how can he ever cease to be himself? If he tries not to be himself, how can he gauge the exact distance he must move outside himself before calling a halt?

What confirms me in this opinion is the unevenness apparent in performers who act from the heart. There is no use your expecting any uniformity in their acting: it is by turns strong and weak, hot and cold, flat and sublime. Tomorrow, they will fail in the place where they excelled today, and the next day they will excel in the place where they failed the day before. Whereas the actor who works from reflection, from a study of human nature, from constant imitation of some ideal model, from imagination, from memory will give uniform performances, all of them equally perfect. Everything has been measured, combined, learned, ordered in his head; there is neither monotony nor dissonance in his delivery. His emotions will be seen to progress, to move in a series of leaps and remissions, to have a beginning, a middle, and an end. The accents, the gestures, the movements are always the same; if there is any difference between two successive performances, it will usually be to the profit of the second. He will not vary from day to day: he is a mirror, always ready to reflect nature—and always ready to reflect it with the same precision, the same force, and the same truth. Like the poet, he continually goes back to replenish himself from the inexhaustible store of nature; whereas if he depended solely on his own resources, he would quickly see the end of them.

What acting could be more perfect than Clairon's?[1] Yet if you follow her performances and study her work, you will soon be convinced that she knows every detail of her performance as much by heart by the sixth performance as she

[1] Clairon: stage name of Claire-Josèphe Léris (1723–1803), famous tragedienne of the Comédie-Française.

does the words she has to speak. Doubtless she has first constructed a model for herself, to which she then tries to conform; doubtless, too, she made it as noble, as great, as perfect as she was able; but this model that she has borrowed from history or summoned from her imagination like some great phantom is not she. If the stature of the model were no greater than that of the actress, how feeble and petty its action would be! When, by dint of hard work, she has come as close to that model as lies within her power, then the job is done: to hold herself firmly at that sticking place is purely a matter of practice and memory. . . .

. . . And why should the actor differ from the poet, the painter, the orator, the musician? It is not in the first furious impulse of inspiration that characteristic traits present themselves; it is in cool and tranquil moments, in entirely unexpected moments. We do not know where these flashes come from: they are a matter of inspiration. For the beauties of inspiration, the fortuitous flashes with which these geniuses sow their works at moments when they themselves are hung suspended between nature and their first sketch—casting alternate and attentive glances at each in turn—these beauties, which often surprise the artists themselves by their sudden appearance, are far more assured of their effect and success than any added in a moment's caprice. It is for tranquil reflection to temper the frenzy of enthusiasm.

It is not the violent man unable to control himself who moves us; that is an advantage reserved for the man in full possession of himself. The great dramatists in particular are diligent spectators of what is happening around them, in both the physical and the moral spheres.

SECOND SPEAKER: Which are one and the same.

FIRST SPEAKER: They absorb everything that strikes them; they store it all away. And it is from these hidden stores, laid up inside them without their knowing it, that so many rare phenomena pass into their works. The emotional, violent, warm-hearted men are on the stage; they give the performance, but they are unable to enjoy it. They are the models from which the genius makes his copies. Great poets, great actors, and perhaps all the great imitators of nature generally, no matter of what kind, though endowed with a fine imagination, a great deal of judgment, delicacy of touch, and infallible taste, are nevertheless the least emotional of beings. They are fitted in equal measure for too many things; they are too busy looking, recognizing, and imitating to be deeply affected by anything within themselves. I see them with their portfolios constantly on their knees, their pencils always in their hands.

We feel; they observe, study, and depict. Shall I say it? Why not? Great genius is scarcely ever accompanied by any great degree of feeling. A genius will love justice, but he will exercise that virtue without tasting its sweetness. It is not his heart, it is his head that does everything. Whereas the emotional man loses his even at the slightest unexpected occurrence; he will never be a great king, a great minister, a great general, a great lawyer, or a great doctor. You may fill the auditorium with such moist-eyed creatures, but don't put any of them onto the stage. Consider women. They certainly outstrip us, and by a long way too, where the emotions are concerned: what a comparison between them and ourselves in moments of great passion! But just as we must yield to them in the sphere of action, so, by the same token, are they an equal distance below us in the sphere of imitation. Strong emotions are always accompanied by some weakness of the nervous structure. The tear that escapes from the eye of the truly virile man will always move us more than all a woman's sobbing. In the great comedy, the comedy of the world, to which I always come back, all the passionate souls are on the stage, and all the men of genius in the pit. The former are called madmen; the latter, who are busy taking notes of the madmen's follies, are called wise men. It is the wise man's eye that seizes upon the comic flaw in all these various characters, depicts it, and makes you laugh both at the tiresome eccentrics whose victim you have been and at yourself. It was the wise man who was observing you both, who was making his comic sketch of both your torment and your ridiculous tormentor.

Yet even if these truths were clearly proved, great actors would never admit them: they are their secret. Mediocre actors or tyros would be bound to reject them; and there are others of whom we might say that they believe they feel, as one says of the superstitious man that he believes he believes, since the latter cannot envisage his salvation without faith, and the former cannot envisage his without emotion.

"Come, now," people will protest, "do you mean to say that the plangent, grief-stricken accents being torn from that mother's very bowels, and so strongly affecting my own, are not being produced by actual feelings or inspired by a present despair?" Not in the slightest. And the proof is that they are being uttered in meter; that they are all parts of a system of declamation; that if they were the twentieth part of a quarter tone higher or lower in pitch, they would be false; that they are subject to a rule of unity; that they have been prepared and led into just as a passage of music is; that they have been made to satisfy all the required conditions only after long study; that they are contributing toward the solution of a given problem; that it was necessary to rehearse them a hundred times in order to make them ring true; and that despite these frequent repetitions, the intended effect is still sometimes missed. The proof is that before saying:

Zaïre, vous pleurez![2]

or

Vous y serez, ma fille.[3]

the actor has spent a great deal of time listening to himself say those lines; that he is still listening to himself at the moment when he disturbs your heart; and that his whole talent consists not in feeling, as you suppose, but in re-creating the external signs of feeling with such scrupulous accuracy that you are taken in by them. Those grief-stricken cries are noted down in his ear. Those despairing gestures are performed from memory and have been rehearsed before a looking glass. He knows the exact moment when he will draw out his handkerchief, the exact moment when the tears will start to flow;

[2] "Zaïre, you are weeping!"
[3] "You will be there, daughter."

watch how they come at that particular word, at that particular syllable, not a moment sooner, not a moment later. That quiver in his voice, those half-finished words, those muffled or long-drawn-out sounds, that trembling of the limbs, that weakening of the knees, those swoons, those attacks of fury—they are all pure imitation, a lesson learned in advance, a pathetic grimace, a sublime piece of mimicry that the actor remembers long after studying it, that he was aware of still even at the moment when he was executing it, that leaves him, happily for the poet, spectator, and himself, in full possession of his mind, and that, like other physical exertions, makes no demand except upon the resources of his body. Once the sock or buskin has been taken off, his voice is weak, he experiences extreme fatigue, he changes clothes, or he goes to bed—but he is left with no depression. It is you who take all those impressions away with you. The actor is tired, and you are sad, because he has been flinging himself all over the stage without feeling a thing, and you have been feeling the emotions without moving from your seat. If it were otherwise, the actor's calling would be the most unfortunate calling in the world. But he is not the character; he plays it—and plays it so well that you take him for the character he is playing. The illusion is all on your side: the actor knows that he is not the character.

. . . The actor's tears come down from his brain; the emotional man's tears well up from the heart. The emotional man's viscera are always producing a boundless turmoil in his head; the actor's head sometimes produces a transitory disturbance in his viscera. His tears are like those of an agnostic priest preaching the Passion, of a seducer at the feet of a woman he does not love but wants to deceive, of a beggar in the street or at the door of a church who shouts insults after you when he has despaired of moving you, of a courtesan who feels nothing yet swoons in your arms. . . .

. . . Reflect for a moment on what is called "being true" in the theater. Does it mean presenting things as they are in nature? Not at all. The true, in that sense, would be merely the commonplace. What is truth on the stage, then? It is the conformity of action, speech, facial expression, voice, movements, and gestures with an ideal model imagined by the author and often exaggerated by the actor. And there lies the miracle. This model does not merely influence the actor's tone of voice; it even modifies his gait, his bearing. That is why the actor on the stage and the actor in real life are two such different people that it is difficult to recognize the one in the other. The first time I saw Mlle Clairon in her own home, I exclaimed quite spontaneously, "But, mademoiselle, I expected you to be a whole head taller!"

An unhappy woman, one who is genuinely unhappy, weeps but does not move you. Even worse, she may display some slight imperfection of feature that disfigures her and makes you laugh, some peculiarity of diction that is discordant and jarring to your ear, or some habitual gesture that reveals her sorrow as petty and ignoble. This is because extremities of passion are almost always subject to distortions of demeanor that the artist without taste will copy slavishly but that the great artist will avoid. Even when he is suffering the utmost torments, we wish man to retain the character of a man, the dignity of his species. What is the effect of this heroic effort? To distract us from the grief and temper it. We want that woman there to fall to the ground decently, gracefully; that hero to die like a gladiator in the arena, drawing the plaudits of the crowded circus, gracefully, nobly, in an elegant and picturesque attitude. Who is more likely to fulfill these expectations? The athlete who is overcome by pain and whose body is distorted by emotion? Or the well-schooled athlete who is in full possession of himself, who remains true to the gymnastic principles he has learned, even as he breathes his last? The Roman gladiator, like a great actor, the great actor, like a Roman gladiator, does not die as people die in bed but is obliged to play another sort of death if he is to give us pleasure. Otherwise, the sensitive spectator would feel that the naked truth, the action itself, stripped of all artifice, was petty and at odds with the poetry of the rest.

It is not that pure nature does not have its sublime moments; but I think that if there is anyone who will certainly have the ability to seize and retain their sublimity, it is the man who has already divined them in advance, with the aid of imagination or genius, and whose head remains cool as he reproduces them. . . .

. . . What I am going to tell you now is something I witnessed myself.

Garrick put his head through the gap between two leaves of a door, and in the space of four or five seconds his face passed successively from wild joy to moderate joy, from joy to composure, from composure to surprise, from surprise to astonishment, from astonishment to sadness, from sadness to gloom, from gloom to fright, from fright to horror, from horror to despair, and then back again from this final stage up to the one from which he had started. Was his soul capable of feeling all those sensations and of collaborating with his face in the playing of that scale, as it were? I don't believe it for a moment, and neither do you. . . .

. . . I regard [Sedaine[4]] as a descendant of Shakespeare—of that Shakespeare whom I shall compare not, indeed, to the Apollo Belvedere or to the Gladiator or to the Antinoüs or to the Hercules of Glycon but, rather, to the St. Christopher in Notre-Dame, a shapeless colossus, crudely sculpted, but between whose legs we could all walk without our heads even touching his baser parts. . . .

Is it at the very moment when you have just lost your friend or your sweetheart that you will compose a poem upon his or her death? No. Woe to him who can use his talents at such a moment! It is when the first great wave of grief has passed, when the sensibility is no longer so excruciatingly raw, when the catastrophe is at a distance, that the soul is calm enough to recall the happiness that has been eclipsed, is capable of appreciating its loss, and that memory combines with imagination, the one to retrace, the other to magnify the sweetness of a time now past. Only then are we in possession of ourselves and able to speak well. We write that we are weeping, but no one weeps when he is hunting for a forceful

[4] Michel-Jean Sedaine (1719–1797), writer of *drames* who followed Diderot's theories on that genre.

expression that is eluding him; we write that we are weeping, but no one weeps when he is busy perfecting the harmony of a line. Or, if the tears do flow, then the pen drops from our fingers, we give ourselves up to our emotions, and we cease to write. . . .

. . . Sensibility, according to the only accepted usage of that word up until now, is, it seems to me, that disposition in beings, always accompanied by a weakness of the organs—a consequence of excessive mobility of the diaphragm, liveliness of the imagination, or irritability of the nerves—that causes them to sympathize, to shudder, to admire, to fear, to be disturbed, to weep, to faint, to help others, to run away, to cry out, to lose their reason, to exaggerate, to despise, to disdain, to have no precise idea whatever of truth, goodness, or beauty, to run mad. Increase the number of such emotional souls and you will inevitably and proportionately increase the number of good and bad actions of every sort, and the quantity of exaggerated praise and blame as well.

Poets, if you are working to please a delicate, tearful, and emotional nation, then do not transgress the harmonious, tender, touching, elegiac limits you observe in Racine; for your audience would run away from Shakespeare's massacres: such feeble souls are incapable of withstanding violent shocks. Take care not to present them with images too powerful for them to accept. . . .

. . . A tragedy, to my way of thinking, is nothing but a noble page of history divided by a certain number of rest stops. A village is expecting a visit from the sheriff of the county. The sheriff arrives. He questions the squire and urges him to renounce his beliefs. The squire refuses. The sheriff condemns him to death and throws him into jail. The squire's daughter comes and asks for her father's pardon. The sheriff accedes to the request but adds a revolting proviso. The squire is put to death. The villagers attack the sheriff and he runs away. The girl's sweetheart kills the sheriff with a thrust of his dagger, and the intolerant villain dies to the sound of curses. A writer needs no more than this to create a great work. Let the daughter go and question her mother's grave as to the debt she owes the man who gave her life. Let her hesitate to make the sacrifice of her honor that has been required of her. Let her, while she tries to make up her mind, keep her sweetheart at a distance and refuse to let him tell her of his love. Let her obtain permission to see her father in prison. Let her father attempt to make her marry her sweetheart, and let her refuse to consent. Let her prostitute herself, and let her father, while she is doing so, be put to death. Let the audience remain unaware that she has yielded to the sheriff until the moment when her sweetheart, coming to tell her of her father's death and witnessing her anguish, learns of the sacrifice that she had made to save him. Then let the sheriff, pursued by the villagers, appear on the scene and be cut down by the lover. Those are a few of the details suitable for such a subject....

. . . In society, when they [actors] are not playing the clown, I find them polite, caustic and cold, ostentatious, dissipated, spendthrift, selfish, and more observant of our follies than moved by our sufferings. They remain quite calm when witnessing a misfortune or when hearing an account of some pathetic adventure; they are isolated, wanderers, always at the beck and call of the great; they have few morals, no friends, and almost none of those sweet and holy ties that associate us with the pains and pleasures of another being with whom we also share ours. I have often seen an actor laugh off the stage, but I don't remember ever having seen one weep. What do they do with it, then, this sensibility they lay claim to and are generally acknowledged to possess? Do they leave it behind in the wings when they walk off the stage and then pick it up again as they walk back on?

What leads them to assume the sock or the buskin? Defective upbringing, poverty, and licentiousness. The theater is a last resort, never a choice. No one has ever become an actor out of love for virtue, out of a desire to be useful to society and to serve his country or his family, or out of any of the right-thinking motives that might lead an honest mind, a warm heart, a sensitive soul toward so noble a profession. . . .

. . . Despite my close observation of these people, I can

perceive nothing that distinguishes them from other citizens, unless it be a sort of vanity that one might term arrogance and a constant jealousy that fills their company with hatred and dissensions. There is perhaps no other kind of social grouping in which the common interest of all the members and that of the public are so constantly and obviously sacrificed to wretched and petty pretensions. Envy is even worse among them than it is among writers; that is saying a lot, but it is true. A writer will more easily forgive another writer for the success of a play than an actress will forgive another actress for the applause that brings her to the attention of some illustrious or wealthy libertine. . . .

. . . Moreover, when I declared that sensibility is a characteristic of good-hearted men and mediocre talents, I was making the sort of confession you do not often hear, for if ever nature molded an emotional soul, it was mine.

The man of sensibility is too much at the mercy of his diaphragm to be a great king, a great statesman, a great magistrate, a just man, a profound observer—and consequently a sublime imitator of nature—unless he can forget himself and stand outside himself; unless his imagination is strong enough, his memory retentive enough to aid him in fixing his attention on the phantoms that serve him as models. But in that case, it is no longer he himself who is performing the task. It is the spirit of another that is controlling him. . . .

—I know what you're going to say: that there will always be the same difference between a man who counterfeits sensibility and the man who really feels it as there is between an imitation and the thing itself.

—Yes, and so much the better, I say. So much the better. because if the actor isn't a man of sensibility in the first place, then he won't have to struggle out of himself; he will be able to raise himself, immediately, in one bound, to the height of his ideal model.

—Immediately and in one bound!

—Now you're quibbling over words. What I mean is that since he has never been reduced to observing the petty model that is inside himself, he will be as great, as astonishing, as perfect an imitator of sensibility as he is of avarice, of hypocrisy, of duplicity, and of any other characteristic that he does not possess himself or of any other passion that is not in his own nature. Whereas what the person who is naturally given to sensibility will show me can only be petty. . . .

. . . But it is said that an orator is better when he becomes excited, when he is angry. I deny that. He is best when he imitates anger. Actors make an impression on the audience not when they rage but when they act rage well. In courts of law, in political assemblies, in all places where men seek to gain control of others' minds, they will feign sometimes fear, sometimes anger, sometimes pity in order to evoke these various feelings in their auditors. What passion itself cannot achieve, passion well imitated will perform.

Do we not say of certain people in society that they are good actors? By this we mean not that such a person feels anything but, on the contrary, that he excels at simulating emotions he does not feel: a role much more difficult than the actor's, for such a man must invent his lines as well. He has two functions to perform, the writer's as well as the actor's. The writer for the stage may produce a better text than the society actor, but does anyone believe that there is any actor on the stage who can feign joy, sadness, sensibility, admiration, hatred, or tenderness better, more deeply, more cleverly than an old and experienced courtier?

But it is growing late. Let us go in to supper.

Bibliography

(*Books in English only*)

CROCKER, L. G.: *The Embattled Philosopher,* rev. ed., New York, The Free Press, 1966.

MORLEY, JOHN: *Diderot and the Encyclopaedists,* London, Macmillan, 1878.

VARTANIAN, ARAM: *Diderot and Descartes,* Princeton, N.J., Princeton University Press, 1953.

WILSON, A. M.: *Diderot: The Testing Years, 1713–1759,* Fair Lawn, N.J., Oxford University Press, 1957.

FELLOWS, OTIS, ed.: *Diderot Studies,* Syracuse, N.Y., Syracuse University Press; and Geneva, Droz, 1949 *et seq.* (a series of volumes containing scholarly articles).

Diderot's correspondence constitutes one of his greatest masterpieces. It is available in French only. The best edition is currently being published under the editorship of George Roth, Paris Éditions de Minuit, 1955 *et seq.*

For other works on Diderot, consult D. C. Cabeen, *A Critical Bibliography of French Literature,* Vol. 4, Syracuse, N.Y., Syracuse University Press, 1951, and the supplement, soon to be published.